A Feminist List edited by
Jo Campling

editorial advisory group

Phillida Bunckle, *Victoria University, Wellington, New Zealand*; Miriam David, *South Bank University*; Leonore Davidoff, *University of Essex*; Janet Finch, *University of Lancaster*, Jalna Hanmer, *University of Bradford*; Beverley Kingston, *University of New South Wales, Australia*; Hilary Land, *Royal Holloway and Bedford New College, University of London*; Diana Leonard, *University of London Institute of Education*; Susan Lonsdale, *South Bank University*; Jean O'Barr, *Duke University, North Carolina, USA*; Arlene Tigar McLaren, *Simon Fraser University, British Columbia, Canada*; Hilary Rose, *University of Bradford*; Susan Sellers, *Centre D'Etudes Féminines, Université de Paris, France*; Pat Thane, *Goldsmiths' College, University of London*; Clare Ungerson, *University of Kent at Canterbury*.

The last twenty years have seen an explosion of publishing by, about and for women. This list is designed to make a particular contribution to this continuing process by commissioning and publishing books which consolidate and advance feminist research and debate in key areas in a form suitable for students, academics and researchers but also accessible to a broader general readership.

As far as possible books adopt an international perspective incorporating comparative material from a range of countries where this is illuminating. Above all they are interdisciplinary, aiming to put women's studies and feminist discussion firmly on the agenda in subject-areas as disparate as law, literature, art, religion and social policy.

A list of published titles follows overleaf

WOMEN IN SOCIETY
A Feminist List edited by
Jo Campling

Women and Spirituality

Voices of protest and promise

SECOND EDITION

Ursula King

First edition 1989
Reprinted 1990, 1992
Second edition 1993

Published by
THE MACMILLAN PRESS LTD
Houndmills, Basingstoke, Hampshire RG21 2XS
and London
Companies and representatives
throughout the world

ISBN 0–333–59471–1 hardcover
ISBN 0–333–59472–X paperback

A catalogue record for this book is available
from the British Library.

Printed in Hong Kong

Series Standing Order (Women in Society)

If you would like to receive future titles in this series as they are published,
you can make use of our standing order facility. To place a standing order
please contact your bookseller or, in case of difficulty, write to us at the
address below with your name and address and the name of the series.
Please state with which title you wish to begin your standing order.
(If you live outside the United Kingdom we may not have the rights for your
area, in which case we will forward your order to the publisher concerned.)

Customer Services Department, Macmillan Distribution Ltd,
Houndmills, Basingstoke, Hampshire, RG21 2XS, England.

'Our work in "secular" feminism reinforces a conviction that a yearning for spiritual dimension is as powerful amongst those who have rejected the church as those who remain.' – **Susan Dowell and Linda Hurcombe**, *Dispossessed Daughters of Eve*, p. 113

'When we are no longer driven by powerlessness to excessive need for power, we can express our human potency in many ways – human sex, human politics, the creative further reaches of the human spirit. The most important effect of transcending those old sex roles may be an evolution of morality and religious thought, as the concrete, flexible dailiness that used to be reserved for female private family life is wedded to the noble grandeur of spiritual vision and higher moral principles as formerly preached from pulpits one hour a week by male priests, ministers and rabbis. In the second stage, that same wedding of the abstract and the concrete will transform the discipline and practice of every profession.' – **Betty Friedan**, *The Second Stage*, p. 322

Contents

Preface to the Second Edition

Ever more women and men are interested in feminist spirituality and theology. Since this book was first published in 1989 debates surrounding women and spirituality have continued to grow. They have become global and worldwide, but also more particular and differentiated, addressing specific concerns in greater depth. Women's voices can now be heard everywhere but they do not receive the attention they deserve. New developments include more women's voices from the third world, and more women addressing urgent ethical and environmental concerns regarding the vulnerability and preciousness of all life on earth.

The tremendous social and political changes of the last few years radically challenge us to reflect and act in a critical, informed and committed way to ensure that we develop all available resources to respond to the great contemporary threats of poverty, violence, war, and ecological disaster. In this context it is absolutely essential that women's voices around the world are listened to and that women take their full part in shaping and transforming the world of today. This is not possible, however, without giving spirituality its central place in our lives.

This new publication represents a revised version of the first edition with a number of amendments and additions, especially a new Epilogue. Bibliographical references have been augmented by about a quarter – itself an indication of the productivity of contemporary women and their active involvement in and concern for articulating a new spiritual vision.

Just a few details about how this book came to be written in the first place. It was originally suggested to me by Jo Campling who is the general editor of the Macmillan series 'Women in Society'. She had heard my Hibbert Lecture 'Voices of Protest, Voices of Promise: Spirituality for a New Age' when it was broadcast on BBC Radio 4

(17 February 1984). Founded at the end of the nineteenth century, the Hibbert lecture is a well known, long established public lecture (or formerly series of lectures) on religion, but mine was the first to be broadcast, and more than 1300 people responded to it by writing in and asking for the text of the lecture. Many people also wrote to me personally, women as well as men from all age groups and walks of life. Some people sent me their books, poems and ideas and I asked permission to quote from some of the material received.

The themes of this book were developed from ideas only briefly touched upon in the original lecture. They have grown over several years by thinking and working with students and teachers, through talking and lecturing in Britain, Germany, Holland, India, Canada, and the USA, and through sharing experiences and thoughts with many women from all over the world. Parts of Chapters 2, 3, 4, and 5 were first presented in the Teape Lectures given at St Stephen's College, University of Delhi, and Bishop's College, Calcutta, in December 1986.

This book is not primarily an academic exercise looking at contemporary feminism from an interested, but detached point of view. On the contrary, its approach is based on a positive identification with the experience of contemporary women, much of which is also my experience. It explores and engages in dialogue with diverse feminist voices in a sympathetic and critical way. The feminist vision appeals as much to imagination and feeling as to the mind. Consequently, this book was written with both my head and my heart.

It could not have been written without the patterns of my experience being shaped by the experiences and thoughts of many other women. Writing this book has led me into a continuous outer and inner dialogue through which I myself have learnt a great deal and have grown in insight and understanding.

I have drawn on the works of many women authors who are acknowledged in the following pages. At a personal level I would like to thank many women friends, both alive and dead, for their great help and inspiration. There is Jo Campling herself, but also the late Magdeleine Leroy-Boy and Charlotte Klein, Mary Kelly, Kim Knott, Ursula Wirtz, Jean Head, Jaya Indiresan and Indira Malani, Airinne Ryan, Barbara Twigg and Sue Davies, the BBC producer of the Hibbert Lecture.

Since coming to Bristol I have had much help and support from Phyllida Parsloe and Iris Tute, and from the women's group which meets regularly at her house. I would like to thank them all most warmly.

In addition particular thanks are due to the library staff at the University of Leeds and the University of Bristol who gave me much help in collecting material for writing and revising this book. Additional material was found at the library of Binghamton University, State University of New York.

As the practice of feminism is of great significance in our family life, I especially dedicate this book to Tony, my husband, and to our four daughters Frances, Karen, Anna and Dominique Nina. I also dedicate it to the women and men students of the Department of Theology and Religious Studies at the University of Bristol who over the last three years have worked with me through the ideas of this book, engaged in their lively discussion and sparked off much further reflection on women's voices of protest and promise.

URSULA KING

Prologue

Much of the experience of contemporary women is similar to that of countless women in ages gone by. Yet in several important ways women's experience today is profoundly different and new, in a sense not experienced by earlier generations. Women ask themselves in a new way who they are, how they relate to others, and what they can do for the world to ensure its survival.

For generations, in fact for most of human history, women have been ascribed a place in society and family by others, by their elders, their fathers, husbands, children and relations. In the manifold web of social interrelations women have been central everywhere, but they have always stood at the intersection of patterns not made or shaped by them. Their role has been narrowly circumscribed by their biological function of producing children and by the associated tasks of nurturing and caring for the young as well as the sick, the old, the infirm. Women's activities have largely been relegated to the private sphere whereas the public domain, where history and culture are actively made and created, has predominantly been the world of men. Women have remained marginal and largely invisible in the public world and seldom, if ever, have their voices been heard. Much of this has changed today, but not as much as women wish.

Showing one's face and finding a voice of one's own

The modern women's movement, especially in its contemporary feminist phase, gives expression to women's active determination to shape their own 'self' and the world around them. Instead of passively conforming to a predetermined role, women want to actively decide for themselves what to be and do, and what to contribute to the life of society. Women have learnt to see the world anew and name and shape it differently. Thus the contemporary feminist quest, concerned with many specific issues, can symbolically be described as showing one's face, seeing a vision and finding a voice of one's own to proclaim it.

In York Minster there stands a stark statue of the Pietà, of Mary in her sorrows as the mother grieving over her lost son, hewn out of the solid, unpolished trunk of a tree. The sculptor, Fenwick Lawson, has shaped the contours of the women's face as if it were growing out of the grain of the wood, as if the features were firmly pressing against the trunk from within, to emerge and become slowly visible to the outside – an image of extraordinary power and beauty. Quite apart from the religious figure it represents, this sculpture of a woman's face emerging, surfacing and finding shape, of a woman in grief and sorrow turning her face to the world with a determination and strength grown out of affliction, powerfully proclaims to me how the face of woman, of all women, is coming into a power and expression of its own. This power also finds expression in a newly found voice.

Finding a voice of one's own has much to do with a newly discovered and newly developed sense of self. It is the expression of a new identity among contemporary women. This is grounded in a new self-awareness, a more critical self-knowledge, a newly gained self-confidence and a strongly expressed new self-assurance. Gaining such self-confidence and awareness is an important part of personal development towards growth and maturity. But today this process of finding a sense of self does not only occur at the personal level. It is happening at the social level to women as a group, in our society and many other societies around the globe. We are witnessing the global rise and surfacing of woman – of woman coming to face her own self, the world and others. In the past, women have almost been like a dumb and deaf person, enclosed in a world of their own, separate from that of most others, with no public voice to express their feelings or communicate their thought. But now women have learnt to speak for themselves. This happens in many different ways, but nowhere more clearly and challengingly than in the feminist movement. It is to this, then, that we must turn as the most articulate and critical voice of contemporary women in order to listen attentively, hear, interpret and understand the experiences of women today.

But of course feminism does not speak with only one voice. There are many different voices, with different stories and sometimes contradictory messages. People unfamiliar with the feminist movement are surprised, stunned and even hurt when confronted with women's array of questions, actions and options which are often little understood.

We hear so many voices in the press, on the radio, on television, but they are mostly the voices of men. Women's voices have been heard much more in public lately, but they are still not yet given the hearing they deserve. Also, a special effort is needed to listen to feminist voices which may be pleading or protesting, aggressive, angry or shrill, but there are also voices which sound wise, strong and resourceful, voices carrying power and calling for response.

To many, feminist voices sound utterly confusing, unconvincing or even plainly wrong. Yet if one takes all these different voices together, one can discern a certain connection between the different themes, an overall pattern and dynamic, and an acute sense of responsibility and concern. Some people consider the voices of feminists as truly prophetic as they express a vision which links together the personal, social, spiritual and political dimensions of human life. The overall goal of feminism is both a 'new woman' *and* a 'new earth' (Ruether, 1975). In other words, feminism seeks a change of consciousness *and* a change of the organisation, power structures and fundamental values in our society – a new culture and civilisation. Feminist voices thus express a powerful vision of new personal and collective forms of life. They are not the only voices to express such a vision of the possibilities of a new age and a new spirit to come, but they speak from an important vantage point. Whether this vision of a profound transformation of self and society will come true will depend on the concerted efforts of many individuals and groups. More than anything else it will hinge on our will and determination to make it come true.

A broad understanding of feminism

Contemporary feminism is not a unitary movement but consists of many different political and ideological orientations. There are liberal, socialist, marxist, radical and other varieties of feminism. David Bouchier in his study *The Feminist Challenge* uses a highly inclusive definition which covers the whole range of feminist beliefs and practices. For him feminism 'includes any form of opposition to any form of social, personal or economic discrimination which women suffer because of their sex' (Bouchier, 1983, p. 2). In the most general terms feminism has been described as a movement to overcome the oppression of and discrimination against women which is deeply embedded in our social and cultural institutions.

If one accepts this view, then feminism can be understood as a *movement for women*, but *not exclusively of women*. Radical feminists would strongly disagree with this. Yet it is possible to argue for a wider, more inclusive approach to feminism whereby anyone, whether female or male, who works for the abolition of women's subordination and oppression, can be considered a feminist (Richards, 1982, pp. 15–17; Midgley and Hughes, 1983, pp. 21–5). There exists no general consensus on who can or cannot be counted as a feminist. A broad understanding of feminism has the advantage of being flexible and inclusive of a wide variety of approaches. It will be acceptable to many women who may otherwise not wish to be associated with the more extreme forms of feminist thought and practice. This is important as the feminist movement, though growing around the world, is numerically still relatively small and needs to gain a much wider support.

Bouchier describes feminism today as 'a universal movement touching every aspect of politics and daily life. In its broadest definition, feminism includes women and men who advocate pro-women issues in governments, political parties, trade unions, schools, universities and the mass media, as well as socialist groups, radical separatists, consciousness-raising groups, peace campaigners and women's centre volunteers' (Bouchier, 1983, p. 177). Like most other writers on feminism, Bouchier is mainly concerned with the social and political aspects of the women's movement. Yet there is another aspect which has received relatively little attention so far. That is the spiritual search and quest associated with some parts of the feminist movement and with some particular individuals within it.

The richness and diversity of feminist literature becomes apparent when one examines the contents of current Women's Studies courses. However wide-ranging, they frequently make no reference to the field of religion and spirituality. Admittedly, comparatively few secular feminist voices are explicitly concerned with this area, yet they are becoming more numerous. Besides these explicit voices, there exists also an implicit dimension and a spiritual quest within modern feminism which require systematic investigation.

Feminism and spirituality

How do feminism and spirituality relate to each other? Feminism is an important social and political movement which has perhaps not yet come of age. Spirituality, on the other hand, has to do with an age-old human quest to seek fulfilment, liberation and pointers towards transcendence amidst the welter of human experience. But today, more than ever before, spirituality is itself at the crossroads. It has become an empty and meaningless word for many people who feel deeply confused and confounded by the sea of changes surrounding us. Many seek a sense of direction and identity amidst the turmoils and divisions of our contemporary world. Many ask what are the fundamental values, the goals and meaning of life. Some claim that our society is suffering from a materialistic world-view where 'things of the spirit' are neglected; they are seeking a profound transformation of society and new paths towards an alternative spirituality.

The term 'spirituality' is easily misunderstood. It is too often associated with an exclusively 'religious' or even 'ascetic' stance separate from the secular world. Many, though not all, spiritual teachers of the past have preached and practised a world-denying spirituality based on a sharp separation of the different spheres of human experience, a separation which has been altogether unwholesome.

However, spirituality must not be understood as something apart from or as something added on to life. Rather, it is something which permeates all human activities and experiences rather than being additional to them. Spirituality can be described as a process of transformation and growth, an organic and dynamic part of human development, of both individual and society. Spirituality has been variously defined as 'an exploration into what is involved in becoming human' or an 'attempt to grow in sensitivity, to self, to others, to non-human creation and to God who is within and beyond this totality' (Scottish Churches Council, 1977, p. 3). Others speak of spirituality as 'the way in which a person understands and lives within his or her historical context that aspect of his or her religion, philosophy or ethics that is viewed as the loftiest, the noblest, the most calculated to lead to the fullness of the ideal or perfection being sought' (Principe, 1983, p. 136). The spiritual has also been described as 'a category of being whose form is the personal, the co-ordinates of which are thought, freedom and creativity and the expression of which is in commitment, aspiration and valuation' (Webster, 1982, p. 89).

These definitions are probably too abstract for practical life. The important point is that they highlight the understanding of spirituality as an integral, holistic and dynamic force in human life and affairs. This is important in relation to contemporary feminism which is not only a strong social movement but also acts as an important critical category in contemporary thought. Its cutting edge dissects all areas of knowledge and culture to show their separateness, partiality and exclusiveness of women in order to seek a new way forward to a more integral and holistic way of thinking and acting.

Feminist thought acts as a decisive critical category for spirituality itself. Negatively speaking, feminist critical thought challenges traditional religions and spiritualities for their exclusiveness, their rejection and subordination of women; positively, it seeks to discover different, more integral world- and life-affirming religious possibilities. The women's movement can be seen as a 'spiritual revolution' (Daly, 1974a, p. 6); it certainly bears witness to a new 'womanspirit rising' (Christ and Plaskow, 1979). At a very decisive moment in human history the search for viable spiritualities is expressed in different but related ways in the writings on both feminism and spirituality. Their themes can be woven together in a criss-cross pattern of search, promise and quest for wholeness and healing in a world torn asunder.

This fruitful and decisive intersection of feminism and spirituality is perhaps best expressed in the title of the essays edited by Charlene Spretnak, *The Politics of Women's Spirituality. Essays on the Rise of Spiritual Power within the Feminist Movement* (1982). We shall have occasion to explore this conjunction of women, spiritual power and politics later in the book. At present it is important to note that I do not connect feminism and spirituality in an exclusive, separatist way as if feminist spirituality were opposed to and different from all other spiritualities. Similar to the broad understanding of feminism, I want to explore the broader connections which exist between feminism and contemporary spirituality, and how these relate to other thinking in this area. Someone might object that I am really dealing with the wider area of women and spirituality rather than with specifically feminist spirituality. To a certain extent this is true. But I am not primarily interested in a historical and descriptive treatment of the spirituality of women; rather, I am looking at those themes expressed by feminist voices which have a bearing on spirituality and indicate a spiritual dimension within contemporary feminism.

Crisis, change of consciousness and choices

The word 'spirituality' has its origin in the western Christian tradition where it has a long history in theology and religious practice (Principe, 1983). But in our times 'spirituality' has become a more universal code word for the search of direction at a time of crisis. In secular society it has become a cipher for the discovery and recovery of a lost dimension. The term 'spirituality' is now used in many different ways. It can refer to a shared reverence for life or to the new thought emerging from a wide range of experiences – from profound social changes to political liberation movements, and to the insights of a new physics and psychology. Some discern the shaping of a global spirituality which may lead to a new genesis (Muller, 1982; King, 1989a), a new becoming so desperately needed to prevent the destruction of our planet and to ensure a better quality of life for all members of the human family.

Looking at contemporary society and at feminism in a global context, as we must, we perceive a profound paradox around the globe between growing diversity and tension created by a self-destructive pluralism on one hand and the genuine search for integration and a new wholeness on the other. We are living at a moment of true crisis, a decisive turning point which has been called a 'hinge moment in history' (Morgan, 1982).

The Greek word 'crisis' originally meant 'discrimination', 'decision' and its wider meaning has been described by the *Oxford English Dictionary* as 'a vitally important or decisive stage in the progress of anything; a turning-point; also, a state of affairs in which a decisive change for better or worse is imminent; now applied especially in time of difficulty, insecurity and suspense in politics and commerce'.

This insecurity is due to the profound changes and fast transformation at work in contemporary society. There are the dominance of technology, the revolutionary changes in communication, the experience of a growing social, racial and religious pluralism at a regional, national and international level. There is the democratisation of human aspirations, desires and hopes, as well as the exponential world population growth with increasing competition for decreasing world resources. Most unsettling of all, there is the continuous threat of war and armed conflict, the unprecedented escalation of the nuclear arms race and the real possibility of a nuclear holocaust on a regional or global scale. But there is also a deep and growing yearning for peace.

The many changes in society have led to a profound change in consciousness. There is a shared awareness that we are one human family with a common destiny, faced by a common threat. There is a search for a new kind of universalism linked to an exploration of the outer world and a new exploration of the inner world, of the complexity and depth of human inwardness. The change in religious awareness cannot be seen in isolation, but is deeply embedded in other social, political, cultural and psychological processes of transformation.

These profound changes are not apparent everywhere and in everybody. But they can be found in many people and especially among the young. A new interest in religiousness is evident, although it is often found at the margin or outside the established religious institutions. This transformation of contemporary religious consciousness is visible in many areas, not least in feminism, but it can also be seen in the new religious movements and in a new interest in religious experience. Everywhere it is linked with the quest for meaningful religious symbols and viable spiritualities.

The American sociologist Peter Berger (1979, 1980) has pointed to the denial of transcendence and repressive triviality inherent in much of the western secularist worldview. He characterises the experience of many contemporaries as a world without windows on the surrounding wonders of life. His perceptive analysis shows that modern consciousness is governed by the imperative to choose. Choices are not optional. They must be made, and the way in which they are made will decide our future. The urgent necessity of decisive choices is nowhere more apparent than in the fundamental issues regarding life and death, the future of our species and that of our planet where we are faced with the ever growing threats of poverty, violence and ecological disaster.

Decisive choices will have to be made at the personal, social and global level. They ultimately imply major political issues. Choice itself is not a matter for choice – we must choose in order to survive. But choices can imply dilemmas and contradictions which are not easy to resolve. The values by which we choose, the goals and visions we hope to realise, are of decisive importance in shaping our choices. The outcome of our choices will much depend on the spiritual power and insight we have into the nature of things, of society, of ourselves and others, and the way we connect these different parts of our experience to each other.

The emphasis on choice for life, for the earth, for a future of humankind is powerfully articulated in feminist thought and practice, especially through women in the ecology and peace movements. Here a new spirituality is being born which is central to feminist self-understanding.

Increasingly one comes across references to ecofeminism, spiritual feminism, metaphysical feminism. These are fluid terms which can be associated with quite different phenomena, but they nonetheless express a unified sensibility and quest. Yet the underlying pattern of these experiences and the dynamic of this transformative vision stretch into a web larger than feminism itself. The promise of feminism holds a prophetic potential for the future of humankind; at the same time, present-day feminism must face some of the dilemmas in its own thinking and make the right choices to ensure its own future (Midgley and Hughes, 1983; Welch, 1990).

Listening to feminist voices

In public discussions about spirituality, usually conducted by professional theologians or religiously committed people, feminist voices on spirituality have so far been little noted. Feminists are perhaps better known for their critique of traditional religion than for their views on spirituality. It has also been shown that on the whole feminists tend to be less religious in a traditional sense than non-feminist women. However, the sharp feminist critique of religion expresses the profound alienation of many contemporary women and challenges important aspects of traditional religious teachings. Yet besides this critique there also exists a genuine religious quest within feminism. This seeks to overcome women's sense of alienation through a profound experience of liberation which extends not only to the external social and political sphere, but also to internal mental and spiritual life.

Why are the intentions of feminists so often misunderstood, misrepresented or simply ignored? Do feminist voices not speak loud enough? Are they perhaps too contradictory and confusing? Or are people simply not patient enough to decipher their messages?

Feminist thought expresses a particular sensibility of the present age which carries the seeds of a new age within it. It is absolutely essential that this thought be taken seriously, even when it needs to be criticised, as it must be on a number of points. Because of the very nature of feminist thought and practice an objective, analytical, detached and non-committed study cannot reveal the full potential of feminism. As feminism is concerned with life issues which demand decisive choices, an imaginative immersion into it, an active engagement with it and a personal response to it are required from both writer and reader. Feminism requires for its understanding what Harvey Cox in a somewhat different context has called a 'participatory hermeneutics' (Cox, 1974).

Over recent years a number of studies have dealt with women and religion in general (Plaskow, Arnold and Romero, 1974; Gross, 1977a; Carmody, 1979; Christ and Plaskow, 1979; Clark and Richardson, 1977; Falk and Gross, 1980; Coll, 1982; Holden, 1983; Sharma, 1987; Cooey, Eakin and McDaniel, 1991) or with particular issues of faith and feminism (Dowell and Hurcombe, 1981; Maitland, 1983; Carr, 1990), or with specialised aspects of feminist theology (Schüssler Fiorenza, 1983; Ruether, 1983; Sölle, 1984; Moltmann-Wendel, 1986; Hampson, 1990; Loades, 1990) or with wider aspects of feminist spirituality (Christ and Plaskow, 1979; Giles, 1982; Garcia and Maitland, 1983; Conn, 1986; Hurcombe, 1987; Wynne, 1988; Fischer, 1989; Plaskow and Christ, 1989; Harris, 1991; Zappone, 1991). All of these will be referred to later. My specific aim in writing this book is to introduce the reader to a global range of feminist voices so that we can listen to what they have to say, explicitly or implicitly, on spirituality and its meaning for us today. This will be deliberately related to new thinking on spirituality elsewhere.

The book gives serious attention to the different and sometimes contradictory voices of women today. It attempts to engage in discussion with them so as to unravel some of the paradoxes inherent in their messages. Feminists have been accused of appealing to emotion rather than argument. In certain circumstances this may be the right thing to do if it is not unreasonable. A more serious flaw of some general feminist writing, including some writing on religion, is the unnecessary and excessive use of jargon only understandable to the initiated or converted. This detracts from the force of emotional appeal as well as that of rational argument. Some voices simply sound too vehement and abusive to be convincing. Their message is branded as ideology or empty rhetoric or even declared a new religion. We shall have to consider these criticisms and face the question of what true liberation means for women as persons.

Listening to the voices of contemporary women we must first of all investigate the feminist challenge to traditional religion. We must also listen to women's claim about the nature and power of their own experience as well as about those experiences from which they strive to be liberated. In relation to religious experience Christian and Jewish feminists have voiced aspects of a new theology more intimately grounded in their experience as women, whereas others explore new spiritualities through the worship of the goddess, in matriarchy cults or in debates about androgyny. Feminist voices of spirituality also speak about our relationship to nature and about peace as a goal of political and human liberation. Women's voices have today entered into a worldwide dialogue which has created a new network and web of experimental thinking from which we hope that a new pattern of individual and corporate life will emerge. Let us then examine these global voices of women and discover what practical spirituality, grounded in new experience, is alive in contemporary feminism. Let us explore how these voices appeal to feeling, imagination, reason and will; and let us enquire how far they can help us to bring about the necessary transformation to create a more peaceful, just and loving world.

1

Voices of protest and anger

'Feminists have charged that Judaism and Christianity are sexist religions with a male God and traditions of male leadership that legitimate the superiority of men in family and society. This new challenge to traditional faiths just confirms the view of some feminists that society has outgrown its need for religion. . . . Other feminists, however, are convinced that religion is profoundly important. For them, the discovery that religions teach the inferiority of women is experienced as betrayal of deeply felt spiritual and religious experience. . . . They are convinced that religion must be reformed or reconstructed to support the full human dignity of women.' – **Carol P. Christ and Judith J. Plaskow**, *Womanspirit Rising*, p. 1

Many contemporaries consider feminism primarily as a protest movement characterised by rage and anger. We have to ask ourselves why this is so. What is feminist protest about? Has it legitimate foundations and if so, how is one to interpret the social, political and spiritual implications of this protest? In particular we want to know why feminists challenge religion and what in religion it is they challenge.

Examples of feminist protest and anger are probably more widely known than the note of celebration and joy which rings through much of feminist writing and experience. People's image of a 'typical feminist', based on either ignorance or prejudice, has been largely shaped by the somewhat one-sided and biased portrayal of feminists in the media. Radical and aggressive feminists especially have been used by critics and opponents as convenient scapegoats so as to avoid the challenge of having to take the real issues of feminism seriously and give full consideration to the alternatives proposed by women. Before we look specifically at the challenge posed by feminists to religion, it will be helpful to unravel some major threats of the feminist challenge in general.

The challenge of anger

Women do indeed speak out in protest and anger; they experience a righteous rage. But what does this really mean? What power and strength is erupting in these feminist outbursts? Many people do not even have the patience to listen, for they find feminist voices too disruptive, unreasonable and shrill. But is the shrillness not there because the voices are still broken, still partially undeveloped and inchoate? They must find a fuller, richer, more balanced and harmonious tone, maybe, to express the full emotional, moral, intellectual and spiritual power which women are now discovering for themselves and proposing as alternative for others.

One must be sensitive to the new spirit emerging and weigh up the positive sides of anger as well as the negative ones. Elsewhere I have described this ambiguity by saying that women

> who were submissive for so long, are now expressing a profound rage and anger. Their dissatisfaction and angry resentment, so far voiced only in private, has at long last been made public: anger with their fathers, mothers, husbands and children; anger with the churches, political and religious leaders, with all the stern gatekeepers of meaningless traditions; anger with the enslaving symbols and oppressive structures of patriarchy. The protest is over the injustices of sexism subordinating one sex to the exploitative powers of another. It is a protest over the history-long exclusion of women from the centres of power and decision-making, their relegation to the spheres of nature and nurture, denying them a full part in shaping the values of culture. Given this history, it hardly seems surprising that some women may now be driven by their anger to seek excesses of power and self-affirmation. It is easy to point to such excesses but more difficult to acknowledge that, most fundamentally, women's protest is over all the separations and divisions which rend our world asunder. (King, 1984a, p. 3)

At the roots of women's protest lies ultimately a spiritual protest. In protesting about discrimination, subordination and oppression, women voice their profound experience of alienation in always being *the Other*

(Beauvoir, 1972) acknowledged, defined, feared and controlled by men. Marianne Katoppo, an Indonesian woman theologian, has proudly written:

> I claim the right of woman to be liberated from being the *threatening Other*. I claim the right of woman to be *the Other* in all her fullness and variety of gifts – *the Other* who is *not* the adversary, the deviation, the subordination of the Self, but the one who gives meaning to the Self. (1979, p. 7)

The power of anger which breaks through in feminist protests is a power which struggles for equality, liberation, and freedom. Looking at anger from its positive side, it can be seen as another face of love – love for authenticity, love for the real, life-sustaining values, love for the fullness of life, love for the earth and its people and, among committed Christian feminists, love for the true church as the people of God.

Thus one must distinguish two kinds of anger, as Susan Griffin rightly remarks. There is the anger which is known and accurately placed, the anger which liberates one in mind and body. But there is also a second kind of anger which is displaced and imprisons. 'It becomes obsessive; it turns into bitterness; it leads to self-defeat; it turns us against ourselves'. But to 'escape from genuine sources of anger is to escape from the self' (Griffin, 1982, pp. 283, 284).

The phenomenon of feminist anger presents a challenge in itself which must be carefully examined and weighed up. Feminists are not exclusively defined by rage and anger as some of their opponents seem to think. Their thinking is not only shaped by reacting to existing situations but is in part truly innovative and creative, as it is grounded in new experience and sustained by visionary imagination. Whilst feminist anger challenges the world at large, the inherent ambiguity of this anger also implies a challenge to feminism itself as it requires a critical self-examination of feminist thought and practice.

The feminist challenge in historical perspective

Feminism is a relatively recent phenomenon. But one must not forget that its roots go back as far as the Enlightenment of the eighteenth century and especially the liberalism of the nineteenth century (Rendall, 1985). It was especially the freedom struggle for the abolition of slavery

which, during the nineteenth century, led to the first wave of the women's movement in the USA and Europe. Perceptive women could
easily see the analogy of their situation with that of unfree slaves. The
initial struggle was much concerned with obtaining the political vote and
equal rights for women, but some early feminists also criticised the
injustices perpetrated by religion.

During the twentieth century many aims of the early women's movement were put into practice. Yet it became increasingly clear that women
had not gained as much as they had hoped for and were far from having
obtained full social equality in all areas of life. During the 1960s new
economic and demographic conditions, especially the wide availability
of birth control, created a new social and political climate. These factors,
together with the protest of the students' movement, were important
influences in the birth of a new feminism. In spite of certain continuities
with the earlier women's movement feminism, as we know it today, is
something decisively and revolutionarily new.

Many critics consider the feminist movement as a passing phenomenon, of significance only for the educated, urban, middle-class women
of the western world. This mistaken impression is due to their very
limited experience of the new spirit which is alive among women in
many different parts of the world. Surveys of contemporary feminism
(Banks, 1981; Evans, 1982; Bouchier, 1983; Eisenstein, 1984; Mitchell
and Oakley, 1986; King, 1986b) often group feminists according to their
major political orientation into liberal, socialist, marxist and radical
feminists. Yet it is important to keep in mind that the fundamental
challenge of feminism, which I consider to be a spiritual as well as a
political challenge, is much wider than any party-political line and is
not restricted to the dominant political orientations of the West. Feminism is about a different consciousness and vision, a radically changed
perspective which calls fundamentally into question many of our social,
cultural, political and religious traditions.

Feminism is not only a social and political movement. It functions
as a critical category in contemporary culture because it challenges and
examines the foundations of our language, thought and institutions, our
social and political power structures and their hierarchical divisions.
Thus feminism has produced a new theory and praxis in most areas of
cultural activity. It offers or at least dreams of challenging alternatives
which seem less divisive, more integral and wholesome. Its critical
perspectives point to the crossroads at which contemporary society
has now arrived, the decisive turning-point we have reached in our
development.

Religiously committed feminists are sometimes somewhat disparagingly called 'soft feminists' by other more radical members of the feminist movement. This is perhaps an indication that religious issues, about which some women care very deeply, are not taken sufficiently seriously by certain feminists. There are a growing number of feminists who, though not religiously committed in a traditional sense, are nonetheless strongly attracted to a wider spiritual quest. They represent what has been called a 'metaphysical' or 'spiritual feminism' which is sometimes criticised for emphasising a path of inwardness to the exclusion of any political commitment. Certain strands of this spiritual feminism are closely interwoven with and influenced by different psychoanalytic theories. These may be criticised in some respects, but women's spirituality as understood in the feminist movement is on the whole strongly action-orientated and has a political dimension in a wider sense, even though it may not be actively involved in party politics.

David Bouchier in his study of the feminist movement in Britain and the USA sees feminism as very much alive, but depicts a two-sided picture of the women's movement by describing it on one hand as 'divided, sectarian, weak and isolated from political power' and on the other as a movement which is 'diverse, creative, full of energy and profoundly committed to the vision of a better life for all women' (Bouchier, 1983, p. 208). He speaks of the smallness and fragility of the movement in Britain where he found about 300 different feminist groups with perhaps 10 000 active members of whom only about 2000 are core members. In North America the numbers would naturally be larger.

Numbers are important, especially with regard to the effectiveness of campaigns about specific social and political issues affecting women. But whatever the numbers are, figures which can be collected by statistical means are bound to mask much of the widespread consent and tacit support which many women, especially young women, students, pupils and women living outside the main urban areas – all unlikely to be organised in strong groups – give to feminist ways of thinking today. It is not only the identifiable feminist core-groups with a strongly pronounced voice of their own, but other, more muted voices too which express significant, transformative experiences in the spirituality of women. These voices are indicative of a changing mood, a growing quest, a newly emerging vision which appeals to thousands more women than can be found in any organised movement.

Feminist critics have unmasked the ideological foundations of much of our knowledge and institutions, including the practice of religion and spirituality. The notion of ideology can be understood in a more general or more specific sense. In a general sense it can indicate the way in which all knowledge, all values and beliefs, are related to actual conditions of human existence, especially economic and political conditions. In a narrower sense ideology can be seen to be related to unexamined thoughts in our lives which we accept as unquestioned. Ideology can hide the truth. The feminist critique of ideology, especially with regard to the understanding and presentation of women, is both necessary and helpful. Yet this critical perspective must in turn be applied to feminism itself, for it is legitimate to ask how far at least some forms of feminism have developed into a new ideology which, far from bringing the promised liberation of women, leads them into a new, though different, kind of slavery. As the feminist writer Susan Griffin puts it in her thought-provoking meditation on 'The Way of All Ideology': 'But when a theory is transformed into an ideology, it begins to destroy the self and self-knowledge. . . . It organizes experience according to itself, without touching experience. . . . Begun as a cry against the denial of truth, now it denies any truth which does not fit into its scheme. . . . All that makes it question, it regards as its enemy. Begun as a theory of liberation, it is threatened by new theories of liberation; slowly, it builds a prison for the mind' (Griffin, 1982, p. 280). Whether feminism will achieve true liberation or create another prison for the mind is certainly the crucial question in the area of spirituality where freedom of the self within and without is the core experience. For many women today the vision of such freedom is first seen and experienced in small groups through a change of awareness brought about by the process of consciousness-raising.

Feminist consciousness and sisterhood

Consciousness-raising has been called the first step in feminist theory. It was originally developed as a method by members of radical feminist groups who helped each other to become fully and critically aware of each other's situation as women. Their encounter took place in small, unstructured and deliberately non-hierarchial groups with changing moderators rather than one permanent 'leader'. This method has spread to innumerable women's groups and caucuses; it has been effectively used on a wide scale throughout the feminist movement. It is intimately linked to the use of story-telling, the sharing of one's own personal story and life-experience of joy and suffering with other women.

This critical sifting and mutual sharing has made women deeply self-aware and has transformed, 'raised', their consciousness. With it comes the experience of women's own power in defining their life and choices rather than their being defined by others. This has led to a sense of independence and autonomy, to a newly found identity and the joy of personal fulfilment. In this deeper sense the liberation of women is not only about economic and social, but also fully personal independence and the discovery of the true self – a discovery of great spiritual importance.

The emphasis on a self-defining, autonomously acting subject and the importance attached to overcoming false consciousness which is ideologically distorted, has much in common with the themes of philosophical existentialism. It is no accident that Simone de Beauvoir's influential book *The Second Sex*, originally published in France in 1949, has remained a classic text in contemporary feminist thought (Evans, 1985). It is important to recognise that the development of feminist consciousness is part of the wider mutation and transformation of contemporary human consciousness. In a book on *Feminist Theory* (Keohane, Rosaldo and Gelpi, 1982) three different forms of consciousness are distinguished as far as women are concerned. There is first of all 'feminine consciousness' which represents for feminists 'an object of analysis rather than a source of insight, it involves consciousness of oneself as object of the attention of another; it arises from the sensation of being looked at and brings to one's awareness what one appears to be in someone else's eyes'. A second form is 'female consciousness' related to 'the deep-rooted, age-old experience of women in giving and preserving life, nurturing and sustaining. Profoundly conservative, it is also resonant with radical possibilities. The notion of women as "close to nature", distorted sometimes to discount the abilities of women to reason and to speak, here becomes the basis for a more fruitful line of argument' (pp. ix, x).

Whilst the first form, in its pure state at least, might be considered an example of what may be called 'false consciousness', the second form of consciousness has been fundamental to the historical experience of women, but in practice it has often been intertwined with the first. Now the third, critical form of consciousness is 'feminist consciousness'. It is described in the following terms:

This is a consciousness developed and defined as we reflect on women's experience, and on the asymmetries in power, opportunity, and situation that have universally marked the fortunes of women. Without denying the importance of 'female consciousness', or the reality of 'feminine consciousness', our 'feminist consciousness' draws attention to the pervasive patterns of subordination, limitations, and confinement that have hampered and crippled the development of the female half of humankind as far back as the species can remember. Concerned about the worldwide situation of women now as well as throughout the past, it develops a vision of an alternative way of living in which individuals of both sexes can flourish in diverse ways, without restraints imposed by rigid and impersonal sex/gender roles. (Keohane, Rosaldo and Gelpi, 1982, p. x)

Feminist consciousness, therefore, does not provide yet another intellectual perspective, one option among many, but it provides a new matrix and orientation to all other perspectives. The deliberately fostered change in awareness among women has sometimes led to radical conversion experiences of such intensity that they have been likened to the profound *metanoia* of a religious experience. This almost ecstatic self-discovery has also led to a new celebration of community, of the bonding among women. The sharing of stories of suffering, oppression and joy, of histories unknown and newly discovered, has created a new sense of solidarity among women expressed as 'sisterhood'. Sisterhood can be both a powerful experience and an equally powerful symbol of the togetherness, the relatedness of all women – their relatedness in suffering and oppression, in giving birth and life, in nurturing and caring, in joy and ecstasy.

Women have written, sung about and celebrated sisterhood in ecstatic and rhapsodic terms as witnessed in contemporary women's poetry, literature, art, films, music and photography. Sisterhood can be, and often is, understood in an exclusive, all-female sense. Mary Daly (1974a) calls it a 'charismatic community' and even a 'cosmic covenant' among women, but sisterhood has the potential of widening out into larger circles of community. For the moment it is important to acknowledge that sisterhood has created and strengthened newly woven bonds among many different women, young and old, wealthy and underprivileged, educated and uneducated, black, white, brown and yellow women. Sisterhood is made up of an immense web of threads of all colours and sizes; its activities consist of connecting and sharing, of speaking and sparking.

This web and its threads has created a women's network far larger and more informal than structured organisations with statistically accessible numbers. The informality and lack of rigidity of the feminist network may appear as weakness from the vantage point of existing political power structures. But as the feminist critique addresses the very nature and essence of these structures, the malleability and flexibility of women's groups – the feminine valley spirit, as the Taoists call it – may prove to be its very strength. As a women's poster tellingly proclaimed: 'Sisterhood is blooming. Springtime will never be the same again'.

Challenging patriarchy

Feminist voices express concern and protest about many specific issues (for an analysis of the major themes see Eisenstein, 1984), but fundamentally all criticisms and campaigns are rooted in an outright challenge to patriarchy, androcentrism and sexism. These are three different, but interrelated aspects of the same basic phenomenon of a false ordering of reality as traditionally understood. With the newly sharpened awareness of feminist consciousness this falsification is now radically called into question and a new order is called for.

What are patriarchy, androcentrism and sexism? These terms are widely used in feminist literature, but are not always clearly defined. If one looks at them in a wider historical perspective, it comes as something of a surprise to learn that their current meaning, implied throughout feminist writings, is of relatively recent origin. Moreover, through their feminist usage these terms have acquired a new meaning they did not have before.

On consulting the *Oxford English Dictionary* (second edition, 1989; hereafter OED) one can find a definition of patriarchy. The new edition now has also entries on androcentric, sexism and sexist whereas the *Encyclopaedia Britannica* (1988) has many entries on sex and sexuality, but none on sexism or androcentrism. Patriarchy is briefly treated, but in a different way from that understood by contemporary feminists.

It is worth reflecting on the fact that the origin of the word 'patriarchy' is an ecclesiastical one, found as long ago as the sixteenth century. Thus the first definition given for patriarchy in the OED is 'the dignity, see, or jurisdiction of an ecclesiastical patriarch' as well as 'the government of the church by a patriarch or patriarchs'. A second usage, found since the seventeenth century, is 'a patriarchal system of society or government by the father or the eldest male of the family; a family, tribe or community so organized' (vol. XI, p. 347). The definition in the *Encyclopaedia Britannica* (Micropaedia vol. 9, p. 200) runs as follows: 'hypothetical social system based on the absolute authority of the father or an elderly male over the family group'. The entry also mentions the theory of nineteenth-century anthropologists who, largely inspired by the example of ancient Greece and Rome, considered earlier cultures as having passed through different evolutionary stages, one of which was patriarchy. But the writer mentions that later anthropologists have largely disproved such evolutionary theories and come to the conclusion that absolute male authority was rare in human societies. Therefore the word 'patriarchy' is said to have fallen 'into disuse among social scientists as a technical or categorical term'.

This discarded anthropological and earlier ecclesiastical usage is obviously of a rather limited application and need not detain us further. But it is clear that there exists an important religious and social dimension in both the concept as well as the reality of patriarchy. Today the world is primarily understood to refer to a male power and property structure in which men are dominant to the detriment of women and, one may add, also largely to the detriment of their own full development.

Patriarchy is widely discussed in feminist theory as it is the central target of all feminist critique. Patriarchy is often contrasted with matriarchy, the rule of mothers, which a considerable number of feminist writers consider as historically prior to the patriarchal system. However, patriarchy is older than written history and so far no definitive answer has been given as to when and why it began. Some radical feminists maintain that the male-dominated family may be an inheritance from our prehuman ancestors whilst others, especially marxist and socialist feminists, consider patriarchy as partly resulting from the institution of private property.

By contrast, the American Steven Goldberg (1977) argues that patriarchy is universal and that there has never been a matriarchy in the history of human societies. Moreover, he strongly maintains that patriarchy was inevitable in the past and will be so in the future. He defines patriarchy as

> any system of organization (political, economic, industrial, financing, religious and social) in which the overwhelming number of upper positions in the hierarchies are occupied by males. Patriarchy refers only to suprafamilial levels of organization: authority in familial and dyadic relationships [between two people, here a man and a woman]

> is a manifestation of the psycho-physiological reality that is referred
> to . . . as *male dominance*. (Goldberg, 1977, p. 25)

The inevitability of patriarchy, rooted in universal male dominance, is
exclusively argued on the grounds of physiological differences between
men and women resulting not from 'obvious anatomical and reproduc-
tive differentiation but a neurodocrinological differentiation' (Goldberg,
1977, p. 64). Specialists in the sexual differences of human physiology
will have to argue with Goldberg on his own grounds, but it seems to me
that emphasising sexual psychophysiological differences is one thing,
whilst vehemently advocating the inevitability of patriarchy as a universal form of social organisation is quite another. The theory seems to be
unduly biologistic, if one may use this term, in determining the social
rôles of men and women on the grounds of their physiological differences. Moreover, Goldberg assumes without much further explanation
that physiological differences also imply fundamental psychological
differences. There is no consideration of the social construction of
role and gender identity created through the processes of socialisation
and formal and informal education. It is not surprising that Goldberg's
arguments, as those of other advocates of a biological determinism of
the sexes, have been strongly criticised (Sayers, 1982; Warren, 1980,
pp. 71ff.).

Goldberg argues at length that his theory is based on a strictly scientific analysis. But if this really were the case, it would have to remain far
more open-ended and could not be so categorical in predicting the
inevitability of patriarchy for the future. His argument is fallacious here,
for whatever may have been the case in the past, there is no reason to
believe that future societies could not be different. Goldberg does not
consider at least the possibility of profound social changes or even leaps
and mutations in the development of contemporary society which are
argued, among others, by many New Age thinkers today – namely, that
we stand at the threshold of quite a different, a new age in the history
of humankind – a vision not unlike that of some feminists.

Goldberg defines a feminist as any person who denies the importance
of physiological factors in sexual differentiation on which he exclusively
builds his argument. However, he seems to be primarily concerned with
strengthening the dominant position of men over and against the demands of contemporary feminists. He even admits that the 'hard evidence for a physiological basis for the female's greater nurturance
tendencies and the female's greater psychological aptitudes is far less

extensive than that for the physiological basis of the male tendencies' (Goldberg, 1977, p. 198). One cannot but suspect that he is far less interested in adducing evidence for females than for males!

As the above arguments show patriarchy, then, implies a theory about both the history and the nature of the human society. It relates to the evolution of societies, but also the nature of the family, the understand-ing and practice of sex roles and the formation of separate gender identity. The term patriarchy is used to describe the situation of women now and in the past, their dependence on and subordination to fathers, husbands, brothers and all men in positions of power, privilege and influence (Figes, 1986). In addition, patriarchy is used as a critical category to pass judgement on contemporary society and its institutions. Consequently, patriarchy is not only the major focus of all feminist critique, but probably also the terms which has attracted the greatest negative emotional charge within contemporary feminism. Moreover, patriarchy is inextricably tied up with deep religious roots and ramifica-tions, not only because of the widely perceived (rightly or wrongly) absolutist rule of a divine father – which must be rejected – but also because of the inherent patriarchal structure of all historical religions.

Wherever one looks in the world, religious institutions are dominated by men. Women are largely invisible, or at least marginal to the public positions of power, authority and hierarchy. There are hardly ever offi-cial 'spokeswomen' of religious institutions whereas at the grassroots level women almost everywhere form the majority of participants in ordinary, day-to-day religious life. Whilst God as all-encompassing Ultimate Reality transcends the differences of sex, this Reality has in many religions been predominantly, and one might say to the point of idolatry, presented as 'father' rather than 'mother'. This is now clearly recognised and found inadequate. As the theologian Sallie McFague has written in a perceptive chapter on 'God the Father: Model or Idol?':

> The issues of idolatry and irrelevance come together in the image of God as father, for more than any other dominant model in Christian-ity, this one has been both absolutized by women and, in recent times, found meaningless by others. The feminist critique of God as father centers on the *dominance* of this one model to the exclusion of others, and on the *failure* of the model to deal with the anomaly presented by those whose experience is not included in this model. (McFague, 1983, p. 145)

In Mary Daly's trenchant critique women's liberation implies moving 'beyond God the Father' (see Daly, 1974a). But whilst not all feminists would wish to draw the same radical conclusions from this position as she does, they would certainly agree with her statement that if 'it is true that human beings have projected "God" in their own image, it is also true that we can evolve beyond the projections of earlier stages of consciousness' (p. 29). Yet this will inevitably involve some forms of iconoclasm – the breaking of the idols of an earlier age.

The perception of androcentrism

Patriarchy is not only about social, economic, religious and political power structures, but is rooted even deeper than that in attitudes, values, language and thought. As Kate Millett has said: 'So deeply embedded is patriarchy that the character structure it creates in both sexes is perhaps even more of a habit of mind and a way of life than a political system' (Millett, 1971, p. 63). Feminist writers are slowly uncovering this hidden dimension of patriarchy by following it through our conscious and unconscious mind and exposing its negative influence in all our thinking.

It is perhaps more appropriate here to speak of the perception of androcentrism which can be defined as 'having man, or the male, at its centre' (OED, vol. I, p. 452). The first usage of the word androcentrism, indicated by the OED, is found as early as 1903. Lester F. Ward (1841–1913), one of the early pioneers of American sociology, seems to have invented the term and first used it in his book *Pure Sociology. A Treatise on the Origin and Spontaneous Development of Society* (1903, reprinted 1914). He deals there with what he called 'the androcentric theory' when discussing the relations between the sexes. In fact, he proposed two theories: 'The androcentric theory is the view that the male sex is primary and the female secondary in the organic scheme, that all things center, as it were, about the male, and that the female, though necessary in carrying out the scheme, is only the means of continuing the life of the globe, but is otherwise an unimportant accessory, and incidental factor in the general result' (p. 292). Ward opposed this theory to another 'gynaecocentric theory', perhaps culling the term from Bachofen (1861). This theory is described as 'the view that the female sex is primary and the male sex secondary in the organic scheme, that originally and normally all things center, as it were, about the female, and that the male, though not necessary in carrying out the scheme, was developed under the operation of the principle of the advantage to secure organic progress through the crossing of strains' (p. 296).

These quotations show that Ward's theory was also primarily based on biological considerations. Influenced by Comte and Spencer and general evolutionary theories of society, Ward maintained that the stage of gynaecocracy was historically primary, but was later succeeded by the stage of androcracy, the rule of men or male supremacy, which resulted in the complete subjection of women. Goldberg, whom we discussed earlier, indirectly refers to one aspect of Ward's theory as well as Bachofen's when he states that 'the term *gynaecocracy* has occasionally been used to describe an (imaginary) society in which government is run by women' (Goldberg, 1977, p. 26).

It is not quite clear from Ward's book whether in speculating about the future of society he considered the current androcentric phase to be superseded by a new gynaecocratic phase. He laconically states: 'The androcentric world view will probably be as slow to give way as was the geocentric, or as is still the anthropocentric' (Ward, 1914, p. 332). He also relates the interesting fact that he first developed his gynaecocentric theory in April 1888 before the Washington Six O'Clock Club in the presence of 'certain distinguished women' who included, among others, the well known American feminist Elizabeth Cady Stanton (p. 297).

The term 'gynaecocentric' did not become widely known in the way 'androcentric' is now current. It is not clear who first adopted the latter term from Ward and then applied it in a much wider sense. From a limited biological, historical and sociological application, the meaning of androcentrism has been expanded to refer to a state of affairs where everything people do and are is now recognised as being one-sidedly defined by the example and experience of men alone. In other words, what is usually thought of as being universally human or a generally valid norm has not been determined by what women and men together experience and understand, but has been exclusively described, analysed, categorised and laid down by men. This is true of the understanding of the family, of society and government, of politics and property, of education and all the disciplines of human knowledge, of the sciences and the arts, of religion and of spirituality.

Men have named things and people; men have thought, invented and shaped the world; they have mapped out reality for themselves and established sharply drawn boundaries within it. Women have been assigned their place and role within the scheme of things made by men

alone. Today's feminists perceive the fetters and limits of these boundaries and wish to redraw the map of reality anew. They claim the right to
do their own naming of things and people, to shape the world, define
language and thought and weave the pattern of their own experience
into the texture of culture and society. Feminists now challenge all the
androcentric assumptions underlying our values, attitudes and beliefs,
including those of religious beliefs. The term 'androcentrism' has become firmly rooted in feminist vocabulary whereas 'gynaecocentric' has
not been adopted, not even by those members of the feminist movement
who plead for an exclusively woman-defined and woman-centred
culture. Some radical feminists may envisage a gynocentric society,
but they are in a minority. Androcentrism cannot be overcome and
replaced by its opposite, for this again would not be inclusive, but
exclusive. The major thread running through the feminist debate is not
sexual exclusiveness and cultural separateness, but a search for a more
integral and holistic way of life. The battle is with dualism in all its
forms, manifested primarily through sexual opposition, but also through
many other aspects of dualistic thinking expressed in concepts such as
body/mind, nature/culture, earth/heaven, black/white, and so on (see
Ruether on 'Androcentrism' in *The Encyclopedia of Religion*, 1987,
vol. 1, pp. 272–6).

Feminist voices criticise all these dualistic divisions and plead for
a new wholeness which can create a more equal and just community
between women and men, a truly full humanity for all. In the words of
Sheila Collins

The wholeness that feminists are proposing is a wholeness based on
a multidimensional vision of the world, rather than on a single vision
which has dominated Western culture and most theological thought.
Such a multidimensional vision means the ability to grasp complexity, to live with ambiguity, and to enjoy the great variety that exists
in the world. Wholeness does not imply the eradication of differences
. . . or . . . the fear of a monotonous unisexual creature. . . . On the
contrary, wholeness of vision may lead to a multiplication of differences, as people are able to choose freely the person they want to be
rather than following a pattern of one they are *expected* to be. Only
through an affirmation and celebration of our differences can we
come to an understanding of the ties that bind the total creation
together. (Collins, 1982, p. 366)

It is precisely this search for wholeness and integration which lies at the heart of spirituality (Zappone, 1991). Seen from a holistic perspective it is painful to discover that most religions are deeply rooted in a patriarchal framework and shaped by an overwhelmingly androcentric point of view. Whilst Christian feminists, for example, have spent much time and effort on reinterpreting the androcentric passages of the Bible, women from other religious traditions, such as Hinduism, Buddhism and Islam are now also beginning to question the androcentric assumptions underlying their traditional religious heritage. This is not surprising as women's consciousness is changing so fast today that more and more women, but more men too, are beginning to recognise what has been called the 'sin of sexism'.

Sexism and the critique of masculinity

Sexism has been defined as an exclusive ordering of life by way of gender. Whilst biological sex is given, gender is socially and culturally constructed and must be learnt. Members of both sexes acquire a gender identity or gendered sense of self which is quite distinct and independent from, and sometimes even opposed to, the biological facts of their sex.

Sexism does not necessarily manifest itself only in an *anti*-woman attitude. It can also be expressed in an inverted manner through being overly flattering and *pro*-woman in certain situations. On closer examination, however, this often turns out to imply a rather condescending and patronising attitude which proves that woman is not really taken seriously as a person in her own right or that her work is acknowledged for its intrinsic worth. This kind of attitude is often found in church circles, especially among clergymen, but equally among art historians (see Parker and Pollock, 1981) and other writers. Goldberg's defence of patriarchy and male dominance, accompanied by paying lip-service to the biological centrality and endurance of women (Goldberg, 1977, p. 193), is another example. Yet the aggressively anti-male attitude of some feminists is just as sexist as the frequent anti-feminist attitudes found among men. In general, however, the word 'sexism' is more often associated with an exclusive attitude towards women than men, as the former is more widespread than the latter.

I do not know who first coined the term 'sexism', but it seems to have been formed in analogy to 'racism'. This is also indicated by the new OED which defines sexism as 'The assumption that one sex is superior to the other and the resultant discrimination practised against members of the supposed inferior sex, especially by men against women; also conformity with the traditional stereotyping of social roles on the basis of sex' (OED, vol. XV, p. 112). The comparison between sexual and racial oppression is often made in feminist writing, but the parallels have their limitations, as Mary Midgley has pointed out: 'For racial disputes there are in principle at least three possible solutions which do not depend on the parties understanding, accepting and learning to live with each other's distinctness. They are assimilation, apartheid and emigration. For sex, there are none' (Midgley and Hughes, 1983, p. 98). The further question arises, of course, whether these three possible solutions offer any genuine solution to interracial strife or whether they represent a further source of it. It seems that for the development of both racial and sexual harmony people have to accept and learn to live with each other's distinctiveness.

At present sexism is endemic in our social, political, educational and religious institutions. Women are kept in subordinate positions almost everywhere whereas men hold most, and often all, positions of authority and power. The sexist premises of all existing disciplines of knowledge are slowly uncovered by many Women's Studies courses which are now developing worldwide. Committed Christian feminists have made great efforts over the years to point out the sexist assumptions in theology and churchlife. In 1974, the World Council of Churches called a consultation of about 170 women from 50 countries to discuss sexism in the churches and examine the discrimination against women among Christians around the world (WCC, 1975). During the opening of that consultation the British theologian Pauline Webb pointed out that sexism is not simply concerned with physical terms, as many people seem to think. She said:

By sexism I take it that we mean any kind of subordination or devaluing of a person or group solely on the grounds of sex. In this sense, it is obviously analogous to racism, and an equally virulent heresy. There was a time when people talked about racism in purely physical terms as though it were all about differences in skin colour. But as we probed it more and more deeply, we discovered much more profound differences – differences of history, culture, identity, and self-understanding. Deepest of all, we traced the entrenchment of racism in the very power structures of society, so that the world today is dominated by white money, white politics, white power.

And the more you think about it, the more you realize that sexism too has these deep ramifications. It is not just a matter of acknowledging physical differences between men and women. . . . It is rather recognizing that alongside this difference there have been different histories, different expectations, a different sense of identity, and an association with the structures of power that have created a male-dominated order in almost all human society and certainly within the Church, making it impossible for the Church to foreshadow the truly human community. (WCC, 1975, p. 10)

Pauline Webb emphasised the need to understand the root causes of sexism and the way it manifests itself in our society today. She also stressed the importance of realising our identity as women and our potential for sharing our experiences with others so that we can bring about a change which will liberate us all. Much of the work of the World Council of Churches in its subsequent project on 'The Community of Women and Men in the Church' has been concerned with getting these aims more widely accepted at a local, regional and international level. Many Christian women from different churches around the world have come together in their work to combat the 'sin of sexism' and put into practice an alternative way of living the Christian gospel. A British example of women's self-examination comes from the Quakers who devoted a whole issue of their journal *The Friends' Quarterly* to 'Sexism and the Society of Friends' (January 1986).

It is not only the churches but many other institutions too which deny full equality and space to women. Such lack of outer and inner space dehumanises women; it warps and maims by not allowing them to develop their full potential – and it harms men too. The feminist protest over sexism, androcentrism and patriarchy implies a critique of countless inequalities and dualities; it also involves a radical rejection of the misconstruction of a traditionally defined femininity. But at its sharpest and most poignant it challenges the very meaning of masculinity in our culture. Feminists (but male critics too) have pointed out that 'the cultural ideal of the competent, aggressive, competitive and emotionally uncommunicative male is a psychological straightjacket which limits men both in their capacity for personal fulfillment and in their moral sensitivity' (Warren, 1980, p. 305).

Feminists see masculinity, as contemporarily understood, practised and projected by the media, as closely associated with the exploitative rape of nature (Griffin, 1984), the manipulative and destructive aspects of analytical science and technology, and the militaristic megalomania of competitive political powers who vie with each other to increase the threat and potential for human extinction. Masculinity is seen to be associated with a falsely praised objectivity which masters and dominates, an instrumental attitude, a cold-blooded, calculating rationality which artificially separates the different spheres of individual and global human experience. Instead of being the human norm for everything, the masculine ideal has become a deformation of being human and is perceived as an ultimate danger for the continuity of life on earth. It is important to recognise that although men may not conform to this as individuals, the negative effects of this masculine ideal nonetheless shape and pervade our culture in countless respects. This trenchant cultural critique finds expression in many aspects of political feminism; moreover, it is an important part of the spiritual side of feminism – of its search for wholeness, integration, balance and sanity in a world wounded by deep divisions.

The feminist cultural critique of the world as it is, with its masculine power structure and competitive spirit, implies a vision of an alternative, a better world which some have characterised as simply utopian. But it needs this utopian quality in order to appeal to and mobilise the creative powers of women and men to bring about the fundamental social change and transformation so urgently required if our highly endangered species is to survive. As Hester Eisenstein has put it:

> But the feminist utopia presents a very different picture, of a society perhaps unrecognizable from where we now stand, but which could emerge, over the very long haul, out of the many changes now being sought by members of the women's movement around the world. In my understanding of the term 'feminist', then, I see an element of visionary, futurist thought. This encompasses a concept of social transformation that, as part of the eventual liberation of women, will change all human relationships for the better. Although centrally about women, their experience, condition or 'estate', . . . feminism is therefore also fundamentally about men, and about social change. (Eisenstein, 1984, p. xiv)

The same author rightly warns against a falsely understood universalism whereby feminists, in their claims about the universal and identical oppression of all women, have been extraordinary facile in their diagnosis through not acknowledging the great diversity of women's experience with regard to race, class, nationality, religion and education at different times and places. Similarly, we must not fall into the trap of a false 'spiritualisation' of the claims of feminism, as if all feminist endeavour had to do with the spiritual goal of self-transcendence and as if there were only one kind of 'spiritual feminism' with clearly perceived aims accepted by all followers. Instead, great diversity reigns here as elsewhere in feminist thought. It is my contention, however, that the multi-faceted feminist enterprise includes many elements which point and pertain to what is traditionally considered as the area of spirituality. If the feminist quest and vision are about wholeness – about how to be wholly and fully human today – if it is about the creative, life-giving powers of individual and social transformation, if it is about the radical revisioning of our ever more complex outer and inner world, then it is at the same time concerned with the dynamics of spiritual experience, growth and liberating fulfilment.

We have looked at the common threads, the shared aims and methods which link all feminists together, even though their political and spiritual options may differ widely and even be exclusive of each other. We must now investigate the specific challenges which feminists voice against many traditional aspects of religion and spirituality. At the same time we must not forget that contemporary feminism includes many creative resources for a rich and powerful spirituality in the modern world. It is this challenge, and its power to nourish and renew the life of the human spirit, which we wish to explore in the chapters that follow.

2

Voices of challenge

'It might seem that the women's revolution should just go about its business of generating a new consciousness, without worrying about God. I suggest that the fallacy involved in this would be an overlooking of a basic question that is implied in human existence and that the pitfall in such an oversight is cutting off the radical potential of the movement itself.

It is reasonable to take the position that sustained effort toward self-transcendence requires keeping alive in one's consciousness the question of ultimate transcendence, that is, God. . . . The new wave of feminism desperately needs to be not only many-faceted but cosmic and ultimately religious in its vision. This means reaching outward and inward toward the God beyond and beneath the gods who have stolen our identity.' – **Mary Daly**, *Beyond God the Father*, pp. 28ff.

Women have always been deeply involved with religious beliefs and practices, but they have rarely held positions of institutional authority in the world religions. Yet many woman in past and present are known for their great moral and spiritual authority which has given them a high status and much prestige within their own community. Many aspects of traditional religion and spirituality have been called into question and deeply challenged by feminist writers. This challenge is not only addressed to religions from without, but also from within, as quite a few women who are strongly committed to a religious faith have developed a growing feminist consciousness. This enables them to criticise religion from within probably more effectively than secular women can do from without.

Women and world religions in a cross-cultural and global perspective

Women have always had a place in religion, but what kind of a place and who determined what that place was to be? By looking at past religious history we can certainly discover a great deal about the image, role and status of women in world religions past and present, and comparative religion scholars have shown considerable interest in the place of women in religion for some time (for example, the German scholar Friedrich Heiler lectured on women in world religions from the 1920s onwards; see Heiler, 1977; also Parrinder, 1980). There is no doubt that such enquiries have brought many data to light which disclose fascinating aspects about women's image, status, and function in ancient and tribal as well as in the great historical religions of the world.

However important and pioneering such studies have been, they appear insufficient and defective from a contemporary feminist point of view. Earlier studies contain much fascinating source material, but they are mainly descriptive without any awareness of feminist consciousness. Thus they give no adequate attention to gender differentiation and do not uncover the patriarchal framework of all religious beliefs and practices. In many ways they only highlight the marginality and invisibility of women as the predominant scholarly perspective remains entirely androcentric. Scholarship on religion still denies full equality and space to women, as do most other disciplines of knowledge. Women are not considered to be a subject or object of study in their own right, but are rather seen and defined from an already given, but unexamined perspective unilaterally established by men.

Thus it is right for contemporary women scholars to call into question much of the accepted interpretation of the history of religions regarding the details of women's participation in and contribution to the past religious history of humankind (Plaskow, Arnold and Romero, 1974; Carmody, 1979; Christ and Plaskow, 1979; Gross, 1977a; King, 1987a; Sharma, 1987; Cooey, Eakin and McDaniel, 1991). This is a growing field where much work still needs to be done, just as much critical analysis is required to challenge the sex-stereotyping in religious education (Trevett, 1983, 1984a). A brief survey of the cross-disciplinary development of feminist theory on women, religion and gender can be found in Constance Buchanan's article 'Women's Studies' in *The Encyclopedia of Religion* (1987; vol. 15, pp. 433–40).

So far, most of the challenge has been addressed to the patriarchal heritage of the Judaeo-Christian tradition, but increasing evidence exists that critical feminist consciousness is growing everywhere around the globe, not only among Jewish and Christian women, but also among women in Hinduism, Buddhism, Islam and other religious traditions. It would be impossible to even attempt a comprehensive survey of recent developments; one could write a separate book on the voices of challenge in each of the world religions. Only a few examples from different religions can be mentioned here in order to illustrate that the feminist challenge to religion must be seen in a global and cross-cultural perspective.

Too many western people mistakenly think that the feminist chal- lenge to Christianity, for example, concerns either the complete rejection of Christian teachings or is primarily about the ordination of women. But the latter is only one particular aspect which has to be seen in a much wider perspective of which even Christian feminists sometimes seem to remain unaware. To realise the extent of the challenge, one has to look at women and world religions in a comparative framework and see how in spite of the many historical, cultural and doctrinal differences of the various religious traditions there are many similarities with regard to women.

It requires courage and the imaginative envisioning of genuine altern- atives to defy the pattern of established traditions. Feminists ask with radical sincerity what in the past of religion is, and remains, usable for women today. This is radicalism in the original sense of the word, in the sense of going back to the roots by returning to the original creative experience in which all religion is grounded. An even greater challenge, however, is posed by the question whether religion can remain meaning- ful at all for women today – whether its spirit is life-giving and em- powering or, on the contrary, deadly and stifling to contemporary women.

Is there *any* room for women in religion? Sometimes one thinks not. It is therefore not surprising that different feminists take a very different stance towards religion. Some reject it outright; they simply see religion as an external institution, authority and power structure which keeps people in a state of dependence and thereby prevents them from ac- quiring autonomy and the will to actively shape their life and take full responsibility for it.

Other feminists, however, have a much deeper insight into the con- tinuing importance of religion in the life of individuals and society. Whilst sharply criticising the negative features, they nonetheless accept certain important parts of religion, especially its spiritually empowering, transforming and healing aspects. But there is a great difference between those feminists who in principle accept the possibility of reforming or revising the sexist characteristics of religion, and others who take a much more revolutionary attitude by seeking religious experience in new religious groups or cults outside the main religious institutions. The important fact which all feminists have in common, whether they be anti-religious, inclined to reform or revolutionary recasting, is the deep conviction that a new spirit is needed, a different approach to symbols, myths and rites capable to reflect and express their new experience of self, world and cosmos today.

The contemporary world is suffering an immense spiritual hunger. In Carl Jung's words people are 'in search of a soul', in search of something that will give them wholeness, a sense of meaning and a purpose which can direct their thoughts and actions. Traditionally much of this whole-ness – of being able to connect and integrate the different experiences of suffering and joy, of growth and diminishment, of being active and passive, of giving and receiving, loving and forgiving – has been grounded in religion as its deepest source and matrix. The springs of faith, whether Jewish, Christian, Muslim, Hindu, Buddhist, Sikh, African, Chinese or Japanese, have given countless millions a pattern and a language with which to make sense of their own selves, of others, of the world around them.

Religious traditions, then, at their strongest, most vital and nourishing – not in their rigidly fossilised forms as we often encounter them now – appeared in the past like a seamless web, a plausible, self-evident whole which made sense and could give meaning and direction to generations. But as the world – the natural world of the cosmos, the human inner world of the self and its uncharted depths, the social world with its pluralistic complexities – has changed so profoundly and so threaten-ingly, and as the sensitivity of our consciousness has changed with it, this seamless web has now been rent apart and lost its unquestioned plausibility and taken-for-grantedness for many, if not most, of those most consciously alive today.

Questions never asked before, problems never encountered in the past, possibilities never envisaged confront us today in most unsettling and perturbing ways. Never before have we sensed the precariousness of our position, the threat to the frailty and dignity of human life, the abyss of life-or-death alternatives with quite the same intensity. This is where feminist consciousness, at its most acute, articulate and critical, acts like a wedge which accentuates and cleaves apart the spiritually powerful from the spiritually empty and pretentious. Feminist consciousness of this kind is not simply one alternative among many, an additional option one can take or leave, but it is a radical transformation of earlier historical perspectives in human consciousness. It is not about the straightforward and somewhat simplistic question 'where are the women?' (as some, even certain feminists, seem to think), of simply adding up numbers on the female side so that once women are 'let in', so to speak, all is well. No, the vision of feminism is much greater, its spirit much stronger and more challenging – and that is why some consider it so threatening.

But if feminism is true to its own holistic perspective, it must strive for the healing of *all* separations, for wholeness and integration wherever needed, not least in the life of the spirit which animates self and society. On these premises, feminism can simply not be separatist, as spirit cannot be divided, but must create and spread a new cosmic web. Whatever attitude is taken towards religion by individual feminists – rejection, reform or revolutionary recreation – the ideas of feminism challenge religion in several important aspects which will now be briefly considered. For the sake of clarity one can group together the numerous voices challenging religion under three different perspectives. The feminist challenge concerns external and internal aspects of religion and implies a progressive level of depth and interiority from the challenge of (1) status, roles and patriarchal institutions to that of (2) exclusive language, androcentric images and symbols in religion to questions regarding (3) the core experience and underlying spirit of a particular religion and the place of women's own religious experience in it. These three concerns frequently overlap in feminist writings, but the challenge possesses both a historical and contemporary dimension as evidence from both past and present is used in the debate.

Women's roles and status in religious institutions

What status and roles do particular religions assign to women? What are the patterns of participation or exclusion from ritual and liturgy? What kind of religious authority can women wield in what kind of religious institution? Are women given equal status in the religious life, i.e. in the priesthood, where it exists, and in various forms of monasticism?

Here the challenge is about the lack of official recognition, the absence of power and status in visible hierarchies, the subservient and frequently invisible role played by many women and the blatant sexism of religious institutions throughout the world.

A cross-cultural historical study of the role and status of women in different religious traditions shows that the less differentiated religion and society are, the greater is the participation of women (Heiler, 1977; Carmody, 1979). The most institutionalised a religion becomes, the more it generally excludes women from positions of authority and power. Thus it is true on the whole that women hold higher positions in archaic, ancient, tribal and relatively non-institutionalised forms of religion (such as shamanism, possession rites, spiritualism, or in non-hierarchical groups such as the Quakers) than in the highly differentiated religious traditions with their complex structures. In both primitive and ancient religions we find the widespread presence of women magicians, shamans, healers, visionaries and seers, prophetesses and priestesses. (For numerous cross-cultural examples of female shamanism see Mühlmann, 1984.) Female visionaries played an important part in Germanic religion, and the women oracles of ancient Greece are equally well known. So are the *sibyls*, the prophetesses and fortune-tellers, considered to be the mouthpiece of a particular god.

Female temple priests and attendants existed in Egypt, Sumeria, Babylonia, Greece and ancient Japan. Roman religion knew the vestals, the consecrated virgins charged with the perpetual care of the sacred fire in the temple of the goddess Vesta. Women's role in the religion of Rome has been summarised as follows:

Women played an essential part in the celebration of Roman religion. The wife shared responsibility with her husband for supervising the household cult. Apart from the Vestal Virgins, whose function was official and important, the wives of two of the major priests were themselves priestesses. Women had cults and ceremonies from which men were excluded (and vice versa). . . . The Christian practice keeping women away from the altar was to be a departure from Roman custom. (O'Faolain and Martines, 1979, p. 88)

In another quite different religion, the Shinto religion of Japan, women have held and still hold important positions. These were admittedly much higher in ancient times, in primitive Shinto, than in the subsequent shrine and sect Shinto, but they are still of considerable significance in contemporary popular Shinto, the religion of the people. A recent study of the position of women in Shinto states:

> Woman appears in Shinto as a female deity, a virgin, empress and ruler, priestess, cult dancer, founder of sects and as a 'shaman' out-side the organised system of Shintoism. These female figures have in common a special relationship with the deity, based largely on the experience of ecstasy. They have always been, and are still, called *Mikos*, literally 'children of God'. This term means a mediator be-tween the gods and men, and is used to designate not only the lower order of priestesses in Shinto shrines and women unconnected with any shrine claiming religious and magical powers, but women in general, who because of their charism have played an important part in religious life from primitive times to the present day. (Okano, 1976, p. 206)

It is undoubtedly a challenge to women that none of the great founders of religion was a woman. Moses, Mahavira, Buddha, Zoroaster, Jesus, Muhammad – all are men. But women founders exist in more recently established religions, especially in sects and cults, and in new religious movements in Japan, India and the West. There is also the remarkable phenomenon that an extraordinary number of important women seem to surround at least some of the male founders of religion. At the time of a new religious breakthrough when a charismatic personality – an enlight-ened being – shapes a new way of life, much is questioned and, one might almost say, new seeds of liberation are sown. In such a period of flux women, in their support of new movements of reform or radical renewal, often have greater freedom than is customary in their environ-ment and play a crucial role in the early development of a religion. One can think of the many outstanding women in the history of ancient Israel (Nunnally-Cox, 1981, pp. 3–96) or of the women surrounding Jesus (Moltmann-Wendel, 1982; Nunnally-Cox, 1981, pp. 97–117) or the Buddha (Horner, 1975; Paul, 1979) or Muhammad whose spouse played a decisive role in early Islam and whose daughter, Fatima, occu-pies an eminent position among Shia Muslims.

The earlier, more undifferentiated religions – whether prehistoric, archaic or tribal – all share a primal vision characterised by a unitary consciousness within which self, society and nature still form a continuum, an uninterrupted whole. The historical religions, with their break-through to individual, reflexive consciousness, lost this basic unity and are all shaped by a fundamental dualism affecting time (past/present; present/future) and space (sacred/profane), cosmos (earth/heaven), self (body/spirit) and society (men/women). From their early origin the historical religions have been male-dominated, cast in a dualistic and patriarchal spirit. With the institutionalisation of religious roles and functions sacred authority, like secular authority, came to rest in men. The exercise of most religious functions, whether sacrifice, teaching, preaching, blessing or initiation, became a male prerogative almost everywhere. We can observe such developments in ancient Mithraism as much as in Brahmanism (where we know of women seers in the early period of the Vedas and Upanishads), Judaism, Christianity and Islam.

The regressive participation of women in religious life historically manifests itself in two different ways. First, there is the general decline of the oracular, prophetic and priestly activities of women if one compares the situation of ancient cultures with that of more recent times. Then there is the specific regression of female religious activity in particular religions if one compares the creative time of a founder with the practices of subsequent ages. Where women founded their own religious communities to follow the highest spiritual ideals of their religion, as did the nuns in Buddhism and Christianity, they were always given lower status than the male religious.

It comes as no surprise that women from very different religious backgrounds today find inspiration and strength in the rich historical data available now on the religious activities of women in the past. They use these materials to challenge existing religious authorities and structures by demanding full participation as well as public recognition of the many-sided and varied work already done by women in religious institutions. Buddhist nuns in the Theravada tradition strongly request the right to full ordination in Sri Lanka and Thailand; in the Mahayana tradition women ask for full recognition as Zen masters (Bancroft, 1987). Hindu women have established the right to recite the Vedas and follow the path of renunciation (*sannyasa*) traditionally closed to them; some also campaign to be gurus in their own right (King, 1984b).

Unless anyone might think that the demands of women's liberation only influence the religious lives of western women, here is a quotation from the 1974–6 Report of a Hindu religious order of women, the Sri Sarada Math, founded as an innovation in 1954:

During the last hundred years women in the West have re-orientated themselves, and the fruits of their labours are now enjoyed by women everywhere in the world. Women, so long regarded, by themselves as well as by men, as inferior, weak and somehow not fully adult, now play a different role as partners and co-sharers.

The rise of woman may be seen as an event of far-reaching significance, an event which links up with the chain of circumstances that characterize the present era and act as propelling forces in shaping the future. . . .

The rise of woman, in both East and West, and also the founding of the Sri Sarada Math, must be viewed in this context. . . . The Sri Sarada Math is part of woman's rise to strength; it is also part of the tidal wave of spirituality set in motion by Sri Ramakrishna and Swami Vivekananda. [Important reformers of modern Hinduism] (Sri Sarada Math, 1974–6, pp. 3, 4, 5)

Whilst Hindu women ascetics are in a tiny minority when compared with the large number of male ascetics in Hinduism, the number of Catholic nuns both in India and in the Roman Catholic Church worldwide is known to be three times larger than that of male religious and priests taken together. Yet women in the churches, and in the Roman Catholic Church in particular, have always been kept in a dependent status. In the words of Susan Dowell and Linda Hurcombe (1981), Christian women have been and still are 'dispossessed daughters of Eve'.

Over recent years, many campaigns have been undertaken to counter-act the public invisibility and lack of recognition of women in the Christian churches. The Movement for the Ordination of Women has gained considerable support in Britain and elsewhere and it represents an important challenge to the established institutions and structures. But the challenge goes much deeper too, as the same authors clearly stated:

we find ourselves continuing to debate the importance of the symbol of female priesthood in the healing role of the church. We began with a question – 'Why?'. Why is the church the last place to initiate the true feminization of the moral order enshrined in its gospel? Why is the church the last place to make the equality of men and women a reality in its structures? (Dowell and Hurcombe, 1981, pp. 112ff.)

To many the issue about the ordination of women appears to be a predominantly contemporary one – and so it is in the larger Christian churches, whether Anglican, Roman Catholic or Orthodox. But many smaller Christian denominations have been far more flexible and innovative at an earlier stage. One must not forget that the first Christian woman minister, the Reverend Antoinette L. Brown, was ordained by the Congregational Church in New York in September 1853. Forty years later, at the famous World Parliament of Religions in Chicago (1893) – the first global gathering of members of different faiths – a considerable number of women speakers took part, seven of whom were ordained ministers. But there must have been considerably more, for by 1921 when Reverend Antoinette Brown died, it was estimated that there were more than three thousand women ministers in the United States (Deen, 1959, p. 396).

These women must have made a considerable impact at the parish level, as did the numerous women from many nations who worked in the mission field abroad and made an essential contribution to Christian missionary activities during the nineteenth and twentieth centuries. By 1928, Methodist women missionaries were talking about 'a world missionary sisterhood' (*A Centennial Tapestry*, 1983, p. 3). Then, as now, women were active in the work of the churches at the grassroots level, but received little public recognition for it. They were also excluded from the main institutions of theological education. This only changed significantly after the Second World War when theology courses became more widely available to lay people in general and to women in particular.

Traditionally, most religions have excluded women from advanced learning and teaching (King, 1987c). Hindu women were not allowed to study the Vedas, just as Jewish women were excluded from studying the Torah and Talmud, which were indispensable for becoming a rabbi. For a very long time Christian women had no access to theological faculties and seminaries. In the USA, Oberlin College allowed a few women to attend its theological school in the 1840s, and some Methodist and Congregational seminaries had a few women students by the late nineteenth century whilst Harvard Divinity School did not admit women until the 1950s (Ruether, 1981b).

During the last thirty years, the number of women theology students has risen exponentially. In many theology courses in the West more than half and sometimes the overriding majority are women. The increasing participation of women in theological debate is one of the crucial factors in understanding the rise of feminism within Christianity and Judaism. To have become theologically literate, however, has brought the inequality and injustice of religious institutions towards women into even sharper relief.

Reformed Judaism ordained its first woman rabbi in the USA in 1972. Ten years later there were already 61 women rabbis and by 1986 their figure had increased to 131. Now even conservative Judaism which opposed the idea for so long has several women rabbis.

' Christian women participate to a greater, though still not sufficient, extent in the work of those churches which ordain women ministers. Women theologians are still in a minority among their peers but they do speak up, not only in the West, but also in Asia (Chatterji, 1979; Katoppo, 1979; Fabella and Oduyoye, 1988; Fabella and Lee Park, 1989; Chung, 1991a) as well as in South Africa (Vorster, 1984). The feminist challenge does not only concern itself with the role and status of women in religious institutions, but calls into question the very concepts, images and symbols embedded in religious language and thought.'

Women in religious language and thought

The power of naming is one of the most decisive human activities in constituting the world as experienced. That power has been an almost exclusive male prerogative throughout most of human history. This power is well illustrated by the Jewish-Christian story of Adam (Genesis 2:19–20) whom God empowered to name all the animals after their creation, which occurred before the creation of Eve. Contemporary feminists rightly claim the power of naming as one of their most fundamental rights for expressing and shaping their own experience and worldview which, in turn, includes the power of transformation. As Mary Daly has powerfully declared,

> it is necessary to grasp the fundamental fact that women have had the power of *naming* stolen from us. We have not been free to use our own power to name ourselves, the world, or God. The old naming was not the product of dialogue . . . partial and inadequate words have been taken as adequate.
>
> To exist humanly is to name the self, the world, and God. The 'method' of the evolving spiritual consciousness of women is nothing less than this beginning to speak humanly – that is, a reclaiming of the right to speak. (Daly, 1974b, p. 130)

Much re-examination is going on regarding the language used in religious teaching, preaching and ritual. It is helpful to distinguish between religious language which makes wide use of images and symbols appealing to emotion and imagination, and theological language which primarily relies on abstract concepts and systematic ordering of thought arising out of critical reflection on religious experience (McFague, 1983). Thus religious and theological language are closely intertwined and yet distinct and quite different in their approach. It is perhaps not too large a generalisation to say that religious language, as found in prayers, songs, devotions, utterances of prophets and seers, and in the accounts of saints and mystics of all religions, is closer to its experiential source. It is thus more open to female imagery and experience than the language of systematised theological doctrine which is always closely controlled by reasoning rather than spontaneity. Theological language represents, without exception, the creation of a male specialist group, whether Brahmans, priests, rabbis, monks or whoever.

In examining religious thought and language one can begin by asking what different religions affirm about women in their sacred scriptures and doctrines. What language do they use in prayers, liturgy and ritual, and how far is this exclusive and anti-feminist? Moreover, can we find examples of female imagery and symbolism, especially in reflections on the nature of the Spirit and Ultimate Reality?

At the heart of the different world faiths there is always the challenge of the spirit in the form of a promise for true liberation and salvation which ultimately transcends sexual divisions. This is the most powerful challenge of all, and one can always ask how far members of each religion do or do not live up to this challenge of the spirit. The belief in the possibility of spiritual equality has been put as little into practice as the teaching about the fundamental oneness of the human community. How often have the ideals of spirituality been taught and practised to the detriment and exclusion of women? One can apply to all religions what has been said about the Christian church, namely, that they possess the message of liberation, but it is others who liberate.

The scriptures of all the world religions – even those which assign a relatively high status to women – contain passages expressing the subordination or inferiority of women, even when the language is not explicitly anti-feminist. Contemporary women look at the different sacred scriptures in a new light and re-examine their teachings in a critical perspective. The most radical critique has been applied to the sacred literature of the Jewish-Christian tradition, especially to the Bible. Most famous is the pioneering effort of the American woman Elizabeth Cady Stanton (1815–1902; see Griffith, *In Her Own Right. The Life of Elizabeth Cady Stanton*, 1984) who took the radical measure of cutting out all anti-feminist passages in her 1898 edition of *The Woman's Bible* (new edition 1985). This was highly criticised and misunderstood at the time, but has been rightly celebrated by more recent feminists for its daring innovation. Contemporary critics use a more differentiated approach in reinterpreting biblical materials by reflecting on the underlying principles of a feminist critical interpretation (see Russell, *Feminist Interpretation of the Bible* (1985); Schüssler Fiorenza, 1983, 1984). They realise that an effective critique of biblical passages must be more concerned with 'depatriarchalizing' the Bible (Trible, 1978b) and 'reconstructing' tradition as customarily taught (Christ and Plaskow, 1979, pp. 131–92; Schüssler Fiorenza, 1983) than with simply cutting out passages which appear unacceptable to women.

Both Jewish and Christian feminists have written on the reinterpretation of the creation story in the book of Genesis, chapters 1 and 2. The figure of Eve in that story has had a far more wide-reaching influence in Christianity than Judaism because of the particular interpretation given to these chapters by early Christian writers. According to a later Jewish tradition the woman whose creation is mentioned first in Genesis 1:27 was not called Eve, but Lilith, said to be Adam's first wife whilst Eve was his third. Lilith insisted on full equality with Adam because of their identical origin (the Genesis passage reads 'God created man in his own image, in the image of God he created him, male and female he created them'). When Adam did not agree to this, Lilith left him in protest and even a group of angels sent by God was unable to make her return. It is hardly surprising that the future of Lilith has caught the imagination of contemporary Jewish feminists. An American Jewish feminist magazine is called after her, and Judith Plaskow has retold the story of Lilith from a contemporary perspective bringing Lilith and Eve together for 'Lilith by herself is in exile and can do nothing. The real heroine of our story is sisterhood, and sisterhood is powerful' (see Plaskow, 'The Coming of Lilith: Toward a Feminist Theology' in Christ and Plaskow, 1979, pp. 198–209).

Much has been written by both Jewish and Christian authors on women in the Bible. The numerous female figures in the Hebrew Bible and New Testament can truly be regarded by contemporary women in the Judaeo-Christian tradition as 'foremothers' of the faith whether they are the matriarchal figures of Sarah, Hagar, Rachel or Rebecca, the women of the Exodus and Promised Land, such as Miriam, Deborah or Delilah, women of the times of the prophets (Ohler, 1987), or women closely associated with Jesus and his disciples (Nunnally-Cox, 1981; Dumais, 1985; Moloney, 1985). By examining the stories and language of the Bible, Torah and Talmud, and the ideas found in the ideological works of the so-called Church Fathers, feminist scholars have discovered many new data which were unknown or simply overlooked before (Aspegren, 1990; Børresen, 1991). Similarly, the language and thought of other scriptures, whether Hindu, Buddhist, Jain, Muslim, Sikh, Japanese or Chinese, require critical re-examination from a feminist perspective, but this has happened only to a limited extent so far.

What images of women can be found in the sacred literature of the world faiths? On comparing writings from different religious traditions two distinct types of images can be met in quite different religions (Gross, 1974). One is the mother image which can often be seen as arising out of male religious activity and projection, as it is an image closely bound up with the fertility and sexuality of women. The other is a non-maternal image which Rita Gross, for want of a better word, simply calls the mate-image. This woman-mate is seen as co-eval and independent or as complementary to males, but not as their adjunct.

The mate image tends to occur in religions where the co-participation of men and women in religious activities is also present, whereas the mother image is linked to religions with much greater sexual exclusiveness and division where women do not take part in ritual. These images relate closely to the way in which both profanity and sacrality are projected on to women. Thus women reflect in a particular way the ambiguity of the sacred so central to many religions where the sacred is a locus of tremendous power which is experienced as immensely attractive and terrifying at the same time.

It has been said that religions are the most important source for shaping and enforcing the image and role of women in culture and society. One must therefore enquire most carefully which images of woman a particular religion has created and handed down from generation to generation, and how far these may be beset with inherent contradictions. One must also ask in what way these images, especially when they are highly idealised and praised, such as the image of Mary in Christianity or that of Sita in Hinduism, may possibly relate to the actual lives and experiences of real women. Some important images of woman in the Jewish and Christian traditions are discussed in the volume on

Religion and Sexism edited by Rosemary Radford Ruether (1974b). The images of woman in the religions of classical antiquity have also been closely examined (Pomeroy, 1976, 1984; Cameron and Kuhrt, 1983; Goodison, 1990) and an increasing amount of work is being done on women in non-western traditions, especially women in India (Jacobson and Wadley, 1977; Leslie, 1989, 1991) and in African traditional religions (Hackett, 1985; Gaba, 1987; Mbon, 1987).

In the theological anthropology of Christianity the biblical affirmation that God created woman and man in the divine image has always been and still is of fundamental importance. Every human being is considered to reflect the *imago dei*. But the interpretation of the Genesis passages on which this belief is based has often been conducted in a most exclusive and anti-feminist manner. Real women in history have been 'not in God's image' (see the title of O'Faolain and Martines, 1979) but rather in man's.

From the earliest days of Christianity male theologians adopted a defective anthropology, largely based on Aristotle's biologically wrong understanding of women as being incomplete males (Horowitz, 1976). Traditional theological sexology – a term used by some writers to describe the theological understanding of the nature and meaning of the two sexes – has been thoroughly androcentric, as a number of studies have demonstrated (Bailey, 1959; Børresen, 1977, 1981). Christian anthropology, i.e. the Christian teaching about the nature of the human being, has not paid sufficient attention to the meaning of sexual differentiation. The 'Christian doctrine of man', as this aspect of theology is still often called, quite literally has been most of the time a doctrine *about man* and *for man* in the sense of the human male. It can be quite appropriately described as 'an anthropology of female inferiority' (Dowell and Hurcombe, 1981, p. 85). The Norwegian woman theologian Kari Børresen writes:

> Traditional theological sexology is androcentric in the sense that man is considered the exemplary human being (*vir = homo*) and woman (*femina*) is defined as differing from this norm. With this assumption, the biblical creation and fall are interpreted as follows: being created in God's image (Gen. I, 27), woman is spiritually equivalent with man (*femina = homo*). But as sexually different, she is created from and for man (Gen. II, 18–24; . . . .) As a community in this world, the church maintains the God-willed subordination of woman as *femina*;

her full equivalence as *homo* will be realized only in the final resurrection. (1977, p. 32)

In other words, in the Christian tradition woman has been seen as subordinate to man in the order of creation, in the here and now. However, in the order of redemption, the order to come, the spiritual equivalence of man and woman has always been taught and affirmed as an article of faith. As is stated in a passage of the Letter to the Galatians much loved and quoted by Christian feminists: 'There is neither Jew nor Greek, there is neither slave nor foe, there is neither male nor female; for you are all one in Christ Jesus' (Gal. 3:28).

But this statement of equivalence, of spiritual equality, which could be matched by others, must be set against many other biblical passages, especially in St Paul, which express the subordination of woman. The entire Bible is characterised by what George Tavard, in his study *Woman in Christian Tradition* (1973), has called the 'double typology of womanhood'. Quotations from scripture are tied to a profound ambiguity as some express subordination and others the full equality of women. However, in the past male interpreters of the Bible have in general preferred to dwell on those passages which can be used to reinforce woman's status of subordination and dependence. A contemporary French theologian has analysed the inherent anti-feminism of much Christian teaching (Aubert, 1975) and speaks about a 'masculinising exegesis' whereby theologians have used passages of the Bible to legitimise the marginalisation of women in terms of their sexual function. This double typology still affects much Christian thinking on women as is evident from an examination of Catholic, Orthodox and Protestant images of womanhood still widely prevalent in Christian churches today (Tavard, 1973, pp. 125–86).

Much that is taught on the image and nature of woman is deeply rooted in a dualistic perspective which sharply divides and opposes to each other the realms of body and mind, nature and spirit, woman and man, earth and heaven. This is not only characteristic of the Judaeo-Christian tradition but runs through all the world religions in one way or another. On one hand there is always a search for wholeness inherent in the quest for the spirit, yet on the other hand much religious teaching is not holistic, but dualistic. The theological issues pertaining to the search for human wholeness and identity have been most thoroughly investigated by 'The Community of Women and Men in the Church', a study group set up by the World Council of Churches in Geneva and supported by worldwide participation (see Parvey, 1983; also the section on 'Women in Church and society' in WCC, 1983, *Nairobi to Vancouver*). In 1980, this group organised a special consultation for women to re-examine the Christian teaching on the image of God and human wholeness. Much of the material brought together then was published under the title *In God's Image: Reflections on Identity, Human Wholeness and the Authority of Scripture* (Crawford and Kinnamon, 1983). The testimonies, poems and reflections of women collected in this small volume provide an excellent basis for group discussions.

The symbol or, as some would say, myth of Eve is still a powerful one in western culture. For many women today it stands for the oppression and subordination of women through past centuries. The images and symbols relating to women are deeply embedded in our language and it is part of the feminist task to deconstruct language in order to highlight its underlying assumptions. For theological language this is increasingly being done, but Christian women also make great efforts to eradicate the many examples of sexist language in rites, hymns and liturgy (Morley, 1984, 1988; Morley and Ward, 1986; Winter, 1987, 1991). However, the symbol of Eve is still so powerful that a German publication calls feminists 'God's new Eve' (Lüthi, 1978). How Christian women through the ages have been oppressed by the story of Eve is symbolically shown by a small sculpture in the Catholic Faculty of the University of Nijmegen (Netherlands) which represents Eve bent to the ground under the weight of a huge apple on her back. Symbols and language are powerful indeed.

We must be aware of the inherent dynamics of language and the way it may be used to persuade, to evoke, challenge or provoke. Language is one of the primary human tools to establish communication and thereby make community and communion possible – or to prevent it by enforcing boundaries, erecting barriers and false dividing lines. The new language of sisterhood aims to establish new links, new connections, and thereby to create a new sense of community and ultimately a new culture. Many feminist writers have addressed the issues of language and gender. From the perspective of religion one of the most important issues is the language used about Ultimate Reality itself which sustains and nourishes us all the way of participation (see the section on 'Feminine Language and Imagery in Constructs of Ultimacy: Cross-Cultural Examples and Theological Proposals' in Gross, 1977a).

For the Judaeo-Christian tradition this reality has always been named as God and although always asserted to be utterly beyond all names and sexual divisions, God has been customarily referred to by the pronoun 'he' and described as 'father', even though images of mother and lover are not absent in the tradition, and are of great importance in some mystical literature and writings on spirituality. Many recent writers have examined the association of the father image with God (see *Concilium* 143 [1981], 'God as Father?') and its implications for the image of woman. The most iconoclastic effort in this direction is the radical stance of Mary Daly's *Beyond God the Father* (1974a) which has provoked a great deal of debate in theological and feminist circles. The issue has perhaps less to do with a particular image as such than with its exclusive and oppressive interpretations in terms of justifying patriarchy as a social system. If God is nothing but the ultimate patriarch, the dreadful authoritarian father figure, then this symbol may well be dead and not be speaking to our contemporaries any more.

However, often enough particular interpretations as well as critiques of the divine father image are based on a false literalness in assigning a rather restricted meaning to a particular word outside the wider context of images, symbols and metaphors in which the entire God-talk is rooted and embedded. One has to be particularly sensitive to many levels of meaning and especially to different models of God or the Divine found in religious language (Chopp, 1989; Wren, 1989). The image of God the father has been more than any other the dominant model in Christianity. Thus the question arises whether the feminist critique of God the father calls into question the root-metaphor of Christianity and whether the Christian tradition possesses resources both for limiting the model of God the father and for permitting complementary models. However, Sallie McFague in her study *Metaphorical Theology. Models of God in Religious Language* (1983) argues that 'the root-metaphor of Christianity is not God the father but the kingdom or rule of God, a relationship between the divine and the human that *no* model can encompass. The divine-human relationship, therefore, demands both the limitation of the fatherhood model and the introduction of other models' (McFague, 1983, p. 146; see also McFague, 1987).

A similar idea is expressed by Rosemary Ruether when she asks:

How can we think about God in new ways that are not sexist? Should we say that God is female rather than male, or both male and female? Maybe we have to go deeper than this. We have to ask why it is that the symbolic relationship of God to the world has been seen in terms of domination and subjugation and so provides a model for a similar social relationship. Can we think of divine transcendence in another way? God's transcendence could be seen not as a 'power over' that reduces creation to a servant status. Rather, it could be seen as the ground and power for created being to exist and to be continually renewed. God is thus both the ground of being and its continual power for aspiration to new being. (Ruether, 1979a, pp. 64ff)

The theological question is really about what the divine father symbolism implies, which aspects of it are utterly misleading or redundant, and which elements we cannot possibly do without. An excessive and impoverishing literalism is evident when some authors argue in a rather unsophisticated way whether God is man or woman. It is far more helpful for contemporary women to explore the feminine dimensions or aspects of God, whether expressed in biblical imagery or other similes relating to specifically female activities such as giving birth, suckling an infant, nurturing and caring or mothering in a wider sense. Many biblical passages, especially in the Hebrew Bible, use specific images of female personhood and activity to illuminate God's own being and doing. Although God is nowhere directly addressed as 'Mother', Isaiah likens God's saving activity to a mother giving birth to a child. Elsewhere God is likened to the protective mother bird or the mother eagle, the midwife or nurse, or to a mother quieting and comforting her child (see Alan E. Lewis's report *The Motherhood of God* prepared for the General Assembly of the Church of Scotland, 1984).

God's activity is not only linked to female imagery, but also to certain words of feminine gender. The Hebrews believed that God was present and acted in the world through his teaching (*torah*), wisdom (*chokmah*), his indwelling presence (*shekinah*), his spirit (*ruah*), mercy and compassion (*rehem*). These are all nouns of feminine gender and the most interesting is the word 'spirit' which remained feminine in its Greek translation 'sophia', but became neuter in the Greek word 'pneuma' and masculine in the Latin 'spiritus'. There are some important Judaeo-Christian speculations on Sophia as Wisdom Goddess, especially in the documents found at Nag Hammadi (Egypt) in 1945, produced by early gnostic groups. It has been argued that the teaching of Sophia in the Wisdom Goddess tradition was masculinised in the name of Jesus Christ (Arthur, 1984, 1987) and suppressed in the New Testament writings.

In recent years, much effort has been devoted to showing how the dominant affirmation of the fatherhood of God is complemented in the

Christian tradition by a whole spectrum of appellations and images relating to the experience of women, especially to motherhood. Julian of Norwich's invocation of Jesus as 'our true Mother' is often quoted. Much less well known are the expressions of other women such as, for example, Mary Baker Eddy, the nineteenth-century foundress of Christian Science, who objected to the sole use of 'Father' as a designation for God and replaced it by 'our Father-Mother God' (Trevett, 1984b). Carol Ochs (1983) has explored with much sensitivity the whole process of infant care and mothering as profounding nourishing our spiritual life whereas Margaret Hebblethwaite, in her book *Motherhood and God* (1984), has drawn on the experience of giving birth as a theological resource for thinking about God (for a critique see Pepper and Hebblethwaite, 1984).

Yet this line of thought is not without inherent contradictions as will become apparent when we look at mother goddesses in a later chapter (see ch. 5). The Anglican theologian John Robinson pointed out long ago that the association of God with motherhood is problematic for contemporary women as it does not so much express the autonomy and adulthood of women as persons in their own right as underline the very role women have been traditionally restricted to and limited by. In wider terms the entire father–mother symbolism with regard to God enforces a parent image for all people and can be seen as a dominant, hierarchical model of God which keeps human beings in a state of dependence as 'children of God'. This parental image of divine reality, however rich in some respects, may be as unhelpful to us today as some other models of God as lord, master and judge. Our egalitarian age is more inspired by images which stress autonomy, independence and equality, such as God the liberator, friend or lover (McFague, 1987). If family relationships are used as analogies for divine–human relationships, the sister–brother or wife–husband image may be more appropriate than the parent–child one.

If we consider the vast resources of religious traditions other than Christianity, we can find very different approaches to Ultimate Reality. In the devotional theology of theistic Hinduism we can find the parental analogy for God, but much is made of God as lover and friend. More important in our context, Hinduism knows the immense power of *Shakti*, the divine cosmic energy which is always thought of as female. There is a strong tradition of goddess worship in Hinduism. This implies profound ambiguities, however, especially at village level where the *matas*, the local goddesses, have to be appeased in numerous ways. The great

Goddess, called *Devi*, appears in many different forms. For those who see in her the highest form of divinity she is the source of all existence, the supreme power which is also represented as consciousness and knowledge. Without this power or *Shakti* the gods are dead, inactive and unknown. It is thought that the origin of the worship of the Goddess goes back to pre-vedic times (before the second millenium BCE) as the Vedas, the scriptures of Hinduism, reflect a strongly patriarchal society with predominantly male gods.

In some Hindu texts the knowledge of the universe is a transcendent knowledge identical with the forms of the all-powerful Goddess. Thus the Goddess is sometimes described as 'knowledge-of-the-Immensity', mother of the universe, pervading the whole world. She is also called 'the Resplendent-One'. Gujaratis worship the Mother Goddess as Ambaji whilst Bengalis address her as Durga and both groups celebrate each year an elaborate festival in her honour. The symbol of divine energy or *Shakti* linked to the 'Mother' played an important role in Indian nationalism and the independence movement when the Goddess came to stand for the country and her power (Ratte, 1985). It is equally interesting that in Mahayana Buddhism supreme wisdom or *Prajnaparamita*, the 'Perfection of Wisdom', is not only feminine in name, but is also represented by many feminine statues and images, although she is not worshipped as a goddess. This feminine principle is wisdom as supreme compassion rescuing human beings from ignorance and suffering. Faith in her will lead her follower to liberation. The Buddhist scholar Edward Conze has described her as follows:

> Like a woman, the 'Perfection of Wisdom' deserves to be courted and wooed, and the Sutras on Perfect Wisdom constitute one long love affair with the Absolute. Meditation on her as a goddess has the purpose of getting inside her, identifying oneself with her, becoming her. . . . And in her ultimate core the *Prajnaparamita* is described as for ever elusive, not possessed by anyone, but absorbing all. (Quoted in Bancroft, 1987, pp. 90, 91)

Whilst the personification of wisdom as feminine, whether as *Prajnaparamita*, *Sophia* or *Shakti*, can be inspiring for contemporary women, one must ask how far these speculations are entirely of male origin and remained exclusively accessible to males in the past. How far has the existence of goddesses, whether in Hinduism, Japanese Shinto, in ancient Near Eastern or African religions had any influence on the lives of actual women, not in the sense of their devotion to these figures, but in terms of real empowerment enhancing women's role and status in society?

If religion is about more than outward ritual or sophisticated doctrinal speculations, if it is the voice of prayer, praise and communion, or the centre point of meditation and true inwardness, if it is about that transformative power that sustains life, nourishes and heals it with the energy of the spirit, then we must in the end come to the question of religious experience and enquire how far the undoubtedly powerful religious experiences of women are expressed and reflected in the practices and teaching of the different religious traditions. The ultimate challenge is about the nature and depth of experience, but also about the question whether religion as traditionally understood and practised can remain meaningful to contemporary women.

Women and religious experience

Ever since William James published his work *Varieties of Religious Experience* in 1902, the phenomenon of religious experience has been much discussed and studied, but until recently relatively little attention has been paid to gender differences. 'Experience' is a difficult term to define. Sociologists as well as scholars of comparative religion have attempted to classify religious experiences according to important variables such as the intensity of particular experiences, their connection with a time dimension pointing to past, present or future, or the relationship which individual experiences bear to the wider social order.

The word 'experience' can refer to a cumulative insight and understanding gained over a span of time (for example, when we speak of 'work experience') or it can mean a sudden event or encounter (the experience of shock, surprise, sudden joy or of someone's death). In the area of religion, too, many examples can be found of the prolonged, continued nature of experience and of its sudden occurrence or breakthrough. Thus much religious experience is related to continuing religious practice such as prayer, going to church, temple or mosque, performing rituals at regular intervals, etc. This may be considered the ordinary kind of experience which represents religious experience most of the time. However, the term 'religious experience' is often especially connected with the idea of extraordinary experiences such as ecstatic or mystic experiences. The question arises then how far this kind of experience is different from ordinary human experience, whether it represents a sharp break from it or whether, on the contrary, it is part of a wider range of possible experiences which form a continuum.

In order to analyse religious experience and define it more sharply, it has often been asked what is significant in religious experience? This question already sets religious experience apart as something separate to be investigated, but a number of writers turn the question around and ask instead 'What in our experience is religiously significant?' In other words, they explore human experience as it occurs, whether in ordinary or extraordinary garb, and ask about the deeper meaning it has for the lives of particular individuals and communities.

The question about the religious significance of contemporary women's experience concerns us throughout this book and will be discussed in more detail later. As to a clearer gender differentiation in the study of religious experience, contemporary women writers have investigated both ordinary and extraordinary aspects of women's religious experience. For example, Pat Holden in her introduction to the volume of papers on *Women's Religious Experience: Cross-Cultural Perspectives* (1983) distances herself from what she calls the 'exceptional' women in religion and emphasises that her book gives particular attention 'to the everyday religious experiences of ordinary women', whether in England, Greece, Turkey, Africa, Hinduism or Judaism. Another approach is found in the anthology edited by Rosemary Ruether and Eleanor McLaughlin, *Women of Spirit: Female Leadership in the Jewish and Christian Traditions* (1979). Here women are considered who were in many ways extraordinary in the spiritual authority and power they wielded in particular communities and the religious example they set to others. Contemporary women speak about the varieties of their religious experience in *Sex and God* edited by Linda Hurcombe (1987). Yet another approach is exemplified in the studies edited by Nancy A. Falk and Rita M. Gross, *Unspoken Worlds: Women's Religious Lives in Non-Western Cultures* (1980) where are brought together different data about women's religious experience which highlight 'the contrast between extraordinary callings and everyday concerns in women's religious lives' (1980, p. xv). The two editors state clearly that at our present state of awareness it is no longer enough to know how religions view women. In order to discover new and meaningful religious worlds and recover lost data, one has to look at the religious lives and experiences of women themselves:

Since most religions' views of women have been recorded and shaped by men, the study of these views all too easily becomes an extension of androcentrism.

To offer a new vision, our volume had to take up women's lives; it had to place women in center stage – as men had been placed so often in the past – and meet them as subjects, not objects, with their own experiences and aspirations. . . . We had to show that women have their own perspectives and claims on religion, even in systems in which men have traditionally done most of the acting and talking . . . we would explore the so-far unspoken religious worlds of women rather than the much more familiar religious worlds of men. (1980, p. xiv)

Women have always been conspicuous in some areas of religious practice such as domestic ritual or shamanistic and possession rituals or in the rise of new religious movements. What is more, women have made a very substantial and most important contribution to the mystical and spiritual literature of world religions, yet their own views are rarely reflected in the systematised articulations of theology or even the recent works of scholarship in religious studies. As in other areas of our culture this scholarship, concerned with *homo religiosus*, focuses in practice quite literally on religious *man* – the males of religious communities who have always held the dominant positions of institutional authority. And yet there are few religious traditions, if any, where men and women's religious lives are indistinguishably the same. Women scholars of religion have seriously questioned the underlying assumptions of such scholarship (Christ, 1976, 1991; Gross, 1974, 1977b, 1983; Gross and Falk, 1980; Ruether, 1981b; King, 1986a, 1990b) and continue to uncover more data on women's religious lives and roles in the past so that not only men's, but the whole human experience in religion is recalled and made known.

However, it is much more difficult to examine the past than to study religious experience in the present. It is difficult to gain access to the past where data about women are often hidden, buried or left unrecorded. Thus it is particularly important to ask what is women's religious experience today and what place, if any, does it have in their lives. For many contemporary women the experiences of subordination and oppression, of violence and injustice have led to a profound alienation from traditional forms of religion which so often seem to justify the status quo. Much public religious practice highlights the invisibility and marginality of women. Contemporary women with a sharp awareness and critical consciousness rarely find a visible focus for their own identity in traditional religious groups and institutions. Yet at the same time there exists a lively search in the area of spirituality, precisely in order to find and give meaning to the experience of being a woman today in a profoundly changed and at times profoundly confusing social order.

The feminist critique of specific religious ideas and practices is becoming sharper, more articulate and detailed at present. It arises out of the cumulative effort of many women around the globe, but as I and many others see it, at the heart of feminism is a spiritual struggle and a new experience which challenges much of traditional spirituality itself. More and more women are coming forth to speak about their religious life and about the understanding of spirituality from a feminist perspective. This new venture has been likened to 'walking on the water' (Garcia and Maitland, 1983). It is a venture on new and uncertain grounds, into wide open and uncharted seas which hold the danger of engulfing us. But the strength of hope and the faith in a new vision can help women to discover as yet unknown shores. We must therefore listen to the voices of women speaking from the depths of their own experience.

3

Voices of experience

'At first it seems that women's experience is a simple thing. Yet as
soon as one begins to study it, one realizes that it is many things.
Black women, white women, rich women, poor women – all share a
fundamental alienation from self, but there are many differences in
their experiences. . . .

The new experience of women in the women's movement is an
important resource for spiritual transformation. For those of us who
were, in a sense, born again . . . the new experience of women is
crucial . . . women's experience must be defined broadly enough to
include all the experiences of women. . . . After we have talked
long and listened long, we may be able to decide which parts of
traditional feminine experience we want to affirm, own, and transform by their incorporation into a new feminist consciousness and
ethic.' – **Carol Christ**, 'Spiritual Quest and Women's Experience',
p. 6

Feminist voices often refer to the importance of women's own experience as a source of self-affirmation and identity. But what is experience?
And what does women's experience mean, especially today? Within
the specific context of this book one must also ask what is of special
religious significance in contemporary women's experience, and what
importance does the feminist experience have for the understanding and
practice of spirituality today?

Experience as simply lived and happening is the raw material and
matrix for reflection. Thus one needs to pay special attention to the way
experience is understood and interpreted. This in turn has an effect on
how it is lived. Women's experience has been both positively and nega-

tively evaluated, and we shall see how it has become a focus of positive strength and power in feminist thinking.

Women's experience does not show a uniform development or pattern as conditions of life, age, social class, ethnicity, religion and culture vary widely and make the lives of individual women or different groups of women very disparate. Each culture also knows widely differing myths, models and symbols relating to women. However complex and disparate the experiences of women through the ages and varieties of cultures may have been, the contemporary feminist debate is patterned by a web of threads which all interconnect and lead to the central focus of woman's experience. Let us therefore follow some of these threads and discuss what women today consider an important part of their experience.

To begin with it may be helpful to make the same distinction with regard to women's experience as the one introduced in chapter 1 with regard to consciousness, namely to distinguish between feminine, female and feminist experience. Each of these is linked to a form of reflection which leads to the different feminine, female and feminist forms of consciousness discussed by Keohane, Rosaldo and Gelpi (1982). In other words, the different kinds of experience are differentiated by the different degree of self-reflection and critical awareness which accompany them. Feminine experience is thus largely concerned with those aspects of life and being which have traditionally been called 'feminine' and which often reinforce women's otherness in relation to men, so that women experience themselves primarily as objects rather than as acting subjects. Female experience concerns the specific experience of women in conceiving and producing human life, in nurturing and sustaining its growth, and in everything that pertains to this at the biological and personal level. This experience may happen to individual women with or without much reflection, whilst the specifically feminist experience is only possible through the critical reflection produced by consciousness raising. The feminist experience is above all an experience of contemporary women, although it has certain historical antecedents. It entails the critical analysis of both feminine and female experience but must proceed beyond these to the further criticism of the feminist experience itself. For it is true that the latter is characterised by a number of yet unresolved paradoxes which become apparent when one examines the diverse and changing patterns of women's experience.

The changing experience of women

The spiritual quest within contemporary feminism is closely linked to new interpretations of both the female and feminist dimension of women's experience which also involve a trenchent critique of traditional images and roles considered as typically 'feminine'. The discovery of the diversity and richness of women's experience in the present and past requires much effort and attention. It is here where women's own stories, revealing their dreams, hopes, joys, sufferings, disappointments and achievements, play such an important role in the contemporary experience of sisterhood and in the reflective analysis of writers on feminism.

I would like to begin with a story from the end of the last century by Olive Schreiner (1855–1920), the Victorian feminist. Born into a Methodist missionary family on the borders of Basutoland in South Africa, she has among her short stories a powerful allegory entitled 'Three Dreams in a Desert' (1890; reprinted in Bruner, 1983, pp. 102–8). Resting in the shade of a mimosa tree during one of her travels on horseback across a hot African plain she dreamt a series of visionary dreams about the changing fate of woman. In the first she describes two figures with heavy loads on their back; one is the figure of a woman lying heavily burdened on the ground unable to move, the other a man standing beside her. Whilst once in the past woman wandered free by the side of man, she was yoked long ago by the 'Age-of-dominion-of-muscular force' and subjected by man with 'the broad band of Inevitable Necessity'. She has carried her burden for centuries with patience and tears, but with wisdom too. She knows she cannot move with the burden on her back, but its band has now been cut by 'the knife of Mechanical Invention', and the 'Inevitable Necessity' is broken once and for all. Woman can now slowly begin to rise, but man cannot help her and does not understand her struggle. Though woman is still weak, she slowly staggers on to her knees and begins to walk.

In the second dream the woman is beside the steep bank of a river seeking the 'Land of Freedom'. She is told that the only way to this land is down 'the banks of Labour' and 'through the waters of Suffering'. The old man Reason instructs her that in order to cross the dangerous waters of the river she must leave behind a small, winged, male child whom she has carried all along asleep on her breast. The woman wants to take him with her so that he will grow up in the 'Land of Freedom' and offer her friendship instead of passion. But Reason insists that the suckling man-child must stay behind in order to learn to open his wings and fly to the 'Land of Freedom' by himself and grow into a man. Now the woman realises that she is utterly alone in her fight with the elements, but in the far distance she hears the sound of thousands and thousands of feet which one day follow her track, and the bodies of these women to come will form a bridge over the river across which the entire human race can pass. Inspired by this hope the woman takes up the struggle with the turbulent waters. The third, concluding dream briefly describes the coming true of this promise which Olive Schreiner sees as a free land with free people:

> I dreamed I saw a land. And on the hills walked brave
> women and brave men, hand in hand. And they looked into
> each other's eyes, and they were not afraid.
> > And I saw the women also hold each other's hands.
> > And I said to him beside me, 'What place is this?'
> > And he said, 'This is heaven.'
> > And I said, 'Where is it?'
> > And he answered, 'On earth.'
> > And I said, 'When shall these things be?'
> > And he answered, 'IN THE FUTURE.'

Clothed in the imagery of her South African experience and using similes drawn from Victorian industrialism, Olive Schreiner's dreams have a strong prophetic element. Woman's age-old burdens have been loosened, but she has to struggle by herself, often in utter loneliness, to find the way to true freedom yet to come. But a new bond is being forged between her and others who follow the same way seeking freedom and equality without fear. Very subtly the dream also expresses that the future bond will not only be between women and men, but also between women and women.

One can interpret the lonely figure of woman and her struggle in the 'Three Dreams in a Desert' as symbolic of contemporary women seeking liberation and equality and as expressing a presentiment of the new experience of sisterhood. Given these emphases here and in her other writings, it is no wonder that recently a dramatic awakening of interest in Olive Schreiner and her 'feminism on the frontier' (Berkman, 1979) has occurred. Schreiner believed not only in the emancipation of women, but in a global concern for women everywhere linked to the great themes of freedom and true equality. In her essays on *Women and Labour* (1911) she wrote: 'We have in us the blood of womanhood that was never bought and never sold, that wore no veil, and had no foot bound, whose realized ideal of marriage was sexual companionship and an equality in duty and labour; who stood side by side with the males they loved in peace and war' (quoted in Bruner, 1983, p. 103).

I have described Olive Schreiner's allegory in order to stress how contemporary changes and experiences are prefigured in the dreams and hopes of women from the past. What Olive Schreiner felt and saw only vaguely, what she expressed in metaphors and images different from those we would use today, we can experience now in various ways and at many different levels. Her story is doubly significant in that it comes from the African continent rather than from North America or Europe from where most of our women stories have originated so far. The changing experience of women includes today so many women from different social, cultural and religious backgrounds; it is closely related to the fast transformation of contemporary society, to profound changes in personal relationships between women and men, women and women, women and children, and to important changes in self-understanding and the quest for meaning and identity in and through personal and social experience.

Change is not something which occurs only externally; the shared reflection on the changing experience of women is an important factor in the further shaping of the contemporary experience and consciousness of women. We must therefore connect the new experience of women to changes in society and self and ask what promise of freedom and what power of transformation women's experience entails.

The international dimension and pluralism of women's experience

Given the voice of many a critic that feminism represents primarily a white, western, middle-class phenomenon, it is important to highlight the global dimension of women's experience. Women's voices are being raised everywhere. The sharing of women's stories and experiences has created a loose web of connections whose threads are slowly encircling the globe. Many examples could be given of this from Africa, India, China or elsewhere, but the most concrete expression of this global dimension was the United Nations Decade for Women Conference held in Nairobi in July 1985. Devoted to 'Equality, Development and Peace' it consisted of an officially sponsored conference and a much more diversified and livelier Forum of Non-Governmental Organisations. It is estimated that 12 000–14 000 women took part in the Nairobi event which represents probably the largest gathering of women from around the globe in history. In spite of its shortcomings and many criticisms, the Nairobi conference is an event of great importance and powerful symbolic significance. For those who took part it will remain an unforgettable experience and source of transformation. Here very different women became aware of each other's individually and socially limited, and yet mutually enriching, experiences, of their variety of life-styles and worldviews, of energy and power, colour and vitality, of their differences and common concerns. Women shared singing, dancing, music, excursions, workshops and projects, and last but not least, a sense of conviviality and humour. Women spoke powerfully about how they and their sisters are being exploited. They called for change and peace, for the sharing of projects, and for more networking between women of developed and developing countries.

Nairobi was a one-time event, unique because of its size and complexity, but its significance transcends the limitations of time and place, for it expressed and confirmed a new spirit among women and made visible the international, global dimension of the contemporary experience of women. Reflecting on the occurrence of this event can help other women, the numerous women not present at Nairobi, to become more internationally aware and foster global bonds among women.

Women's experience is global in a historical and a contemporary sense. It has its roots deep in history and everywhere feminist writers and researchers are uncovering and discovering the multiple ramifications of these roots around the world. Today, the awareness of the universally oppressive conditions of women and the need for change is growing internationally. Many feminist journals and agencies such as *CHANGE* in London and *ISIS* in Geneva are publishing reports on women from all over the world. The growth in international awareness also affects traditional religious institutions. An example of this is the informative report on 'The Situation of Women in the Catholic Church – Developments since International Women's Year' published in 1980 (*Pro Mundi Vita Bulletin*). It documents the growing feminist consciousness among Roman Catholic women around the world, whether in USA and Canada, Asia, Latin America, Africa or Europe. Another example is John C. B. and Ellen Low Webster's book on *The Church and Women in the Third*

World (1985) which looks at the impact of the church on the status of women in different third world countries and includes a bibliography on women in Africa, Asia and Latin America. Other bibliographies on women and religion in the third world are found in Carroll, 1983; Fenton and Heffron 1987; Russell, 1988.

But the most powerful voices come from third world women and black women themselves bringing about a further change in feminist awareness. They decry the denial of differences and the inherent racism found in parts of the white feminist movement. More than any other source they highlight the extraordinary pluralism and rich texture of women's lives. Some writers have described all women as a 'fourth world', the most oppressed section of the poor and oppressed everywhere, but nowhere is this more true than among black women. Feminist consciousness among black women has grown considerably in recent years, especially in South Africa and in the USA; bell hooks, in her study *Ain't I a Woman: Black Women and Feminism* (1983), has traced the history of black women from the female slave experience to the continued devaluation of black womanhood and to contemporary issues of racism and feminism. She speaks of the initial

> silence of the oppressed – that profound silence engendered by resignation and acceptance of one's lot. Contemporary black women could not join together to fight for women's rights because we did not see 'womanhood' as an important aspect of our identity. . . . In other words, we were asked to deny a part of ourselves – and we did. Consequently, when the women's movement raised the issue of sexist oppression, we argued that sexism was insignificant in light of the harsher, more brutal reality of racism. We were afraid to acknowledge that sexism could be just as oppressive as racism. (hooks, 1983, p. 1)

Black women were doubly enslaved, but they are now fighting with courage and resolution to gain personal and political freedom. Especially in South Africa women are deeply involved in the freedom struggle (see Lipman, 1984 and the *ISIS* 1978 report on African women under apartheid). Coloured women in the USA have come together and expressed their anger, their pain, their 'hunger of soul and stomach' in the powerful anthology *This Bridge Called My Back* (Moraga and Anzaldúa, 1981). It contains the writings of women from many different ethnic groups and includes a valuable bibliography on third world women in the USA, whether Afro-American, Asian/Pacific American, Latin American or Native American. The fears and tears, the hopes and dreams and joys of the many women who walk through this book provide a bridge for other women – not unlike the bridge across the 'waters of suffering' which Olive Schreiner once saw – not a bridge to simply walk over, to walk by and around, a bridge to span a dreadful gap created by others – but a bridge to pass through into togetherness.

This bridge is also the bridge of a dream and a vision, a passage through to a new land where women learn each other's way of seeing and being, where their very vulnerability becomes a source of transformation and power:

> we women on the bottom throughout the world can form an international feminism . . . we must struggle together. *Together*, we form a vision which spans from the self-love of our colored skins, to the respect of our foremothers who kept the embers of revolution burning, to our reverence for the trees – the final reminder of our rightful place on this planet.
>
> The change evoked . . . is material as well as psychic. (Moraga and Anzaldúa, 1981, p. 196)

This is a very radical book concerned with 'the oppression of women of color' and 'Third World Revolution', but the power of its vision and new connections is rooted in faith. It also expresses a spiritual struggle, not one artificially divorced from daily life but rooted in concrete material, economic, political and social conditions of women's complex experience. Traditional religious faith, here mainly seen as habitual external practice unconnected to one's real life and problems – 'an upward turn of hands', 'a vicious beating of our breasts' – is no longer a real source of strength for these women. And yet they are fuelled by the fire of faith and nourished by the courage to be – the courage to be themselves. (The wide range of black women's religious experience is documented in Marilyn Richardson's annotated bibliography on *Black Women and Religion*, 1980, covering almost 900 books and articles.)

Each gathering and group of women, each initiative and activity brings further into relief the great diversity and pluralism of women, not only in terms of their background, but also in terms of their ability, achievements and potential. At a conference of mainly third world women held at Harvard Divinity School on 'Women, Religion and Social Change' one participant observed:

The women who came were unique and remarkable. They had suffered, yet they had great strength. Many had acquired an education, or reached where they were now, against all odds. I shall remember the quiet vision of the Hindu women; the outrageous individuality of the Muslims; the continued humour and hope of black South Africans; and the amazing courage of women from Central America. Here one felt was 'the other half' of humanity. What if one could bring their common sense, their ability to work together, and their non-hierarchical ways of thinking into play on a world scale? I became aware that the greatest potential which we have yet to put into the balance in the attempt to save our world is perhaps the potential of women. Here were exemplified alternative ways of thinking and acting. (Hampson, 1984, p. 20)

The wide-ranging experience of these women – from Central America, South and Central Africa, Israel, India, Indonesia, Mexico, Egypt, USA and Europe – is now fully documented in *Speaking of Faith: Cross-cultural Perspectives on Women, Religion and Social Change*, edited by Diana Eck and Devaki Jain (1986). Another stimulating book with a similar emphasis developed out of a symposium held at Hartford Seminary (USA) which looked at the images and roles of women in different religions, past and present. Published under the title *Women, Religion and Social Change* (edited by Yvonne Yazbeck Haddad and Ellison Banks Findly, 1985) it shows again how richly varied women's experience can be. It is not only the religious background, but the entire social, political and cultural context which shape women's lives and mould the patterns of their experience.

Women's social and work experience

Women's experience in a wider sense is shaped by the status and treatment given to them by society at large. Feminist writers have analysed in great detail the social, economic and political factors responsible for women's oppression and those necessary for their liberation. The rise of the contemporary feminist movement is closely related to important social changes and to economic development. Many women have discovered the decisive value of paid work and money as a source of autonomy and independence. Yet at the same time one must realise that the financial and personal independence women seek is not always

available to all men in western societies either. With the rise in unemployment many men, too, have to seek new sources of identity and
meaning other than their traditional work experience from which women
were often excluded in the first place. In the third world both sexes,
women and men, suffer exploitation and deprivation, and yet the experience of women is always one of further oppression.

Looking at the experience of black women in the United States,
Rosemary Ruether criticises American feminism from within by writing:
'The women's movement fails to integrate the experience of poor and
non-white women. Much of what it means by the "female experience" is
in fact class-bound, restricted to the experience of a fairly atypical group
of white, usually childless, women who are blocked in their efforts to
break into the bastions of white, male, upper-class privilege' (Ruether,
1979c, p. 176). Whilst a considerable amount of feminist writings and
activities may only reflect the experience of a particular group of women,
one must nonetheless recognise that more and more women from
other, less privileged groups are coming forward to speak out about
their own experience and perspective on life.

The sharing of stories often highlights the suffering and the dark
sides of women's experience, that of violence and violation, whether it
occurs inside or outside the home, manifesting itself in assault, rape,
pornography, physical abuse, wife battering or other crimes against
women. Our society seems to be scarred by an epidemic of violence, and
much of it affects women. Many women writers have forcefully spoken
out on these negative, dark sides of women's experience, especially on
the social and cultural roots of sexual violence, and have thereby brought
women's exploitation and suffering through physical, mental and structural aspects of violence into greater public visibility.

Here, more than in other areas, a passionate plea for change and for
concerted action has been made. Here, too, the awareness of the
commonality of woman's experience, the realisation that women from
very diverse backgrounds suffer similar experiences of humiliation, violation and pain, has created and strengthened a bond of sisterhood among
many women.

Women's personal and social experience is moulded and patterned by
the influence of many different institutions and agencies: the family in
which they grow up and the one they may raise themselves, their education and that of their children, the church or other religious bodies,
expectations of physical and mental health, the world of sport, the
powerful image-building activities of the media, social and political

events of local, national or international importance. One of the most central concerns of our society is organised, paid work and economic productivity. Women have always worked, and worked excruciatingly hard, but often not in the sense of paid employment. According to UN statistics, one third of all families in the world are supported by the work of women and for every eight hours worked by men, women work sixteen.

Yet women do not hold the key positions which are the source of power, prestige and wealth in our society. However, like 'experience' itself, 'work' is a notoriously ambiguous concept as the same word performs a dual function: it describes the activity of doing something, as well as the result or end product of that activity. In a more specific sense 'work' always implies some kind of result which distinguishes it from mere activity, from simply 'doing something' like pottering about, playing, relaxing or whatever.

Women's experience today includes the world of organised, paid work so long closed to them. This is an important development in the new consciousness of women. Many types of work possess negative, oppressive and enslaving features, but in its positive sense human work is a source of worth and strong identity, and occasion for creativity, self-expression and a sense of achievement. Work thus understood and undertaken is an act of self-transcendence which can provide important moments for personal growth and spiritual insight. To experience satisfaction, enjoyment and fulfilment in doing one's work and seeing the fruits of one's labours carries its own reward quite apart from the question of payment. Work in this sense is an integral dimension of the experience of being human, and countless women have found a sense of satisfaction, strength and joy from doing their work, however humble and unrecognised by others it may have been.

In modern large-scale industrialised societies work has become increasingly specialised and differentiated in terms of professional and career structures. Women have gained access to most, if not all, work situations but they still remain underprivileged as they often do not enjoy equal status and pay, nor do they receive advancement, promotion and public recognition in the same way as men. Thus the contemporary world of work has opened to women many exciting possibilities of new experience. At the same time it has also created a further source of frustration and anger in that equality, whilst legally acknowledged, is often far from being practised and many instances of discrimination against women at work can be found.

However, many obstacles have to be overcome within women themselves. Women often undertake paid employment out of necessity rather than choice and consider work merely as an adjunct to personal relationships rather than of worth and importance in itself and for their own self-development. Much has been written on the woman at home, how she is the captive wife, chained to the continuation of the species and the maintenance of the family unit. At its worst, this can be seen as an existence rooted in immanence whilst other work, at its best and most rewarding, points to successive possibilities of acts of transcendence, of continually transforming that which is possible into what is actually real. As Ann Oakley (1982) has pointed out in her discussion of domestic work, family life and work at home represent for many women the only work conditions they know and 'housework has prevented women from pursuing many avenues of self-development open to those who do not do it. . . . Housework remains an incredibly important limit on what women are able to do and become' (p. 186).

Another writer puts it like this: 'women face two major obstacles to developing an identity as worker, maker, producer. One is the mythologizing of the mother/home-maker role, and at the same time, its devaluation in the "real" world. The other is the failure of women to see work as a necessary component of identity and autonomy' (Kolbenschlag, 1979, pp. 38ff.). A further obstacle is not so much the lack of skills but the frequently perceived passivity of women or rather, to express it differently, women's passive mode of acting by doing things because they need to be done rather than actively taking up things they want to do or enjoy doing. Participating in the world of work outside engages women in an active mode of doing things which can give a sense of achievement and fulfilment, a deep sense of satisfaction which is the same for women and men. Working then, in this sense, becomes a mode of being. In her reflections on women's work Madonna Kolbenschlag speaks of the 'spiritual sense of work' as important for women as well as for society as a whole:

Recovering of the spiritual sense of work is imperative if women are to be liberated rather than automated by it. The idea of work as a 'command to self-transcendence' is rooted in the Judaeo-Christian heritage. Greco-Roman, biblical and medieval sources alike confirm this consciousness. It is one of the distinguishing characteristics of Western civilization as a whole. . . .

Recovery of the spiritual sense of work and the moral imperative it contains demands that women not abdicate – as men once did – from the nurturant, hearth-centered labor that they have known, but that this be integrated with the achieving, world-shaping enterprises they have generally avoided. Likewise, their liberation can be fulfilled only if men integrate their one-sided, competitive, worldly pursuits with the private sphere of home maintenance and child rearing. . . .

There are no models in our civilization to inspire this change. It will perhaps be more difficult for men than for women. Ultimately, we must evolve an ecological model of work – one that sees all functions as equally important in sustaining an equilibrium in society as well as in personality. (Kolbenschlag, 1979, pp. 86–7)

Without having gained the full battle for equal work and pay, women are now badly affected by the current economic recession. Many short-term, part-time or low-paid menial jobs are held by women and are being phased out first during a time of economic crisis and industrial reorganisation. However, the wide general rise in unemployment has made many people think of re-defining work and of looking for new patterns, whether those of job-sharing, self-employment or cooperative ventures, or of finding alternative resources for creating work which provide an opportunity for developing one's gifts and potentials. Thus 'work', as distinct from employment, is again beginning to be seen as an activity which can bring people together in a new way by sharing their skills and resources and by providing them with a sense of direction and meaning. Many people enjoy taking early retirement so that they can undertake alternative activities precisely because they find them fulfilling and rewarding in a sense their paid employment work never was.

It would seem that whilst women have to go on campaigning for further access to work positions in all areas and at all levels, their old and new experience of work in a wider sense and of sharing the fruits of their labour with others can also be an important source of insight for contemporary society in rethinking and restructuring human work in an age of fast change.

The relationship between women and work has been analysed in great detail in the literature of the women's movement, but is not my main concern here. I simply wanted to remind readers of two points which are perhaps less often mentioned, namely, that work is an important aspect of women's experience which can be a rich source for personal growth, identity and self-understanding as well as the occasion for experiencing transcendence. In addition, women's very different historical experience of work in the widest sense may provide an inspiring resource for thinking creatively about the changing understanding of work in contemporary post-industrial society. Both points require far fuller exploration than given so far and than can be entered into here.

Exploring women's experience and realising the complex texture of its diversity, one must ask how far there can be an experience common to all women? Is there anything specific about women's experience which distinguishes it from human experience in general and from man's experience in particular? 'Woman's experience' has acquired a powerful normative status in feminist writings, especially those of radical feminism but this expression, far from referring to all the diversity and complexity of experience, has come to be especially linked to woman's particular experience, to her biological specificity grounded in her female bodily existence.

Female bodily existence as a source of women's experience

The pains and joys of being woman are deeply grounded in woman's bodily existence. Woman's body creates and cradles life in a way a man's body doesn't. It is much more difficult for women to keep their thoughts neatly apart and separate from their bodies as much of their experience is closely intermingled with bodily functions and events.

In exploring the source of woman's difference from man some feminist writers have evaluated female bodily existence quite negatively in seeing it as the root cause of woman's oppression and inferiority, the real reason for her age-old subordination. Others however have come to recognise the different stages and crises of 'becoming woman' (Washbourn, 1977) – from menstruation to coition, conception, parturition and motherhood – as a source of great pride and strength. Woman's biological make-up is seen as her true source of power, the basis and ground for her feminine qualities of gentleness, tenderness, insight and compassion, her ability to link together and connect people and things. Thus it has been argued that female differences are not only worth preserving, but ought to be celebrated and closely studied, as woman's specific experience can contribute valuable insights for the necessary transformation of the dominant values of contemporary culture.

It is easier for a man to lose himself in abstract thought and become separated from the sources of life; for women life itself is more organically interconnected. In traditional religious thought this has often been negatively evaluated when women have been described as being 'material', more 'physical', more 'flesh' than men.

Religion and sexuality have always been closely interlinked, whether in the sacralisation of sexual activities or their denial in celibacy and chastity or the manifold taboos associated with sexual life (Parrinder, 1980). It is worth mentioning that the World Council of Churches has conducted a study on 'Female Sexuality and Bodily Functions in Different Religious Traditions' (see Becher, 1990). Helpful insights into the relationship between women's sexuality and spirituality can also be gained from the personal reflections found in Linda Hurcombe, *Sex and God – Some Varieties of Women's Religious Experience* (1987). One of the major taboos in religions, from the most archaic to the most sophisticated ones, is connected with menstruation, a truly unique experience of women. The flow of blood, often perceived as the very locus of life and thus a symbol of fertility and abundance as well as of sacrifice, is profoundly ambivalent. Dangerous, impure, powerful, magic and sacred, it had to be shunned or surrounded by special rituals. It also often endowed women with a special sacral power from which men had to keep apart.

The various rites associated with menstruation and its symbolic significance have raised a great deal of interest among women scholars. In some tribal groups first-menstruation rituals for girls parallel initiation rituals for boys to mark a new stage of life and recognise the transition into adulthood (Gross, 1980). Among some people, for example the Anlo in West Africa, women can only fully participate in all religious rituals when they have reached the menopause and become 'like men' by leaving their specifically female experience of bleeding and giving birth behind (Gaba, 1987).

Much critical work still needs to be done in this area, but however fascinating past and archaic beliefs and practices may be and however much they may help us in understanding cultural and religious attitudes to the cyclical pattern of women's life, what can contemporary women make of menstruation, so often simply seen as a 'curse', in terms of their own self-understanding?

Penelope Washbourn, in her study *Becoming Woman. The Quest for Wholeness in Female Experience* (1977) has explored the meaning of woman's bodily existence and its relation to personal maturity and identity with much sensitivity and perceptiveness. She writes about the experience of menstruation as crisis and occasion for transcendence:

> The impersonality of menstruation needs to be integrated into *personal* self-understanding in order for the next life-crisis, a girl's expression of sexuality in relation to others, to be defined creatively.
> . . .
> To emerge enriched from the life-crisis of menstruation implies finally trusting and liking one's body. Trusting it means being peaceful with it, knowing its potential, relaxing with the new experience of menstruation, understanding the possible good offered by the female body structure.
> . . .
> To emerge enhanced from the crisis of menstruation is to receive an increased sense of value as an individual. . . . It heightens rather than diminishes personhood. (1977, pp. 16, 17, 18)

The same author writes later about the experience of pregnancy and birth:

> Perhaps no change in a woman's life is more radical than the experience of being pregnant and giving birth. It is a relatively short experience in terms of time, and though it may be repeated, each pregnancy raises the question of a woman's self-understanding in a new way. . . .
> Fundamentally, pregnancy and birth locate a woman in an experience of the body and a perception of the self that is uniquely female. That uniqueness can bring both pride and fear; it links her unalterably with those who have experienced pregnancy and childbirth and separates her from those who will never experience it.
> Pregnancy and childbirth is a spiritual crisis for a woman, not only in the sense that it raises questions about the interpretation of her femaleness, but also because it implies making a decision about the meaning of the creative power of fertility. (1977, pp. 94, 95)

All too often pregnancy and birth have been looked upon as passive experiences to be endured by women whilst now they are praised and celebrated as active processes which women help to create and shape and wherein they can find an enriching experience for spiritual growth and transformation. Birth and motherhood belong to the central experience of most women's lives, but what meaning they assign to it and what strength they draw from it is open to infinite variations. It links women most closely to the joy of creation where birth, with all its pain and travail, can break into exhilaration and ecstasy. The power and mystery of life, its graceful abundance and utterly gratuitous gift can fill a woman with a deep sense of gratitude and completion and create a strong bond between her and all else that is living.

However, the experience of being a mother is also full of ambiguity, especially in relation to others. All too often women have been seen by society and religious institutions only in terms of their function and role as mother, a role which has defined them in a much more exclusive sense than men are defined by their role of being a father, always only one of the many roles in a man's life. Much comparative work has been done on the different cultural meanings of 'mothering' and on the history of motherhood in western culture. This has created a greater aware-ness about the profound changes in the practice and understanding of mothering in modern times. One of the most significant developments for the liberation of women is the conscious choice of motherhood, a freedom not given to most of our foremothers in history. Women today have far fewer children, and a much higher intensity of personal care and attention, intimacy and personal relationship is expected between a mother and each child than was the case in the past.

Whilst traditionally the role of woman in society was overridingly determined by her biological function of being a child-bearer and mother, today, with changing patterns of life and new choices, a new conscious-ness has developed that there is no role-specific life for women any more than there is a role-specific life for men. Women may choose to be mothers or they may not. Women are no longer restricted to being primarily wives and mothers, although women will continue to be also wives and mothers, just as men continue to be husbands and fathers, besides assuming many other roles and tasks in private and public life. As men have chosen to marry and beget children or not to marry, or not to have children, to pursue a career or devote themselves with greater concern to their families, or to do both, so can women.

Apart from the physical acts of childbearing, giving birth and breastfeeding – all very enriching experiences and important human activities – there does not seem to be any role which belongs specifically to women. From the moment of birth, the rearing of children and the special care given to them throughout their infancy and youth need not be an exclusively female occupation. In fact, it would be a positive factor in the development of men if they took a more active part in the care of the young, as many already do nowadays. It will develop new sides of tenderness and care, of patience and humility – characteristics which will emerge in any sensitive, thinking person who is in daily contact with growing life in all its vulnerability and precariousness (King, 1977).

Especially in the area of personal relationships the task of fathering is as important as mothering, but the word 'fathering' is at present still largely restricted to the act of begetting a child rather than connected with the long drawn-out process of being intimately associated with a child's development and growth into maturity. As many fathers are already closely involved with their children, our language may well lag behind our fast changing social reality here. What matters most is the need for close parenting, something that women and men must do together. The interest in the role of the father in bringing up children is growing and in a few families fathers have deliberately chosen a nurturing, 'mothering' role, but this is not yet generally accepted by society and does meet with opposition (Pruett, 1987).

As Penelope Washbourn has pointed out, children represent an opportunity for psychological and spiritual growth for both women and men:

> Women *need* children in the same manner that men need children, not to be their ultimate fulfilment but to be the possibility for revealing the nature of the mystery of life in its wonders and tragedies. Living in relation to children may be self-revealing as we see ourselves for what we are, accept that knowledge, and find hope in the very ongoingness of life both in ourselves and in our children. (1977, p. 129)

The family has come in for much radical criticism in feminist literature. Perhaps we now know more about its oppressive and destructive influence on women than about its sustaining potential and creative aspects. Sociologists and anthropologists have written about the widely varying family structures and different patterns of relationships in human cultures, but feminist thinkers and theologians have perhaps not yet sufficiently reflected on the personal and social meaning of partnership marriages and of the family as a community of persons where many moments of self-development, self-realisation and self-transcendence can be experienced.

Feminist voices speak most forcefully and movingly about the experience of motherhood, often seen outside a wider personal and social context. Motherhood is greatly celebrated and even worshipped, for it is seen as a profound analogy of the creative power of divine reality, so often symbolised in religions in the form of the goddess. But the mother goddess, like human motherhood, is not without ambiguities as we shall see later (King, 1989b).

In the Christian tradition, where feminine symbolism for the Divine has not been absent but male images have dominated language and thought about God, the experience of human motherhood can become a rich experiential source for theological thinking, as Margaret Hebblethwaite has shown in her reflections on *Motherhood and God* (1984). Her experiences of giving birth to three children and caring for them every day were transformed into creative occasions of meeting and coming closer to God, always courageously named as 'she'. The grace of divine life, of the transforming power of the ever-present spirit becomes transparent here in the spiritual sustenance drawn from ordinary daily events and encounters, from the joys and difficulties of a mother living with and caring for her young.

But many such insights might also be gained without actually giving physical birth – by people who have a close relationship to children without being their biological mothers, such as teachers, doctors or social workers. 'Mothering' as an experience can be extended to cover a wide range of activities and relationships, including spiritual ones. In several Christian groups women religious are addressed as 'Mother' whilst ordained priests and men religious are addressed as 'Father'. This indicates the recognition of and the respect given to a spiritual affiliation and authority analogous to or greater than that accorded to one's biological parents.

In metaphorical terms one can also think of artistic and intellectual creativity as involving the 'nurturing' of an idea which often requires a long period of 'gestation' to come to 'fruition', all terms taken from the biological sphere and the growth of life, but used for both women and men. We have to 'mother' our selves, our interior life; we have to feed and nourish our thoughts, our dreams, our hopes, our prayers – the life of the spirit within us – so that we can be a source of giving and mothers to others.

Gandhi is often described as 'the father of the Indian nation' but, as has been pointed out, there was also something of the mother in him, especially in his desire to preserve the best of Indian truth and tradition and his profound reverence for life. Indians see their country as a 'mother' sustained and nourished by the divine energy of the mother goddess. It would be interesting to explore which nations refer to their country as 'motherland' and which ones speak of the 'fatherland', as Germans are wont to do.

These few examples illustrate that motherhood is a rich and widely ramified concept linked to biological birth, to culturally learnt patterns of mothering and to expressions of metaphysical and spiritual insights in human experience. It carries a rich resonance due to its close association with early human experiences of intimacy, comfort, nourishment, assurance and support patterned by relationships of tenderness, care and love which all of us need to become and be fully human.

One of the most fundamental paradoxes in feminist thought relates to the new normative status assigned to the experience of women. The problem involved is twofold. First, it consists of finding a satisfactory way to relate women's specific experience to general human experience. Women's experience is different; it is distinctive, incredibly rich and diverse, but its full strength and value have often remained hidden and unacknowledged in the past. General human experience, predominantly described by men, silently subsumed women's experience under it. With great pain and struggle we have now come to realise that women's experience must be looked at separately and on its own terms. That will make our understanding of general human experience more complex and complete.

Women's experience must be fully explored, known and described; politically, culturally and religiously it must become an integral part of our total human experience, a rich storehouse to draw upon for all, both women and men. But now the second, more difficult part of the problem arises.

A considerable amount of feminist writing seems to idealise and narrow down women's experience in terms of a uniqueness grounded in female bodily existence. An exclusive insistence on the special experience of womanhood does seem to give biological dimensions a priority over all other considerations of human experience. Why not equally emphasise other spheres of women's experience, especially those of work and creativity? Why not consider all dimensions of the self-creating, self-defining and self-transcending activities of women?

Some feminists seem to be unduly insensitive to the diversity of women's experience and women's needs. The place of biology in feminist theory is certainly one of the difficult philosophical issues facing feminism (see Midgley and Hughes, 1983, ch. 7). How can women maintain on one hand that biology is not destiny, but insist on the other that woman's richest and most specific experience is so exclusively tied to the biological conditions and processes of her body? Is this not biological determinism in another disguise?

I consider the excessive importance placed by some feminists on the experience of birth as dangerously romantic, especially as most women in the western world give birth far more rarely than women in the past or women in the third world. Some feminists are alienated from the birthing process altogether and their rhapsodies about women's special experience make little sense. As a counter-argument to woman's narrowly conceived 'experience' one can also think of many single women who have never borne a child and yet their experience has made great contributions to the social, religious, political and cultural life of the human community.

In addition one might observe that an excessive insistence on the experience of motherhood can be considered as a form of 'retraditionalisaton' emphasising, admittedly in a new fashion, what women have so exclusively experienced for far too long, often to their own regret and at the loss of a wider human experience of self-development and greater fulfilment. How far is the contemporary concern with 'woman's experience' far too body-dependent? Is it not most characteristic of human experience as human that it always transcends the biologically given? But in this, as in other matters, feminist thinking in all its radical critique and revolutionary intentions still follows the major mould of current western thought with its excessive obsession with the body and sexuality, to the exclusion of many other human concerns. It could well be that the voices of women from the third world and from non-western cultural and religious traditions, with their very different history and experience, will eventually provide a healthy corrective and complement to current feminist debates.

Women's experience in all its rich, joyous and painful aspects cannot be exclusively governed by the biological. Female bodily existence is a primary source of woman's self-image and identity, but not an exclusive one. In and through it spiritual power and transformation can be found, but only by going beyond, by transcending it. In other words, whilst human experience is grounded in and bound by the conditions of physical existence women's experience, like all human experience, must ultimately be body-transcendent rather than exclusively body-

dependent. This is not a facile and false universalism in order to evade
the real difficulties of female bodily existence, but it points to a central
concern of the feminist quest: women's search for her true self and for
authentic existence which implies autonomy, freedom and transcendence. An important clue for understanding contemporary women's
experience is found in the changing consciousness of women, their
newly-found sense of self and a differently shaped identity in their
relation to others.

Women's experience of the self

Contemporary feminism is misapprehended if it is only seen as a social
and political movement. Its own crises, struggles and divisions are
linked to profound crises and changes in women's own consciousness
as ultimate ground and matrix of their experience. This transformation
of consciousness has deep repercussions on society at large and on men
in particular.

Authentic experience as lived, loved and suffered by women must
encompass a healing of the divided self often experienced as separated
within and without, inwardly and outwardly, enclosed like a walled city
whose walls must be scaled and pierced to make connections with the
outside world. The need for connections, so much stressed in feminist
thought, presupposes that there exist many separations, opposing tendencies and dualities which have to be overcome and transcended. At the
deepest level the self is severed from the world, from others and from
the life of the spirit. It has to retrace its roots in the cosmos, its connections with the natural and human world, in order to discover the
dynamic continuum of life energised by the power of the spirit. This is
true of any self, but one must ask '*why* the world-sense of the dis-
connected self parallels historically the ascendancy of patriarchy, in
order to grasp . . . how its severed, wounded state can only be healed
through an explicit embrace of the project of gender re-creation. This is
happening within feminism' (Keller, 1987, p. 237).

The American psychologist Carol Gilligan, in her study *In a Different
Voice: Psychological Theory and Women's Development* (1982; see also
Gilligan, 1977), has argued that developmental psychology has not given
adequate attention to the concerns and experiences of women. If women's voice were heard and integrated into the discussions about concepts of self, morality and human maturity, an expanded conception

of adulthood would emerge. Gilligan emphasises the centrality of relationships in the lives of women which is different from 'the bias of men' towards separation. Women experience the interdependence of self and other both in love and work. Women's sense of integrity appears to be entwined with an ethic of care 'so that to see themselves as women is to see themselves in a relationship of connection'. Gilligan also argues that accounts which measure women's development against a male standard ignore the possibility of a different truth 'that women's embeddedness in lives of relationship, their orientation to interdependence, their subordination of achievement to care, and their conflicts over competitive success leave them personally at risk in mid-life seem more a commentary on the society than a problem in women's development' (p. 171).

The process of consciousness-raising has awakened women and expanded their awareness of their own situation, their history, their own resources and the potential of women's shared experience. Such expansion of consciousness enhances self-consciousness and becomes a new source for women's further knowledge about themselves and the world. Self-realisation is always linked to an experience of autonomy and freedom in making decisions over one's own life, in experiencing the power of self-determination. But there exist many obstacles for women on the path to self-actualisation. To accept others and relate to them in a positive manner a person must first accept herself and be truly integrated and centred in herself. A great difficulty arises here because many women are in fact far too other-centred, that is to say, too self-effacing and self-forgetting rather than concerned with self-determination. Here the ambiguity of the self becomes apparent. Women often suffer from a low self-regard; too often they see their task as one of giving, of self-sacrifice, rather than of fostering their self-esteem and own sense of worth which a person needs for mature relations with others. This difficulty is connected with the whole problem of women's passivity created by the tyranny of gender roles in our society. Too often women have accepted the notion of simply 'being' rather than 'doing' as a rationalisation for their exclusion from the actions and decisions of the real world. Superficially this may give the impression of greater self-acceptance and maturity, even of greater religious capacity in women, but at a deeper level it often masks a vulnerable sense of dependence, insecurity and self-refusal. Traditional religious institutions whose activities are so often supported by women can turn out to be hiding-places from women's wholeness. A wrongly understood self-denial cannot lead women on the road to genuine spiritual freedom and self-transcendence.

To find freedom women have to create space for their own self-determination rather than be determined by the images and wishes of others. To achieve this goal, the spell of feminine myths and models which still shape so much of our thinking has to be broken. Myths mirror as well as model human existence and in her critical examination of pervasive feminine myths the American writer Madonna Kolbenschlag (1979) has chosen 'Sleeping Beauty' as the symbol *par excellence* of women's passivity and, by extension, as a metaphor for the spiritual condition of women cut off from autonomy and transcendence. To find true selfhood women must *Kiss Sleeping Beauty Good-Bye*, as the title of her study says, and abandon other legends enshrined in well-known fairy tales which proclaim the passivity and dependence of women. Kolbenschlag begins her thought-provoking study with the challenging remarks:

> The ancients debated the question of whether or not woman could have a soul. Today the 'woman question' is one of removing the barriers that prevent woman from *becoming* a soul.
> . . .
> Much testing, much reflecting, much living must intervene before we can say, 'My soul is now my own'. This is finally what *liberation* means, that I have rescued my spirit from repressive coercion, from inner compulsion and from the hazards of freedom itself. (Kolbenschlag, 1979, p. xiii)

The hazards of freedom are many indeed. Besides the deep damage that has been done to female and male selves by the dominance of masculinity in our culture, there exists also a new danger for women arising out of the contempt for the feminine implicit in some feminist writing, leading to what Helen Luke has called 'the tragic alienation of women from their own femininity' (Luke, 1981, p. 10), often apparent in counselling. But the question then arises, what is the truly feminine within us and how can we realise its potential as women and men? It is far too simple a statement, and no help at all to women struggling for a self-identity and a sense of fulfilment, to say that 'the instinct of the feminine is precisely to use nothing, but simply to give and receive' (Luke, 1981, p. 11). This can easily be misunderstood as yet another example of accepting traditional gender definitions whereas the real problem consists in finding an answer to the question: how can women find their true self and realise the potential of the feminine side of their being too?

Much of the answer to this depends on what kind of self-concept women are able to develop beyond what is traditionally available in our culture. Too many people go on depending on sharp gender divisions created and shaped by social conditions very different from our own. Apart from biological factors gender differences have been explained by different childbearing and mothering practices whereby girls in our culture are parented by a person of the same sex and thus come 'to experience themselves as less differentiated than boys, as more continuous with and related to the external object-world'. The difference is summed up as 'The basic feminine sense of self is connected to the world, the basic masculine sense of self is separate' (N. Chodorow quoted in Oakley, 1982, p. 274).

If the boundaries of the female self are more permeable, this may go some way in explaining why women as a group seem to have developed a heightened sensitivity to other people and often find it both easier and more rewarding to attend to human relationships than men in general do. However, contemporary feminist consciousness calls traditional gender identities radically into question and seeks the emergence and growth of a new female self. Ultimately, this also implies a new male self and a new relationship between the two sexes – in fact, nothing less than 'an explicit embrace of the project of gender re-creation' (Keller, 1987). In other words, the questions raised and the personal and social tensions created by the rise of feminism involve a profound paradigm shift in the understanding of human selfhood. From the perspective of women seeking a new self-understanding and independence one can ask

> whether many of the crises currently emerging in male/female relationships and in family life are, in fact, symptomatic of woman's need for ethical autonomy and her struggle to achieve it. If so, what many look upon as the disintegration of 'feminine' identity should rather be viewed as a moral imperative. What for men is a given, a self-transcending capacity imbued by socialization and cultural conditioning, is for women a quality that must be acquired, seized – painfully and often traumatically – sometimes very late in life. The contemporary migration of women into the marketplace suggests that meaningful work may have a significant effect on the achievement of ethical autonomy. (Kolbenschlag, 1979, p. 30)

Besides her experience of work and of a wider social network woman's newly emerging identity and selfhood is profoundly shaped by
and closely connected with a revisioning of relationships. Our society is
characterised by strong gender polarisation which an increasing number
of people, but most of all women, find no longer acceptable nor helpful
for living. We have reached a kind of 'boundary crisis' in the understanding of gender roles and of the relationship between the two sexes.
For some women relationships with men have become less important to
their own development and self-understanding than relationships with
other women. To experience and acknowledge love for another woman,
with or without sexual intimacy, can bring liberation and transformation.
The experience of friendship, of trust, of mutual acceptance and encouragement, of sharing one's joys and depressions can be a deeply enriching
encounter and bond between women irrespective of whether they also
have close relationships with men and children.

Women ministering in mutuality form an integral part of the joys of
sisterhood so often celebrated by feminists. Such experiences are not
necessarily identical with, but also not totally different from, the strands
of thought found in contemporary lesbianism which some of its adherents do not primarily see as a question of sexuality but as one of identity
and total commitment to women in a completely male-dominated society. Lesbian couples and communities demonstrate the possible pluralism of human relationships; their experience can be seen as a valuable
source of knowledge and female self-affirmation for all women, whilst
it provides an explicit counter-identity for some. However, women have
to be aware of the danger of separatism. If feminism is to make a
decisive contribution to the transformation of the social order, it has to
remain open-ended and not set itself up as a new, exclusive absolute.
The liberation gained by women's new consciousness must not lead
to another kind of bondage, namely that of a separatist ideology instead
of true inner and outer freedom. To revitalise our culture women need
to create a 'gynergetic continuum' (Keller, 1987) which flows out only
through all women, but also into all touchable men. This continuum
can heal the severed self and release as yet untapped psycho-political
and spiritual power in the world.

Self, identity, relationships and the value of the acting, self-reflective
subject are all of central importance in philosophical discussions about
the nature of the human person as an individual and social being. Philosophers have speculated on these issues since ancient times, but feminists today call into question many of their speculations. By probing

women's experience cross-culturally and historically, our knowledge of ourselves, our world and our social life has to be newly framed and constructed – the knowledge of both women and men that is. It is not our task here to pursue philosophical questions of a technical nature, as has been done by others (see Davaney, 1981, *Feminism and Process Thought;* Harding and Hintikka, 1983, *Discovering Reality – Feminist Perspectives on Epistemology, Metaphysics, Methodology, and Philosophy of Science*; Keller, 1986, *From a Broken Web: Separation, Sexism and Self*) but to consider another question which is now being asked more and more, namely, what is the spiritual dimension of women's experience in all its rich variety?

The articulation of spiritual questions has only come of late in the feminist movement and many women writers do not yet mention this subject. Ann Oakley in her book *Subject Women* (1982), described as 'A powerful analysis of women's experience in society today', lists ten different feminist positions in a table on 'Tendencies in the women's liberation movement' (see Oakley, 1982, pp. 336–7). These are classified according to their social, political or cultural orientation, but there is no reference whatsoever to 'spiritual feminism', 'metaphysical feminism', 'feminist theology' or 'feminist spirituality movements', all tendencies which exist within the wide compass of the contemporary women's movement. Nor is there any mention of women's growing interest in questions of spirituality and mysticism in the sixteen units of the Open University course on 'The Changing Experience of Women' (1983). This is more than simply an omission or oversight. It leaves out a major note, a depth dimension and key to meaning, without which the new consciousness and self-understanding of women remains incomplete and a central aspect of their experience unacknowledged and unexplored. We must ask then what inner strength and spiritual power can women draw from their rich experience, newly explored, articulated, praised, celebrated and reflected upon today? What is the spiritual dimension inherent in women's experience and in feminism as a whole?

The spiritual dimension of women's experience

Experience has much to do with what happens to us through encountering others. In an outward sense it includes social pressures, constraints and opportunities, all of which shape our lives. But our inner thoughts and feelings are part of our experience too, and at the deepest spiritual level we must enquire what meaning we can discern in the intricate web of our experiences, and whether we can find in it a pattern, a direction or an orientation which seem to make sense.

I am suggesting that women's contemporary experience with all its choices, all its variety and diversity, encompasses important occasions for the disclosure of meaning. It can open up decisive moments of revelation which point to transcendence and spiritual liberation. This is true in the lives of individual women, and it is true for feminism as a whole. The encounter with feminist thought and the experience of her sisters can reveal to an individual woman what she is and can become. It opens up a new horizon for individuals, for groups of women and, potentially, for the whole of society. To share other women's experiences, struggles and thoughts is a catharsis, a cleansing and strengthening process whereby a woman can gain greater clarity of vision and become more transparent to herself.

Critics of the feminist movement often maintain that contemporary women are primarily interested in seeking to snatch outward power from men rather than fulfilling themselves through service and self-giving. There may be some truth in this, but for reasons not always easily understood. Women do seek power in its outward forms and need to obtain it to find true space for freedom and self-determination, for a full self-development and higher self-regard, without which true service and self-sacrifice are not possible, for how can one give up what one has never had? At the same time it must be said that giving, nurturing and caring must not be restricted to women alone. Selfless service must be performed by men too if we want to create a truly caring society. However, outward power and authority must ultimately be grounded in and sustained by inner energy and strength, by authentic existence and spiritual power. Kolbenschlag rightly points to the subtle interdependence between outer and inner power with regard to women earning their own money:

> Making money is a supreme act of personal power in our society. To reject the opportunity to make money out of fear, inertia or guilt is to sacrifice an important source of autonomy and commitment. To reject the opportunity to make money for other transcendent motives may also be a supreme act of autonomy. (Kolbenschlag, 1979, pp. 104ff.)

Money can be of great importance for spirituality, if only in order to abandon it! Acting in such a spirit of detachment represents a further step towards transcendence, but it goes beyond the ordinary experience of most people who must follow a path in and through the things of this world. But in doing so we can learn to see that the spirit addresses us through the events of our lives, through what we do and what is done to us. Spirituality is thus not added on to life as a separate pursuit, but grows out of the very tensions, the fibres of our experience. The spirit comes forward and meets us not only in and through the events of our personal lives, but also through the movements and events of our time, not least through feminism.

The spiritual dimension within contemporary feminism has much to do with the determined quest for wholeness and integration, the attempt to heal deep divisions and overcome all dualisms. But the central pivot of it all is the notion of freedom and everything this entails, from the experience of personal autonomy and authentic self-existence to a new vision of interpersonal relationships built on equality and partnership, to an altogether different, new social order for the world. At its heart feminism is grounded in and empowered by an act of faith. One could describe this as a vision quest carried by the faith in the possibility of another reality, a hope which goes far beyond current social and empirical evidence. Precisely for this reason feminism is considered as unrealistically utopian by some, whilst others see it as strongly prophetic and vitally important in shaping our global future. This dynamic faith at the heart of feminism seems to me one of the most important and precious qualities, the true source of its inspiration, a source of immense worth, in fact if one so wishes to see it, a sign of the spirit itself.

Spirituality has both personal and social aspects. It touches and transforms self and society alike. At first woman's search for a liberated self appears to be an utterly inward quest, a very lonely personal journey to 'the land of freedom' and self-determination. But like the waves of the ocean, the effect of self-transformation touches many wider shores although, as Robin Morgan has remarked, it is difficult to imagine at present 'what the ripple effects might be from that single dropped pebble releasing the creative energy of more than half the human species after so long'. If one considers feminism in a larger context, as one must, one realises that

> The profound potential of feminism lies not only in those aspects of its vision expressed now and in the past by women, individually and collectively (and by a few men), but even more in the chain reaction of events set off by its most minute accomplishments. This chain

reaction can't yet be predicted by those of us – women and men – still groping toward that vision through the pain and confusion of the present. We can only begin to imagine the results, and the results of the results; only being to glimpse or intuit them. . . .

What we imagine, glimpse, intuit, is that feminism is not only about women (which *would*, remember, be sufficient cause for it), or even about women and men and political/emotional/spiritual/economic/social/sexual/racial/intellectual/ecological revolution, or even about the above plus a revolution in sentience on this planet. All that. And more. (Morgan, 1982, p. 282)

Feminism is for Morgan the call for the next step in human evolution, the very key to our survival and transformation as a species. Even though not all feminist writers are aware of these wider perspectives, one must see feminism in this larger context which raises some of the most challenging issues for us today – issues which are intimately connected to personal, social and global aspects of spirituality.

Questions of spirituality appear in contemporary feminism both in this wider, more universal sense, but also in a very particular way. As mentioned in an earlier section of this book, the contemporary search for an authentic, world-transforming spirituality takes many different forms. In feminism it is especially concerned with the experience of women, in particular with their experience of exploring, finding and affirming their own self. This search is often bound up with finding a greater and deeper reality, a transcendence beyond the self as well as a new community beyond one's own individuality. Today, in feminism as elsewhere, spirituality is not an exclusive exploration of interiority and inwardness, but closely interwoven with all other dimensions of human experience, including social and political life. Thus spirituality is not a permanent retreat from the world into the monastery, the desert, the cave, or even the silence of one's own heart and mind, but arising out of the midst and depth of experience, spirituality implies the very point of entry into the fullness of life by bestowing meaning, value and direction to all human concerns.

Authentically lived experience, rooted and grounded in wholeness and greater reality, radiates power, the power of spiritual energy and strength, of a large, continuous life web and rhythm of which the individual person forms an integral part. Women today seek more participation and power in all areas of activity, but they also experience a tremendous power from within their own being. Looking at the contemporary experience of women from the perspective of spirituality, we must ask what resources women possess to live an authentic existence and find the strength to create a more caring community. To put it differently, which experiences and exemplars provide important sources for the spiritual identity, authority and power of women? To answer this we need to be attentive to the numerous voices of spiritual power found among women in past and present.

4

Voices of spiritual power

'For too many women, unfortunately, the myth of a divided spirituality survives, and too often it is equated with that antisexuality ram-
pant in the ancient world. . . .

We can counter the myth of a divided spirituality by reclaiming a
history of women's experience and emphasizing a theology that centers
on ourselves and God as beings who relate one with another. . . . If
the self-concept is the single most important component of our behaviour, including our spiritual lives, then women, with centuries of
conditioning about inferior spiritual capabilities, now must fight back
and liberate ourselves from the mythology and inadequate theology
that deprive God of meaning and ourselves of expectations of
sanctity.

In reclaiming our own experience, we see clearly that authentic
spirituality must be eminently social. . . .

History has shown us women whose mystic experience in what I
call the 'mystic circle' moved from contemplative prayer as learning
love into intensive social involvement. . . .

Valid mystical feminism reaches out, then, to our neighbor; it is
social, rooted in love and ablaze with concern.' – **Dody H. Donnelly**,
'The Sexual Mystic: Embodied Spirituality', pp. 125ff.

Reading this quotation one can immediately ask whether there is something like 'mystical feminism' and 'feminist spirituality' and what are its
main characteristics. The emphasis lies undoubtedly on a new self-
concept and new relationships, on a breakthrough in consciousness and
on a spirituality which is embodied and undivided, that is to say integral
and holistic. Traditionally, spirituality is so often conceived as apart

from the world and apart from the body, especially the female body. If one examines the literature on spirituality in different religions, spiritual advice seems often to be given irrespective of gender, addressed to seemingly asexual beings. In practice, however, most spiritual advice available from the past is addressed to men and often implies explicitly negative evaluations of women. Manuals of asceticism have much to answer for, as male models of holiness and perfection are often built around the rejection of and utter contempt for female bodies and their natural biological functions. In many, though not all, religions of the world women are considered as spiritually inferior and incapable of the same spiritual attainment as men. Supported by the institutional structure and power of office, men have seen and acknowledged spiritual authority as primarily invested in themselves.

Unfortunately this has little changed today. And yet we know of many women of great spiritual authority and power who have provided spiritual leadership and inspiration for others, but often in an informal, non-hierarchical and non-institutional sense. Women have found spiritual empowerment in small groups or through literary and artistic creations which have given them a sense of their own worth, a sense of mastery and achievement. Yet it is quite extraordinary that in spite of the patriarchal cast of all religions and the male dominance and pride in spiritual matters, powerful women of the spirit, women saints and mystics, have emerged in all faith communities known to us. Women around the globe possess a rich spiritual heritage of which they can truly be proud and feminists must help all women to become more aware of this. With rising spiritual awareness it is important to ask what spiritual resources can women draw on and enlist in meeting the crying needs of our contemporary world?

Spiritual resources within women themselves

In answering our question we must emphasise first of all the rich resources which women possess within themselves and which they have manifested frequently enough throughout history. These are resources primarily linked to women's biological, emotional and psychic attributes and abilities. There is perhaps first and foremost the immense resource of suffering as a source of strength to overcome adversity and affliction. There are the pain, the tears, the agony, the immense labour in bringing new life into the world and attending with equally immense patience to its slow and imperceptible growth. These are the roots for women's resources of compassion, of insight, and ultimately of wisdom.

There is also women's attention to detail, to the *minutiae* of life, the faithfulness to the daily round of duties which ensure personal and social wellbeing and make the smooth running of ever so many activities in the world possible and bearable. Then there is women's power of listening, of pacifying, of soothing and healing many a wound and settling many a quarrel and dispute. There is the strength of an encouraging smile and the gentle touch of love, the experience of generous selfless giving, of comfort, warmth, patient encouragement and recognition, the adaptability to people and their personal needs, the caring concern and understanding of others.

Peace, love, joy and harmony are all fruits of the spirit found in people of spiritual power and presence. They are not qualities unique to women but women, by the very nature of their traditional tasks and experience and by the social pressures and constraints put upon them, have often developed and embodied these qualities to an unusual degree. It is perhaps for this reason that the French religious thinker Pierre Teilhard de Chardin (1881–1955) expressed the view that on women 'life has laid the charge of advancing to the highest possible degree the spiritualization of the earth' (1975, p. 84). Others have said similar things before. For example the famous Islamic mystic Ibn Arabi (13th century CE) engaged in wide-ranging speculation about the role of women for the spiritual life of humankind (Schimmel, 1975, 1982). Our world would certainly become radically transformed if the spiritual qualities which have often been seen as specifically 'female' or 'feminine' were accepted and practised as a general human norm.

Today many women in the feminist movement experiment with new ways of understanding and practising spirituality. They thereby seek to evolve a new pattern of behaviour and relationships, not only for themselves, but for all people. One of the most critical and agonising issues of our times is that of peace, and no spirituality can evade it and remain convincing. Women have been traditional peace-makers in the personal and private sphere, but today they have taken their peace-making capacity into the public domain by struggling and campaigning for peace and justice in an entirely new way. This is evident from women's deep involvement in the peace and ecology movement to which we shall return later.

To put into practice the spirit of peace, of friendship and love, humankind must become fully aware of all the potentials of our global spiritual and moral resources, an essential part of which is represented by the spiritual heritage and resources of women. More than anything else this heritage of women consists in the celebration and affirmation of all life – the life that flows in our veins, the force that lives in nature all around us, the life that animates us within, and the life of the spirit which continually renews us. This is a most precious heritage for the renewal of our world and the life of all people, but women in particular can draw great strength not only from the spiritual resources within themselves and their sisters, but also from a rich and diverse heritage of symbols, beliefs and exemplary lives in the cultures and religions of the past.

The spiritual heritage of women

Whilst the past can never provide a complete blueprint for the shaping of the present, it contains many spiritual treasures which can help us in living today. More and more people are becoming aware of the rich spiritual heritage of women which must be recovered from the past. This means we have to uncover much that has been hidden, left out or forgotten; it means we have to remake, rewrite and reinterpret much that has gone for the history of our religious traditions. Innumerable women throughout history have lived a life of faith and have been a source of strength and fortitude to their contemporaries and later genera-tions. It would be impossible to list all the great 'women of faith', the 'women of wisdom' known and praised in different religions, but let us look at just a few examples from the rich storehouse of history which can provide sources of inspiration for women and men today.

What is, in brief, the spiritual heritage of women? There is first of all the amazing heritage of all the resources of the primal, the archaic and the tribal experiences with their diverse worldviews wherein the inter-dependent unity of earth and sky, of day and night, of the female and male halves of human existence are still intuited as an integral whole lost to us today, a harmony of interdependence, mutual relationship and complementarity we have to forge again in a new, but different way. There is, for example, the Babylonian and Maori myth of the birth of all living forms from world parents who, in their sexual embrace, represent primal completeness and unified totality lost through their separation, a loss which must be overcome in order to regain unity. Contemporary women can learn a great deal from the balance and coherence of the primal vision, not only as it existed in the distant past, but as still found intact in some small-scale societies today. One can admire and feel inspired by the 'daughters of the dreaming' (Bell, 1984), the Australian Aboriginal women whom a woman researcher encountered as:

> a strong, articulate and knowledgeable group of women who were substantially independent of their menfolk in economic and ritual terms. Their lives were not ones of drudgery, deprivation, humiliation and exploitation . . . nor was their self-image and identity bound up solely with the child-bearing and child-rearing functions. Instead I found the women to be extremely serious in the upholding, observance and transmission of their religious heritage. Religion permeated every aspect of their lives. (Bell, 1984, p. 231).

Another important aspect of women's spiritual heritage is the widespread experience of mother earth, the matrix of all life, the *Terra Mater* or cosmic mother widely worshipped throughout the world, whether we think of traditional African religions, of aspects of early Indian and Greek religion, of Celtic religion or so many others. What does the widespread existence and worship of an earth and fertility goddess teach us today? We have the 30 000 years old statue of the Venus of Willendorf, the oldest sign of fertility in the western world and a key symbol of life and creativity. Yet today we are looking for a new kind of fertility, not so much a fertility at the physical as at the spiritual level. Many women and men are discovering today a new kind of spirituality through their realisation of the interdependence of all living forms on earth. They are developing a new 'spirituality of the earth', a 'creation spirituality' whereby they recognise and celebrate the gift of life animating the earth and they acknowledge and venerate its sacredness.

A still richer heritage of women is represented by the numerous goddess figures found in Northern Europe, Europe, Africa, India and the Far East. It is not only the earth-centred, nature-oriented worship of the mother goddess who creates and sustains all life which many contemporary women have rediscovered as a powerful inspiration for their spirituality, but especially the figure of the independent Great Goddess. Less linked to motherhood and female bodily existence, she above all expresses female independence and power in her own right. She is seen as a feminine symbol of Ultimate Reality and reflects the great metaphysical truth that all is one at a higher level of existence. In the ancient

Near East this figure is also known as *Sophia*, the great Wisdom Goddess, a divine being different from that of the patriarchal Father God (Long, 1992). She is not so much a symbol of life as a symbol of spiritual plenitude, fullness of insight and understanding, a source of spiritual rather than physical birth and generation.

In the Far East we have *Kannon*, a female image of the Bodhisattva of compassion and mercy whose figure has attracted widespread veneration through the ages. The gracefulness and serenity of *Kannon* is sometimes understood as transcending the sexual distinctions of male and female, but she is also a figure who has assumed within herself several aspects of other female divinities found in China and elsewhere.

The awareness of the differentiation between male and female as well as the search for a higher unity has led in many religions to the concept of an androgynous godhead as the ultimate symbol of the unification of all opposites. We find the image of the androgyne as a symbol of unity and completeness in Indian religion, in the classical religions of Europe, in early Christianity and elsewhere. For many feminists the androgynous model is of central importance for their spiritual and social life, as we shall observe in the next chapter.

Can one see in these developments a progressive spiritualisation of female experience from the physical level to aspects of the spiritual such as wisdom, truth, love and integration? At the level of symbol and myth, of story and thought about the creation of the world, the nature of life and of Ultimate Reality we find a wealth of female imagery which can inspire not only the newly found identity and awareness of women today, but of men too.

A further source of inspiration and strength can be found in the lives of women saints and mystics from East and West, many of whom provide viable examples for a dynamic, world-oriented spirituality today. This does not require their slavish imitation, as we can no longer live under the same conditions as women in the past. Yet powerful past 'women of the spirit' can none the less provide rich resources for the psychic, intellectual and religious life of our own times. Who is not inspired by the ardent love of the Islamic mystic Rabi'a and the many women in Sufism who followed in her path? Who does not admire the singlemindedness of Akka Mahadevi, the great Shiva devotee, or Mira Bai, the famous poet-princess of Hinduism who worshipped Krishna above all else, or Bahinabai who combined her life for God with a life for the family? Closer to our own time there is Sarada Devi, the wife of the late nineteenth-century Hindu saint Ramakrishna, who became a guru in her own right and subsequently inspired the foundation of Hindu women convents (see Ramakrishna Vedanta Centre, *Women Saints East and West*, 1955). We also know of innumerable Buddhist and Christian nuns, of women founders of religious groups, sects and new religious movements in different parts of the world. How did all these women of the past experience their vocation and find their identity in responding to a call of the spirit? How did they pursue a life of intense religious devotion and deep spirituality, often against the most incredible odds of their social and cultural environments?

All the resources of our creative imagination are called upon to stretch far back into the past and rejoin the lives of women through the ages. In retracing the pattern of their struggles and choices we can begin to sense the vivid texture of their lives and breathe the strength of their spirit. Women today can rejoice in the many spiritual 'foremothers' we possess and can discover a great company of women who can inspire their own search for identity and freedom. This is a powerful connection, a web of universal sisterhood far stronger than just the experiences of today.

This connection with the past is a tissue covering all aspects of women's lives, but it is of particular significance in the area of spirituality. Whilst numerous details of women's past religious beliefs and practices may have an intrinsic fascination for us, not all are of equal importance for women's spirituality today. More than anything else it is the figure of the woman mystic who provides an outstanding example of personal autonomy, deep commitment and spiritual power. As many feminist writers remain unaware of the importance of religion as a powerful source of identity and freedom and are unacquainted with the spiritual heritage of women, they tend to ignore the inspiration and strength that women can draw from the example of religiously committed women in the past. One only needs to look at Simone de Beauvoir's influential work *The Second Sex* (1972) to realise that her far-reaching analysis of women's role and subjection in society takes little account of the independence reached by some religious and lay women in the Judaeo-Christian tradition, for example, who pursued the spiritual life with extraordinary singlemindedness and often gained positions of great moral and spiritual authority in their communities, and this is true of many women in other religious traditions too. Contemporary feminists would do well to listen to the powerful voices of the women mystics who provide us with a paradigm of female spirituality and authority of greatest interest for us today. Let us examine the reasons for this.

The paradigm of the woman saint and mystic

People interested in spirituality may object to looking at women mystics separately from male mystics. This may be taking gender differentiation too far, for surely what matters first and foremost is the mystical experience, the spiritual life, rather than the sex of the person who pursues a particular spiritual path. Thus might argue many a contemporary writer on spirituality. However, on closer enquiry some surprising perspectives emerge when one combines the current interest in mysticism as an important religious phenomenon with a feminist perspective (King, 1981b).

Before we look specifically at the woman mystic, a few words on the contemporary understanding of mysticism will be helpful. Whilst mysticism is a notoriously difficult phenomenon to define, it is clearly present in all religious traditions of past and present. It occurs inside and outside religion and can be seen as an integral part of the ongoing history of the human spirit. In fact, one can consider the recurrence of mystical experiences as a testimony to the continuing breakthrough and disclosure of the divine spirit within history, within the world and within ourselves. Whilst there is always a vision and apprehension of underlying or overarching unity, the different mystical experiences are very varied indeed and do not conform to an overall pattern, but fall into divergent types.

It is important to realise that the comparative study of mysticism in its different varieties is largely a modern development which, for reasons that cannot be discussed here, belongs mainly to the twentieth century (King, 1982). The rediscovery of the life and work of many women mystics of the past has also occurred during this period. Although this recovery has by no means been the exclusive achievement of women, it is striking how many women scholars have made outstanding contributions to our present knowledge and understanding of mysticism in general and of women mystics in particular. To name only a few, there are Evelyn Underhill, Grace Warrack, Geraldine Hodgson, Phyllis Hodgson, Hope Emily Allen, Emily Herman, Hilda Graef, and for Islamic mysticism Margaret Smith and Annemarie Schimmel.

Mysticism is always embedded in a wider social, cultural and religious context. It cannot be accounted for purely in terms of individual experience nor in merely philosophical or scientific terms, but it invites above all a religious and theological interpretation, a unifying vision and exploration beyond analysis. The more we differentiate and analyse, the more we encounter that which cannot be grasped or got hold of, but which we can only embrace in love and surrender. We meet here the ultimate mystery of life itself which has to be lived, loved and celebrated, and experienced as lodged in the womb of the spirit.

The challenge of mysticism is the challenge of the oneness of the spirit. This is an integral and most precious part of our global religious heritage. But this challenge has rarely been realised in terms of the sisterhood and brotherhood of all people, in the form of an actual, concrete unification and practical oneness of the human community. Ultimately, the challenge of the spirit is a trans-sexual one pointing to wider connections and greater sharing beyond all differences. But what can we especially learn from women mystics?

Mysticism can be seen as a path to a summit or centre, a journey with many stages and difficulties, a call to a supreme adventure. Many women of the past and present have taken up the challenge of this call. The adventure of following a call to the spiritual life, under whatever form and in whatever way, gave women in the past a freedom from social ties which makes them stand out among their contemporaries. This freedom sometimes went so far that the distinction between women and men became obliterated. Women of great spiritual authority were recognised as persons in their own right who were given wide recognition, even by otherwise anti-feminist ascetics. This can be seen in the early Muslim reactions to the mystic Rabi'a who introduced the concept of pure love into Islamic mysticism (Smith, 1928) or in the attitudes of the contemporaries of Margery Kempe or St Teresa of Avila. The dominant androcentric perspective required, however, that women of such strength of spirit were likened to be 'as men' who had transcended what were perceived to be the innate limitations of womanhood.

In the Christian tradition this attitude goes as far back as St Jerome who maintained that a woman who does not follow the path of wife and motherhood, but devotes herself to a life of virginity by serving Christ more than the world, ceases to be a woman and 'will be called a man'. In the context of a very different religious tradition, namely late nineteenth-century Hinduism, Ramakrishna too is quoted as having said that if a woman follows the path of complete renunciation or *sannyasa*, she 'is really a man', not a woman. Similarly, Teresa of Avila appealed to her nuns to be 'courageous like men'. This theme of the 'male woman' can be traced right back to early Christianity (Aspegren, 1990). In Islam too, the great women mystics were said to have reached the lofty stage of 'Man of God' (Schimmel, 1982, p. 146). Many similar statements could be cited which provide evidence for the extraordinary limitations of the traditional understanding of women's roles and abilities. They highlight the sexist presuppositions in correlating certain roles, attributes or qualities with one sex rather than the other. Why should women not be courageous as women? Why should they not embody certain religious and spiritual ideals within all the conditions and potential of their own sex and on their own terms rather than be compared to and measured by an extraneous norm, that of men?

Although there is a great diversity among the women mystics of the past, in most religions women's spiritual attainment was often, if not always, linked to a life of sexual abstinence and renunciation. In Christianity it was usually either virgins or widows free from family ties rather than married women who followed the spiritual path, and many did so as nuns. The history of women's asceticism and spirituality still needs to be written so that one can assess its precise importance for women today. Communities of nuns and religious sisterhoods have been important in the development of Buddhism and Christianity. Christian religious orders of women are found from the fourth century CE onwards whilst single women ascetics have a long tradition in Hinduism and Jainism (Shântâ, 1985). However, women living in organised religious communities are rare and relatively recent in Hinduism (King, 1984b) whilst in Buddhism the number of nuns has never been large. In Christianity, by contrast, nuns have been very numerous and have made decisive contributions to its development and spread. The investigation of the contemporary diversity of activities and lifestyles found among Christian nuns provides a fascinating area of research (Bernstein, 1976). Less than twenty years ago, the number of Roman Catholic women religious alone was more than 1 million worldwide which was three times the number of all male religious and priests put together (Moorehouse, 1969, pp. 253ff.) The number of vocations has declined since then, but more recent statistics still list a world total of 946 398 Roman Catholic nuns (Barrett, 1982, p. 836).

These figures indicate that religious sisterhoods, wherein women follow a vocation by living in separate communities, were by no means a phenomenon restricted to the Middle Ages, a time which produced so many outstanding women mystics. However, their achievements have often been obscured as in the transmission of the tradition more attention has been given to the works of male mystics who were less numerous in some periods than the women whose writings had to be 'rediscovered' in modern times.

Women mystics in medieval times

During the eleventh and twelfth centuries CE the phenomenon of women recluses developed in western Europe, a typical women's movement which seems to have had no parallels among men. Women from well-to-do families renounced marriage and devoted themselves to a solitary religious life in cities by living in a cell attached to a church. Such life of solitary confinement was taken up after several years' preparation which culminated in a religious ceremony conducted by the bishop of the town and attended by many people. It concluded with the words 'requiescat in pace' – 'rest in peace' – words normally uttered over someone who is being buried. From her cell the woman recluse could follow through a window all the services in the church and much of her day was devoted to prayer, meditation and spiritual reading. But there was time for other activities too, such as spinning, weaving, sewing and embroidery. The cell might have a small enclosed garden where herbs were grown for medicinal purposes and some recluses undertook the copying and illuminating of manuscripts. Although isolated, these women recluses were far from separated from the world as they enjoyed high esteem and were sought after for advice and counsel. They undertook spiritual direction, some even heard confessions and aroused the jealousy of the clergy, whilst others gave instruction to girls (Aarnink, 1983).

One still gets a feel for the kind of life that these women lived when one reads about Mother Julian living in her cell at Norwich. It is possible that the movement of Christian lay women represented by the medieval beguine communities developed from the women recluses. Due to the death of thousands of men during the crusades and other wars, women far outnumbered men during the thirteenth century. The existing convents were overcrowded and would not accept new novices. Also, traditionally they were mainly open to women from aristocratic families who could bring a substantial dowry. Thus women were challenged to take their spiritual life into their own hands. Instead of living alone by being attached to a church or hospice, women came together in small groups and formed communities of Christian lay women who showed great fervour in devoting themselves to a life inspired by the ideals of the gospel. They also accepted women from wider social strata than did the convents (Bowie, 1989; Zum Brunn and Epiney-Burgard, 1989).

The beguines have been called feminists before their time but, unlike with the recluses, the idea of living Christian spirituality in lay communities also took root among men who are called 'beghards'. This movement of lay spirituality flourished during the thirteenth and fourteenth centuries CE by spreading from the Low Countries along the Rhine valley to Germany and France. The women and men in this movement

> sought the *vita apostolica* – the 'apostolic life' of poverty, mendicancy, and preaching. When this ideal was voiced and practiced in the twelfth century by unlicensed itinerant preachers who were dissatisfied with the laxities they found in the hierarchical Church it seemed heterodox. . . .
>
> Beghards and beguines organized themselves in a half-secular, half-religious fashion. . . . The women called beguines vowed themselves to chastity and most lived in convents known as beguinages, earning their livelihood by manual labor or taking alms. Though females unquestionably predominated in the movement, it is a mistake to underestimate the role of males. (Lerner, 1972, p. 36)

Many contemporaries considered the beguines and beghards as the most devout Christians of their age. It is possible that the Dutch mystic Hadewijch (thirteenth century CE) was a beguine. But there were also charges of hypocrisy and heresy, not for reasons of laxity and indifference, but based on insubordinate religious zeal. The basic criticism was directed against their intense, unlicensed lay piety and some of their sharpest critics came from among the male friars. From the early fourteenth century CE onwards the beguine movement was attacked for its unauthorised and excessive pursuit of the apostolic life and many members were accused of proclaiming the heresy of the Free Spirit (Lerner, 1972).

This heresy certainly seems to have found many adherents among women, not all of whom were necessarily beguines. It taught that men and women could attain perfection on earth through a direct personal relationship between God and the soul which made the mediation of the church unnecessary. Many beguines are also reported to have had visions of an impending third age in which the Holy Ghost would be incarnate in a woman. Women played a large part in a number of medieval heresies, but the reasons for this are not always entirely clear. Some have been stated as follows:

> Putting aside the male prejudice the females are particularly susceptible to religious enthusiasm . . . there were genuine sociological

reasons for the attachment of women to the *vita apostolica* and psychological reasons for their leaning toward mysticism in the later Middle Ages. Because of the higher male death rate and the large number of unmarried clerics there was a surplus female population. To make matters worse, there was a scarcity of legitimate female vocations and comparatively few women could gain entrance into nunneries. The beguinal life was thus a perfect avenue for the unmarried to obtain occupation and a modicum of communal security. Many . . . wanted no more than that, but it is easy enough to understand why a good number of women, some of whom were not beguines, turned to radical mysticism. The medieval relegation of women to an inferior status was as severe as their material problems. Women could not become priests, but Free-Spirit doctrine offered them something better than that: full union with divinity. (Lerner, 1972, p. 230)

One can see the 'proto-feminism' of the late Middle Ages (1200–1500 CE) as one of the most startling developments in history (Clark and Richardson, 1977, p. 102). Some of the highest flights of mystical poetry produced during that period came from the pens of women. They created a rich heritage of devotional and spiritual literature which made wide use of allegories and visions clothed in intense, dramatic and often erotic imagery. It expresses a profoundly affective spirituality, born out of and true to the experience of particular women. If one examines the wide range of mystical literature produced by women, often the only source of knowledge for us about their life and experience, a number of interesting differences are apparent when compared with the mystical literature written by men.

In examining *Medieval Women Writers* on both secular and religious themes Katharina M. Wilson (1984) has stressed the pronounced difference between the writings of medieval men and women:

Both groups write from their respective but collective experiences: men often write of the physically heroic pursuits of men at war; women write of the spiritually heroic exploits of love and devotion. Moreover, women often depict women characters more frequently, more sympathetically, and more convincingly than do male authors. (Wilson, 1984, p. xx)

The same author maintains that 'With women mystics the presence of female consciousness is less pronounced, but they . . . tend to emphasize the female aspect of divinity (that is, Christ's role as mother) more than do their male contemporaries' (p. xxi). It is also interesting to note that in later reflections on texts of female mysticism medieval and Renaissance writers invariably seem to emphasise

> the woman's talents for prophecy, inspiration, Christian devotion, and genuine religiosity, not her acuity, erudition, or literary gifts. She is depicted (and frequently depicts herself) as a vessel of divine inspiration, not as a creative genius, and the scriptural injunction that God often elects the weak to confound the strong is frequently invoked to explain the phenomenon of lay and female mystical inspiration. (p. 17)

All mystics see their role as passive before God, but with women this seems to be doubly so. Many mystics, whether male or female, made wide use of bridal and nuptial imagery to describe the soul's intimate relationship with God, the radical nature of their yearning and belonging, but the writings of women mystics are often expressed in a particularly strong emotional and sometimes even ecstatic tone. They reverberate with the intensity of an experience which is nothing less than an all-consuming love affair with God.

Specialists in the comparative study of mysticism have pointed out that mystics in different religions tend to emphasise either the objective reality of God's greatness and transcendence or the subjective element, their inner religious experience. Thus there is not only an element of sexual differentiation, but also one of different emphasis in the different religious traditions. For example, mystics of the Jewish Kabbalah (always male rather than female) or of eastern orthodox Christianity emphasise the objective side by writing mostly about God rather than their personal experience of divine reality. The mystics of western Christianity, by contrast, have made wide use of the spiritual autobiography since the Middle Ages, and this is particularly true of women mystics. It is indicative that the first autobiography in the English language is *The Book of Margery Kempe* (Butler-Bowdon, 1936) wherein a fourteenth century illiterate lay woman from King's Lynn in Norfolk – mother of 14 children – describes her religious experiences, pilgrimages, thoughts, feelings and impressions with great vivacity and directness. From this book emerges a 'clear, vivid picture of an immensely vital, honest, and intense human being . . . , a woman who is at times reminiscent of Saint Paul and at others of the Wife of Bath' (Wilson, 1984,

p. 300). Only discovered earlier this century. Margery Kempe's story also 'illustrates the new woman who assertively dominates her husband on the basis of her experience of being married not to him, but to God. (Margery actually experienced this marriage with God and wore, thereafter, a wedding ring inscribed "Jesus Christ is my love.")' (Clark and Richardson, 1977, p. 103). A rich resource for understanding the world of Margery Kempe and female sanctity in the late Middle Ages is Clarissa Atkinson's study *Mystic and Pilgrim* (1983).

That women mystics express greater subjectivity and stronger feelings in describing their experiences may have something to do with the fact that women were officially excluded from theological education and teaching. Not being schooled in objectifying modes of thought, they were freer in expressing their own feelings and cast their ideas in a subjective mode. It has also been observed that male mystics often describe the stages of the mystical path as the ascent of a mountain, as a path towards a summit or goal, whilst female mystics make more use of images of inwardness such as the cave or the rooms of a mansion or of a castle (as in Teresa of Avila's *The Interior Castle*; see Green, 1989).

All these differences seem to indicate that women mystics stress subjectivity and personal experience more than external factors and objectivisation. Given the vivid directness of expression and the wide prevalence of love mysticism among women, one wonders whether women embody a more concrete, emotional and perhaps even romantic type of mysticism rather than the intellectual and abstract type found among men. The affective piety and devotion and the call to holiness and spiritual perfection open to medieval women in the Christian west gave many a woman an authority and empowerment rarely equalled in the history of womankind.

We still need to study the specific contributions and achievements of women mystics in much greater detail. There is much to be learnt from the very positive role women played in mystical Islam or Sufism (see 'The feminine element in Sufism' in Schimmel, 1975, pp. 426–35). Women are found in almost every avenue of Sufism. They have acted as patrons of Sufi orders, been in charge of certain Sufi convents, are venerated as saints and accepted as spiritual guides. As mothers, many mystically inclined women deeply influenced their sons in becoming Sufis who, unlike Christian monks and ascetics, did not have to remain unmarried. Women married to Sufis also exercised a strong influence on Sufism, especially during its formative period. Sufism offered women greater possibilities than Islamic orthodoxy to participate actively in religious and social life and many Sufi women teachers are known, especially in Turkey and Egypt, even in modern times. Annemarie Schimmel, an outstanding authority on this subject, has compared the Muslim and Christian woman mystic. Referring to Islam she writes:

> It might be difficult to find many unmarried women who pursued the Path. For, contrary to the Christian ideal of the virgin saint, the nun or recluse who experienced the highest ecstasies in her lonely cell far away from the bonds of husbands and children, most of the Islamic women saints were married and usually had a family. It was thanks to them that their children grew up in the atmosphere of perfect trust in God and piety as we can still observe in the villages of Anatolia and Pakistan. (Schimmel, 1982, p. 150)

In some ways women mystics in Islam may provide a more suitable model for women today than the women religious of medieval Christianity but, unlike in Christianity, women in Islam did not excel as authors of works on mysticism. One reason for this may be the different attitude to learning and education and the lack of access to the language and thought of the Koran. But we know that the classics of mystical education in the Persian, Turkish and Urdu languages were read and taught in the women's quarters of pious families of the upper classes. The Muslim women of the Indian subcontinent in particular were also the addressees of mystical folk poets who were able

> to explain the secrets of the mystical path in simple, easy verses which the women could sing while spinning or grinding grain so that their household chores were transformed into symbols of spiritual activities. Just as by unceasing spinning the thread becomes fine and so precious that it can be sold at a high price thus the heart becomes refined by the constant repetition of religious formulas or the names of God so that God will 'buy' it at Doomsday for a high price. (The relation between the constant murmuring of the sacred words and the humming sound of the spinning wheel makes this image particularly fitting). (Schimmel, 1982, p. 150)

Much more research is needed on particular women figures in the history of Islamic mysticism, but we can see from these few references that contemporary women can draw inspiration from the examples of the past which illuminate many different aspects of the spiritual quest among

women. The awareness of women's importance in the global history
of spirituality and mysticism is growing. So much so that some years
ago a male author who produced a fine anthology on mysticism
(R. Woods, *Understanding Mysticism*, 1981) found it necessary to apolo-
gise for the relative absence of female contributions to his work. Yet
there is certainly no lack of material!

A helpful introduction to the life of several women mystics of the
Middle Ages is found in the essays and selected readings of Katharina
M. Wilson's anthology *Medieval Women Writers* (1984) which has
already been mentioned. It brings together the achievements of outstanding religious and secular women writers who lived between the ninth
and fifteenth centuries CE. They include the great women mystics
Hildegard of Bingen and Mechthild of Magdeburg from Germany,
Hadewijch from the Netherlands, the politically active St Bridget from
Sweden and St Catherina of Siena/Italy as well as Julian of Norwich
and Margery Kempe from England, not to forget the 'French heretic
beguine' and follower of the Free-Spirit Movement, Marguerite Porete,
whose mystical treatise *Mirror of Simple Souls* enjoyed a high reputation
through several centuries, in spite of Marguerite's being burnt at the
stake. It was handed down anonymously and at one time even considered
to be by the famous mystic Ruysbroeck. (See also Dronke, 1984, *Women
Writers of the Middle Ages: A Critical Study of Texts from Perpetua
(+203) to Marguerite Porete (+1310).*) Full length editions of Christian
women mystics can be found in the series *The Classics of Western
Spirituality*, especially the text of Julian's *Showings* (1978) and *The
Complete works of Hadewijch* (1981). For specialised studies on the
beguines, Hildegard of Bingen, and Julian of Norwich see Zum Brunn
and Epiney-Burgard (1989), Newman (1987) and Jantzen (1987).

Medieval women were kept out of the universities; they could not
become scholastic theologians, but many achieved distinction through
becoming powerful writers on spirituality and mysticism, providing
spiritual leadership and counsel to others. These were women of great
independence and power, not so much in external terms, but in terms
of moral authority and spiritual perfection. These were women strong
enough to resist the pressures of family, society, and even the church at
times, out of a deep commitment to a higher calling. This also often
empowered them to enter into much freer relationships with men, some
of whom publicly recognised the authority and spiritual power of their
women contemporaries.

In her essay 'Women, Power and the Pursuit of Holiness' Eleanor

McLaughlin shows through the lives and stories of medieval women how the pursuit of holiness seemed to empower them. She writes:

> I hope to show how the spirituality of the women who were called holy by their friends, their neighbors and the Church was a source of wholeness, meaning, power and authority. The effectiveness of these women was rooted in their holiness. Power out of holiness.
>
> A second theme suggested by the lives and work of some medieval saints, both men and women, is the possibility that the ideal of human nature they exemplified – or their biographers set forth – represent a range of human possibility, a richness of human expression, that has been particularly hospitable to women and to whatever is meant today by the 'feminine'. . . .
>
> This more 'feminized' human nature was *not* seen as 'feminine' by men and women of the pre-Reformation Church but rather as Christian, typical and in the image of God, who was Mother as well as Father, Love more than Intellect. Holiness called forth a Christian theology and an anthropology radically *less* androcentric than that which dominates Christian piety today.

And towards the end of her essay the same author concludes:

> Yet it may still be possible for us today, seeking to discover meaning at the center of the self and the cosmos, to quicken the imagination and enrich our symbolic vocabulary by listening once more to the stories and the vision which lie readily at hand within the Western Christian tradition shaped by powerful, holy women. (McLaughlin, 1979, pp. 102 and 126ff.)

It is not only in Christianity, but also in other religions that we encounter the powerful voices of women saints and mystics. We have to rediscover the global heritage of women's spirituality and draw inspiration from the enabling power women possessed in the past. Yet this important task must be undertaken in a critical spirit not subject to false idealisation.

Mysticism and feminism: some questions for the feminist mystic

Having emphasised the importance of women mystics as a paradigm for contemporary women, it would be wrong to consider all saintly women of the past, whether in Christianity or elsewhere, as 'feminists' or 'proto-feminists' simply by virtue of their belonging to the female sex. On the contrary, when looking more closely at the life stories of some women saints from a contemporary feminist perspective, one realises the ambiguity of some women's example and also the ambivalence inherent in the pursuit of spirituality. 'What does one do today with obedience, passivity, contemplative enclosure as a flight from the world, and the apparent loss of self in the pilgrimage toward dependence on God?' How much can we really learn from these women saints and mystics when one realises 'that the female holy ones were not quite as equal as their brothers' (McLaughlin, 1979, p. 101) and when one becomes aware of the blatant fact that throughout the history of religions patriarchal male spiritual guidance remained the order of the day and that, exceptions apart, religious traditions have on the whole legitimated a rather restrictive spirituality for women, namely a spirituality of dependence, obedience, passivity and heteronomy. Whilst it would be falsifying historical evidence and perhaps even constitute sexism in disguise if one ascribed feminist modes of thought and behaviour to all women of the past, solely because they were women following a path of self-realisation, one can none the less look at past instances of female mysticism from the critical perspective of feminist consciousness. One can then discover and accentuate the liberating qualities of mysticism which gave particular women not power *over* but power *for*, enabling power, to seek spiritual, personal and social freedom which entailed further power for advising, teaching, writing, counselling and helping others as well as power for building and transforming communities.

Female mystics thus exemplify to an extraordinary degree women's struggle for autonomy and self-affirmation, crowned by the liberating experience of self-transcendence. The multiple threads of their life's journeys and stories provide a rich tapestry of the spiritual life which above all is a proof of women's powers of radical love and self-surrender to a reality greater than themselves. Caroline Walker Bynum (1982) has emphasised the affective quality of the spirituality of the high Middle Ages typical of both women and men, but particularly found among women, especially in the thirteenth century when

> women were more likely than men to be mystics, to gain reputations based on their mystical abilities, and to have paramystical experiences (such as trances, levitations, stigmata, etc.). Moreover, these women mystics were primarily responsible for encouraging and propa-

gating some of the most distinctive aspects of late medieval piety: devotion to the human, especially the infant, Christ and devotion to the eucharist (frequently focused on devotion to the wounds, blood, body, and the heart of Jesus). (pp. 171ff.)

This is a specific example from the Christian tradition which shows how women's spirituality is often linked to a concreteness, a directness, if not to say 'physicalness', of experience far removed from the abstract flights of theological speculations. Similarly one can find in Hinduism a rich spirituality and deep devotion to the divine child Krishna, often practised by women. The close relationship to children is so much part of women's experience that it is here transferred to a divine and symbolic level.

The same concrete physicality of women's spirituality appears in attitudes to food studied by Caroline Bynum in *Holy Feast and Holy Fast: The Religious Significance of Food to Medieval Women* (1987). Such spirituality can be nourishing for us today as it is an integral part of women's historical heritage and experience whose empowering aspects more and more people are beginning to discover. Whilst the women saints and mystics of the past were not necessarily 'feminists' in any contemporary sense of the word, women today can legitimately call for and undertake the feminist appropriation of female mystical experience and thereby discover resources for pride and praise as well as spiritual power.

Being more conscious of a web of interrelationships and connections, women are perhaps less tempted than men to see spirituality as something apart from life. If spirituality is considered an intrinsic dimension and potential of human consciousness, a path to a higher, fuller life which explores the furthest limits of being human, then it implies a horizon of transcendence which affects the very texture of life and provides it with its ultimate meaning and essence. Spirituality is thus the very leaven of human life. But in its traditional religious forms spirituality has often become rather stale, unable to act as a true leaven to transform life and make it rise. So many spiritualities of the past can no longer give us the energies and vision we need and feed our zest for life in a world clouded by danger and despair. Many individuals and movements today, not least contemporary feminism, are taking soundings to discover a new spirituality for a new season.

Given the pressing needs of the present, there is a real need for the emergence of what has been called 'the feminist mystic'. If one understands the mystic as primarily someone withdrawn into inward experience, this would seem rather contradictory. But if there is a connection between inner and outer transformation, as there must be, if the inward transformation of self is linked to outward social transformation, then the conjunction of feminism and mysticism is not as contradictory as it might at first appear. Anne Bancroft has described such contemporary women mystics from very different backgrounds in her *Weavers of Wisdom* (1989).

But the meaning and path of the feminist mystic is not always an easy one. Mary E. Giles prefaced several contributions on *The Feminist Mystic and Other Essays on Women and Spirituality* with the following words:

> There are no sure voices to guide us. . . .
>
> We are a present, suspicious of the past, uncertain of the future. We are the women of solitude, being taught the art of living in and through the Spirit, and it is not easy.
>
> It is not easy precisely because the assured voices of religious and social institutions and traditions which we believe instructed women in the past seem still. . . .
>
> We may not yet hear . . . harmony, but it is there. . . . Women who know the solitude of the solitary endeavor are open to it, this music of oneness to which mystics of all times and traditions attend and upon which they play, each one a unique variation. . . .
>
> Such women are not creations of pious fancy; they were women who laughed and loved, wept and despaired. Like us, they were women for whom living was a daily encounter with pettiness and bigotry. But they did not submit to discord; the harmony of love prevailed. (Giles, 1982, pp. 1, 2 and 3)

In Mary Giles' book the emphasis is very much on the personal journey required for spiritual transformation. But this journey has important implications for relationships with others and for the shaping of community. One of the recurrent themes in feminist spirituality is women's need to find their true self, a topic already touched upon in the previous chapter. Women are so accustomed to living for others, whethers partners, husbands, children or ageing relatives, that they frequently subordinate their own identity and self to the needs and interests of other people. Their service to others, to their loved ones, which is so much needed for the maintenance of community, has in practice often developed into a caricature of true service by becoming excessive female subservience with the result of women's own spiritual deprivation. Such female subservience has often been encouraged by religious and spiritual authorities who have helped to condition women into what has been called a 'merger self' rather than to foster and nourish a 'seeker self'. But in order to grow to maturity women have to make their own journey along the spiritual path and undertake their own vision quest to answer the call of the spirit.

This need, so fully articulated, now raises the question which aspects of past female and feminine experience women wish to affirm or to reject. The many choices open to women today – the choice of gender role, the choice of work, the experience of relationship, of motherhood, of self-affirmation and identity as well as the choice of an authentic existence empowered by a horizon of transcendence – require 'the courage to be alone' (see Giles, 1982, pp. 84ff.). The experience of separateness can help women to enter into stronger relationships and to create new connections in their lives. For many women voluntary or involuntary separation from others can be a dark night marked by the mystery of suffering and pain which may contain within it a mystery of personal and spiritual transformation.

This requires the recognition and wrestling with what some feminist theologians have called the specifically 'female sin' of woman's underdevelopment of self, of her unconscious passivity and receptivity which can lead to aimlessness and drift and utter superficiality rather than the active shaping and direction of her own life. Such a sin is a much greater temptation for women than the sin of pride, hybris, ego aggrandisement and self-sufficiency more often found in men. Whilst women need to fight the 'sin of sexism' inherent in the structures of society, they must equally well fight this debilitating 'sin' within themselves. Shaking off one's shackles and being caught by the grace of anger can be a transformative experience leading to spiritual awakening.

Mysticism is often defined as an experiential knowledge of God, a knowledge based on experience rather than rational deduction and suffused with love. The German theologian Dorothee Sölle has explored the dynamic interrelationship between 'mysticism–liberation–feminism' (Sölle, 1984, pp. 79–105; also Sölle, 1981a). Although we do not yet have a feminist description of mystical theology, Sölle argues that mysticism provides a greatly useful resource on the long road to liberation, especially for feminist Christians, but one can legitimately expand the argument to apply to mysticism in general, wherever it is found. Sölle gives three reasons for this: '(1) Mystical theology is based on experience, not on authority. (2) Explicitly or implicitly, mystical theology speaks of a God whose essence is *not* independence, otherness, might and domination. (3) Mysticism helps us learn the great surrender' (Sölle, 1981a, p. 179).

Like other theologians, Sölle argues that the traditional language about God is locked up and caught in a 'prison of symbols' which has to be opened for the power of the spirit to become effective. In this context it is worth noting that the language of the mystics often draws on symbols and experiences from nature rather than on abstract concepts, and this is particularly true of women mystics. It is thus closer to the rhythms and patterns of life as lived and experienced rather than thought.

For a feminist reflection on mysticism the lesson of self-surrender can be liberating too. For the mystic the self yields completely to the higher power of the spirit, the dynamic presence of divine life. The medieval mystics often distinguished three stages in the process of self-surrender: leaving the world, leaving the self, leaving God. Sölle refers to numerous trends towards mysticism in contemporary counter-culture and youth movements where many have 'left the world' and seek alternatives to the existing social order, but only few perhaps have also left their own ego behind. There is a fine dividing line between self-awakening and autonomous self-identity, so much needed in women, and the many manifestations of selfishness and egocentricity. Yet at the same time it is important to realise that one cannot surrender a sense of self one has never possessed.

Striving for a spiritual ideal and true holiness embodied in daily life requires that a person is God-centred rather than self-centred or, to use a more neutral terminology, that one is 'Reality-centred', that is to say oriented towards a greater reality than one's own life. Women as a group are on the whole known to be more other-centred than self-centred and whilst it is sometimes possible to detect a selfishness in inverted forms here, this other-centredness has often been seen as the main reason why women seem to possess a greater capacity for spirituality, self-surrender and sacrificial love. Many writers, not only in medieval times, have praised the special sanctity achieved by women. This other-centredness is perhaps women's greatest strength and at the same time the main reason for women's weakness, for their frequent lack of personal, emotional and spiritual autonomy. Women need to reflect critically on the inherent ambiguity of both self affirmation and self-surrender in seeking to develop their own independence and identity.

To return to the last stage of surrender on the mystical path, to 'leave God' is the most difficult of all for the mystic as this implies abandoning the embrace of God, the solitude of the spirit, to return to the world and its burning concerns to help our sisters and brothers. Many mystics of the past have been socially very active and many writers today stress the important connection between mysticism and social action or even militancy (Curle, 1976). This connection between mysticism, social action and politics is an important issue for the spirituality of the women's movement today (Collins, 1974; Christ, 1975; Spretnak, 1982). To be viable and convincing women's spirituality needs to be active, dynamic and forceful; it needs to be what some have called a spirituality of combat, a spirituality which is militant yet non-violent. But what are the necessary conditions for it to grow and develop?

Space for women's spirituality

Many women today can no longer find the inspiration for an active spirituality in traditional religious institutions, but they frequently seek it through literature (Christ, 1986) and art, through free experimentation and new kinds of community. As Joann Wolski Conn has commented in her discussion of women's spirituality:

> Because the spiritual tradition of women is often carried on in recent times outside the official context of religion, studies of women's fiction offer helpful resources for women's spirituality.
>
> This literature demonstrates how women's spiritual quest concerns women's awakening to forces of energy larger than the self, to powers of connection with nature and with other women, and to acceptance of body. For women, conversion is not so much giving up egocentric notions of power as passing through an experience of nothingness finally to gain power over their own lives. (Conn, 1980, p. 303)

Women's quest for spirituality includes the discovery that we have to shape spirituality for ourselves independently from male models and male spiritual guidance. Trusting their own experience and being attentive to the voice of the spirit within women can find the powers for healing, wholeness and love, for ministry to others. We do need women map makers of the interior country, as Sara Maitland (1983) has forcefully argued, but we need more than that. The problem is, how to connect inner and outer freedom, how to interrelate spiritual and social power? How can women find a truly creative balance in these matters?

Listening to powerful spiritual voices of the past one must ask oneself how far the spirituality and culture of women requires a place and space apart to flourish? Whether one thinks of the allegory of a separate 'city of ladies' created by the early fifteenth-century writer Christine de Pizan (1983; see also Wilson, 1984, pp. 333–63) or the separation of the sexes among the Australian Aboriginals where women follow elaborate rituals of their own and find continued meaning for their self-image as independent and autonomous members of society (Bell, 1984), whether one looks at the separate communities of religious and quasi-religious women of the Middle Ages or the women's groups today, one can always see that women gain self-affirmation, strength and spiritual power from within themselves and from each other by being on their own and in their own separate group. The question of physical and spatial separation, of a time and a space of their own – at least as a temporary and recurrent measure – is of the utmost importance for women's self-development and spirituality.

Such an experimental approach to spirituality, beginning with women's need for self-development, is sensitively explored in Kathleen Fischer's *Women at the Well. Feminist Perspectives on Spiritual Direction* (1989) and Katherine Zappone's *The Hope for Wholeness. A Spirituality for Feminists* (1991). Both write from a Christian perspective whereas a wider treatment of spirituality is found in Maria Harris' *Dance of the Spirit. The Seven Steps of Women's Spirituality* (1991) and the numerous contributions to the excellent Reader edited by Judith Plaskow and Carol P. Christ, *Weaving the Visions: New Patterns in Feminist Spirituality* (1989), a sequel to their earlier work, Carol P. Christ and Judith Plaskow, *Womanspirit Rising* (1979).

Women need room and space in their lives which gives them the freedom to develop their own gifts and follow their own calling. Olive Schreiner in one of her dreams lets a woman choose between 'Life's Gifts' of love and freedom, and the woman chooses freedom rather than love, a new calling rather than the traditional one which has so many ties attached to it. But in Schreiner's allegory woman is assured that one day life will give her both freedom *and* love, rather than love without freedom (Schreiner, 1895, pp. 115–16).

Women need the freedom to be alone. They need empowering space in their lives which often means time and silence for themselves to pursue a deep quest within themselves, to reflect on the sources and forces of their own lives and their own particular vocation. To gain liberation and find freedom requires detachment – detachment from immediate economic, social and emotional pressures; it requires the capacity for introspection and self-awareness as well as self-conscious choice. Such creative space is more than freedom in a personal and psychological sense as it can open up into a larger spiritual freedom which overcomes bondage and discloses a wide horizon which may range from joy and love to an awareness of divine splendour and glory. Women must create such space where there is room for friendship and celebration, for adoration and praise. Only then can individual people and communities find a sense of wholeness and integration.

This is where the mystics can help us, and women can learn from women mystics in particular. It has been said that the ecstatic religious experiences of women in the past, or of women of other societies and cultures, only existed in a total context which women today would find unbearably restricting (Bregman, 1977) and therefore cannot possibly provide suitable models for us. But I have tried to show that the powerful voices of past women saints and mystics, in spite of certain limitations, speak to women today with greater force and persuasion than they did to many of our ancestors.

5

Voices of a new spirituality

'We dare to raise the issue of spirituality for women, to begin to redefine it, and to say it is of vital importance to the women's movement.

Feminist spirituality has taken form in sisterhood – in our solidarity based on a vision of personal freedom, self-definition, and in our struggle together for social and political change. The contemporary women's movement has created space for women to begin to perceive reality with a clarity that seeks to encompass many complexities. . . . We choose the word spirituality because this vision presupposes a reverence for life, a willingness to deal with more than just rational forces, and a commitment to positive life-generating forces that historically have been associated with a more limited definition of spirituality. . . .

In its broadest context, spirituality is being open to reality in all of its dimensions – in its rational, irrational and superrational complexity, and acting on that understanding. This requires a radical departure from the present compartmentalized ways of perceiving and determining action.' – **Judy Davis and Juanita Weaver**, 'Dimensions of Spirituality', pp. 368ff.

Many different dimensions and definitions of spirituality exist, even within one single religion. Feminists, too, vary widely in their understanding of spirituality, but there is no doubt that the issue of spirituality provides an important focus for the thinking and being of contemporary women. 'Women talk about Spirituality', 'Women's Spirituality Rediscovered', 'Discovering Spirituality for Ourselves', 'In Search of the Feminine' are only some of the titles given to women's workshops and publications in Britain. In the USA the interest is much greater still and began much earlier. Some of this is associated with the so-called free spirituality movement which links women's spirituality with a separate women's culture. There is also the journal *Womanspirit*, published since 1974, which insists that spirituality is not just the pursuit of a privileged or fringe group but that 'womanspirit lives in the lives of all women'. It is a matter of women trusting their own experience and evolving their spiritual consciousness, power and strength within and among themselves.

In one of the early numbers of *Womanspirit* the editors wrote: 'Our intention is to put women in touch – in communion – with each other and ourselves. . . . We feel this is a time for searching and sharing, for something *is* stirring the inner space of women. We do not know, cannot guess, what direction it will take. . . . We believe that many women, like us, need space to get in touch with their energy, wisdom and strength' (*Womanspirit*, 3, 1975). This underlines the experimental and experiential character of contemporary women's search for spirituality which is a quest for personal and social wholeness often powerfully expressed through the medium of art and literature.

As far as traditional religions are concerned, many feminists find the historically available models of spirituality too restricting and oppressive, too onesided and male-dominated for their new understanding of self and community. They see all existing religions as irrevocably cast in a patriarchal mould which remains dualistic and therefore cannot give women the vision of wholeness they need. Whilst traditional, patriarchal forms of spirituality are vehemently rejected, new forms of spirituality are eagerly sought, created or recreated through the use of ancient symbols, rites and beliefs. The result is a new kind of spirituality which as 'feminist spirituality' or even 'a religion for women' sees itself as altogether different and separate from other forms of spirituality.

Throughout this book spirituality has not been understood in this separate sense. Instead I have tried to explore a wide range of different dimensions which link the experience of women with that of spirituality or point to the spiritual implications of contemporary feminism. It is important, however, to realise that a separate feminist spirituality exists among particular individuals and groups who practise and voice it in different ways. Mary Ann Warren discusses this development in her encyclopedia *The Nature of Woman* (1980) under the heading of 'spiritual feminism', a term which according to her refers to that segment of the women's movement which is concerned with the development of an explicitly feminist religious awareness. . . . Some spiritual feminists hope to discover in the ancient worship of the Great Goddess not only an empirical refutation of the misogynist assumptions fostered by patriarchal religion but a source of authentic religious vision, a woman-centred world view free from the patriarchal taint. Some feminists have investigated (and even revived the rituals of) ancient and medieval mystery religions and witchcraft traditions. . . . Those who draw religious inspiration from such nonstandard sources constitute what might be called the revolutionary or heretical portion of the spiritual feminist movement. (Warren, 1980, p. 441)

This assessment is made from the perspective of traditional religion which spiritual feminists might well question, for far from seeing themselves as 'heretical', they consider themselves perhaps more as innovative and truly creative or in some cases as carrying on an ancient tradition relating to women rather than men. This spirituality is seen as truly woman-centred; it is a vehicle for their self-enhancement and revitalisation, a source of energising power, but also an inspiration for collective identity.

This is an important point not mentioned by Mary Ann Warren. Separate feminist spirituality is not only linked to a personal search for meaning and greater inwardness, but is often closely connected with the acceptance of social responsibility and political activism. Whilst individual women may have found a sense of identity and spiritual empowerment in spiritualist groups (Haywood, 1983), theosophical circles (Burfield, 1983) or other movements which provided an alternative to established main-stream religion, some feminists see their new spirituality not only as important for themselves, but even more so for the construction of a new social order and the destruction of the old one. This is where their approach is truly revolutionary, at least in spirit.

However, many concerns of the separatists overlap with those of other feminist groups. Mary Ann Warren also refers to a more inclusive meaning of 'spiritual feminism' when she goes on to say:

The majority of spiritual feminists, however, are not revolutionaries. Instead, they seek to work within the various Christian, Jewish, and (in a few instances) Islamic churches, to increase the participation of women, to gain entry for women to the priesthood or clergy and other church offices, to alter the antifemale elements of the church's teachings, and so on. Some even hope eventually to eliminate the presumption that the deity itself is male, or exclusively male . . . so long as the patriarchal aspects of these major religious traditions persist, reformist efforts by the spiritual feminists will be important as a way of making feminist ideas accessible to women whose religious convictions might otherwise preclude their sympathizing with, or even understanding, feminist demands. (Warren, 1980, pp. 441ff.)

In many ways the 'new spirituality' of feminists cannot be easily defined or circumscribed as there exists no strong embodiment or institutional core yet, but only small cult groups (see the addresses and resources listed in Patrice Wynne's *The Womanspirit Sourcebook*, 1988). Expressions of the new spirituality are varied and diffuse; attempts to describe them are more like capturing a mood or pointing to a potentially powerful transforming vision than discussing particular beliefs and practices, although these exist too. At the same time feminist voices on spirituality express many concerns shared by other contemporary movements seeking personal and social transformation. Above all they share an empowering holistic vision pointing to a richer sense of reality, a reverence for life, and a commitment to new forms of community.

But in spite of this common orientation feminist spirituality has developed distinctive elements and themes of its own. These include especially the veneration of the Goddess in diverse forms and, linked to Goddess worship, the emergence of matriarchy groups and a new witchcraft movement. Much use is also made of the symbol of the androgyne which seems to express for many the new forms of wholeness and integration women are looking for. Each of these strands consists of a wide variety of phenomena, often not without contradictions. Some of these will be examined in the following sections.

In search of the Goddess

The voices of a new spirituality draw their inspiration from a great number of different sources which are newly interpreted from within the perspective of contemporary feminism. Reality in its fullness, the source of all life within and without is today experienced, envisioned and conceptualised by many as Great Goddess. Her presence and power are affirmed in their own right, as different from and prior to the appearance of the traditional figure of God who has become almost completely identified with the male norms of patriarchal tradition. The Goddess is associated with an earlier matriarchal age of ancient times which, it is claimed, was superseded and suppressed by the ascent of male supremacy in all fields of human endeavour. Contemporary worshippers of the Goddess often refer rather indiscriminately to goddess figures and symbols of different periods and religious traditions which tend to get fused in a new understanding of a female form of ultimate Being.

But who is the Goddess and what does she stand for? Is she primarily a powerful symbol corresponding to a deep psychological need of human beings? Or is she a metaphysical reality in her own right? And what historical evidence do we have for the worship of goddesses in earlier times? And how does this relate to goddess figures in contemporary religions in Japan, India or Africa for example? Most important of all, what can the Goddess possibly mean for women today?

So much is written about the Goddess, both for and against her, that one can be truly bewildered as to her meaning and significance. Many works are published in praise of particular goddesses of the past, sometimes with relatively little critical assessment of the available evidence. The development of a feminist perspective of enquiry has encouraged a number of women scholars to undertake historical studies on goddesses which present us with new data of great importance for women's self-understanding and that of the cultures of the past.

Yet it is important to realise that most contemporary women's interest in the Goddess is less concerned with historical evidence than with the existential significance of her presence in their lives now. Thus quite a few publications on the Goddess are primarily confessions of faith in the strength of the feminine principle symbolised by numerous goddesses of different religious traditions, whether living or extinct. The return of the Goddess is seen as 'a way of initiation for women', a path 'for renewal in a feminine source-ground and spirit', 'a vitally important aspect of modern woman's quest for wholeness' (Perera, 1981, p. 7). The power of the Goddess is something that women, traditionally marked by powerlessness, can experience in the pattern and rhythm of their own lives. As one of the authors of the book *The Ancient Religion of the Great Cosmic Mother of All* wrote: 'For a woman now to be able to recognise and love the Goddess she must also be able to love herself and the Goddess in other women. Women's ancient love for each other has been diverted and has been forcibly directed exclusively towards the male as representing the Godhead. . . . Feminism means the rebirth of the Goddess in us.

She the One universal and infinite Self' (Sjöö and Mor, 1981, p. 5; also Sjöö and Mor, 1987).

How is this rebirth taking place? Let us look more closely at the return of the Goddess into contemporary religious consciousness and trace the emergence of a new Goddess spirituality and worship. As recently as 1982 a review of publications on 'Feminism and Spirituality' could still begin by affirming that 'Feminists often react with hostility, or at least, with hesitation, to the concept of "female spirituality", discussions about a female deity, or to "matriarchy" (Long, 1982, p. 103). By now these subjects have entered much more widely into the general discussions of feminists, though not necessarily those of the public at large. More and more women have begun to explore the heritage of the Goddess and ask about its meaning for us today. As the same reviewer went on to say:

A new era of feminist research is delving into prehistory, history, theology, anthropology, archaeology and many other disciplines and showing there is ample room for reconsideration. They are claiming that female deities, reflecting women's culture and women's power, were universally accepted by humankind until the modern era of immediate pre-industrial societies; that women's lives were not subordinate, and that women's values were indeed uppermost. Such values linked the physical with the spiritual, and were monist and holist rather than split and dualist. There is, claim the researchers, a huge area of female-defined spirituality which generates and feeds into feminist philosophy and activity.

Side by side with this comes an explosion of interest in the participation in women's rites and rituals, both those assumed to come from the past, and other re-created for the present. (Long, 1982, p. 103)

A pioneering work written several decades ago from a psychoanalytic perspective and often quoted today is M. Esther Harding's *Woman's Mysteries Ancient and Modern* (first published in German in 1949, translated into English in 1955 and reprinted many times since). It discusses many aspects of the feminine principle as portrayed in ancient myths, stories and dreams and draws out their significance for contemporary women. Details chosen from Babylonian, Assyrian, Egyptian and other sources of the ancient Near East highlight the symbolism of the Mother Goddess and other figures in ancient times. These provide an inspiration not so much for a new religious cult as for the reflection on woman's deepest nature and the development of the feminine self. Esther Harding's primary aim is to lead her readers to the inner development of the much neglected emotional realm and feminine side of human nature without which spiritual life will be atrophied. Writing from the perspective of the 1950s, she assesses the significance of the Goddess for her own time as follows:

> In the image of the Mother Goddess – ancient and powerful – women of olden times found the reflection of their own deepest feminine nature. . . . Today, the goddess is no longer worshipped. Her shrines are lost in the dust of ages while her statues line the walls of museums. But the law or power of which she was but the personification is unabated in its strength and life-giving potency. It is we who have changed. We have given our allegiance too exclusively to masculine forces. Today, however, the ancient feminine principle is reasserting its power . . . men and women are turning once again towards the Moon Mother, not, however, through a religious cult . . . but through a change in psychological attitude. For that principle, which in ancient and more naive days was projected into the form of a goddess, is no longer seen in the guise of a religious tenet but is now sensed as a psychological force arising from the unconscious, having, as had the Magna Dea of old, power to mold the destinies of mankind. (Harding, 1982, p. 241)

The feminine principle is indeed asserting its power, but since Esther Harding wrote her conclusion, modern women's interest in the Goddess has grown beyond psychological explanations into a new religious cult. This development has been strengthened by newly available historical evidence about goddesses of the past whose worship has been linked with theoretical explanations about the nature of society and women's power within it.

Widely acclaimed has been Merlin Stone's work *When God was a Woman* (New York, 1976), published in Britain as *The Paradise Papers* (London, 1976; new edition, 1979) with the subtitle 'The Suppression of Women's Rites'. Some consider this book a feminist classic which, among other things, defends the matriarchal theory first put forward by Bachofen in 1861. Stone examines wide-ranging archaeological and mythological evidence for the veneration of the Great Goddess in the ancient Near East. She may have been worshipped as early as 25 000 BCE and her worship was certainly well established throughout the whole area by 7000 BCE and prevailed for many centuries until it was superseded by a patriarchal deity introduced by Indo-European invaders. These established the dominance of their own religion by the third and second millennia BCE, yet the earlier Goddess worship continued to survive for many centuries thereafter.

The book also argues that Goddess worship was coexistent with a matrilineal family system, that women were priests and prophets and worshipped the Goddess through sexual rites which were later misunderstood by male scholars who described these worshippers disparagingly and wrongly as 'temple prostitutes'. They were equally wrong in describing the Goddess religion as 'a fertility cult' and the Goddess as an 'earth mother' whilst she was in fact the Queen of Heaven, creatrix of the universe, giver of life and death, the supreme deity of sexuality and childbirth. She was often associated with a consort who was her son and lover.

Unlike the earlier matriarchy theorists of the nineteenth century, Merlin Stone does not consider matriarchy as a universal, but relatively primitive stage in the evolution of human society and culture, later to be superseded by higher stages, but as a condition highly conducive to culture creation and progress, as the cultures where the Goddess was worshipped developed agriculture, architecture, writing, mathematics and law.

Yet all this material raises a host of further questions, some of which are difficult to answer. Is the worship of goddesses in ancient times – or in living religions today for that matter – in any way a proof for the existence of female power and the high status of women or does this worship ultimately rest on male projection? If earlier societies were matrilineal, that is to say descent was counted through the woman's rather than the man's family line, does this imply that they were also truly matriarchal, i.e. that the main economic and social power rested in the hands of women rather than men? Were women really better off in matriarchal and matrilineal societies, and did the worship of goddesses enhance their own position and power?

A good deal of further research is needed to clarify historical evidence so that the significance of ancient and classical goddesses can be more fully elucidated for earlier periods of history as well as for today when feminists are reappropriating the insights of an earlier age for their own needs. Sarah Pomeroy (1976) has studied the goddesses of classical antiquity whilst Charlene Spretnak (1981) has attempted to reconstruct the 'lost goddesses' of early Greece from a collection of pre-Hellenic myths. She contrasts the goddesses of classical Greece from the seventh century BCE onwards with the Great Goddess of pre-Hellenic culture whose mythology was matriarchal whilst that of classical Greece was patriarchal. Spretnak's interest in ancient historical materials is mainly motivated by the current interest in spirituality. She considers mythology as a helpful path in the spiritual quest, and pre-patriarchal Goddess tradition is a rich source from which women and men may draw great benefit whilst searching for new paths of inner growth and spiritual awakening. She also stresses the limitations of a Jungian interpretation of Greek mythology and of the widely quoted 'feminine principle' which may be far from large enough to be equated with the all-encompassing power of the Great Goddess. Spretnak also makes a clear distinction between pre- and post-patriarchal spirituality and maintains that the work done by contemporary women writers and artists on the myths of the Goddess has as its goal 'not the reinstatement of prehistoric cultural structures, but rather the transmission of *possibilities*' (1981, p. 41).

One of the most detailed and widely cited historical works of recent years is Marija Gimbutas' new edition of *The Goddesses and Gods of Old Europe 6500–3500 BC* (1982). By 'Old Europe' she understands a 'pre-Indo-European culture of Europe, a culture matrifocal and probably matrilinear, agricultural and sedentary, egalitarian and peaceful. It contrasted sharply with the ensuing proto-Indo-European culture which was patriarchal, stratified, pastoral, mobile, and war-oriented, superimposed on all of Europe . . . between 4500 and 2500 BC. During and after this period the female deities, or more accurately the Goddess Creatrix in her many aspects, were largely replaced by the predominantly male divinities of the Indo-Europeans' (1982, p. 9). She mentions the persistence of Goddess worship for more than 20 000 years from the Palaeolithic to Neolithic and beyond. After a thorough examination of the sculptured figurines, shrines and mythical images of Old Europe Gimbutas provides a detailed interpretation of the Great Goddess of life, death and regeneration (see especially ch. 8) who 'is associated with moon crescents, quadripartite designs and bull's horns, symbols of continuous creation and change. The mysterious transformation is most vividly expressed in her epiphany in the shape of a caterpillar, chrysalis and butterfly. Indeed, through this symbolism our ancestor proclaims that he believes in the beauty of young life' (1982, p. 237). The Great Goddess appeared in different manifestations as 'Virgin Nature Goddess' reflecting the free, untamed and savage forces of nature, its brilliance and wildness, its guiltless purity and strangeness whose dark roots could cause madness and death, or as 'Earth Mother' who gives birth to life, sustains it and in the end receives it back into her bosom. She is distinct from the 'Pregnant Vegetation Goddess' who is able to influence and distribute fertility. In the figurine art of Old Europe each of the feminine aspects, virginity, birth-giving and motherhood, as well as the Terrible Mother aspect, are represented. All are linked to nature's life cycle concerned with death and regeneration and all were worshipped as symbols of exuberant life. Gimbutas' examination of the mythical imagery of Old Europe leads her to the following conclusions:

> The new discoveries have served only to strengthen and support the view that the culture called *Old Europe* was characterized by a dominance of woman in society and worship of a Goddess incarnating the creative principle as Source and Giver of All. In this culture the male element, man and animal, represented spontaneous and life-stimulating – but not life-generating – powers. . . .
>
> The pantheon reflects a society dominated by the mother. The role of woman was not subject to that of a man, and much that was created between the inception of the Neolithic and the blossoming of Minoan civilization was a result of that structure in which all resources of human nature, feminine and masculine, were utilized to the full as a creative force. (1982, pp. 9 and 237ff; see also M. Gimbutas, *The Language of the Goddess*, 1991)

Besides our growing knowledge about the goddesses of Old Europe, Ireland, Greece, and the ancient Near East (Condren, 1989; Goodison, 1990), materials from other cultural and religious sources are now becoming more widely available to reveal the many facets of goddess worship. An example of this is *The Book of the Goddess Past and Present. An Introduction to Her Religion* (Olson, 1983) which sets the cult of the Goddess in a cross-cultural context. This collection contains several essays on goddesses in India, China and Japan as well as in the religion of North American Indians on which far less information is available than on the goddesses of the ancient Near East and classical times. The Hindu tradition in particular has developed the ritual, devotion and theology of the Goddess perhaps more profusely and profoundly than any other religious tradition and can provide a rich resource for the contemporary rediscovery of the Goddess. On the great Goddess or *Mahadevi* see especially David Kinsley, *Hindu Goddesses. Visions of The Divine Feminine in the Hindu Religious Tradition* (1986); additional material is found in J. S. Hawley and D. M. Wulff, *The Divine Consort. Rādhā and the Goddesses of India* (1982); for a general overview see the article on 'Goddess Worship' in *The Encyclopedia of Religion*, 6, pp. 35–59.

The above discussion demonstrates that several different perspectives are possible in interpreting earlier goddess-worshipping cultures from a contemporary point of view. There is first of all the question of the cumulative evidence of historical facts and of the appropriate criteria by which we can explain them in a meaningful way. There are psychological and psychoanalytic levels of meaning that can be given to historical data about the Goddess, and there is also another possible interpretation at the level of spiritual awareness and religious practice. In many writers these different levels are not clearly distinguished or are simply confused, for the current cult of the Goddess, though still comparatively small, uses materials rather eclectically by drawing inspiration from very different sources.

The contemporary rediscovery of the Goddess cannot do without historical data, yet the main significance of the Goddess for a growing number of women today is not historical, but religious. In any case, perceptive feminist writers are well aware of the problematic of historical reasoning with regard to the status and power of women and the nature of a female deity since the past cannot provide us with ready-made, adequate solutions for the religious, social and political needs of the present. The contemporary search for the Goddess takes many different forms. Some may seem extreme, heretical, deviant, or simply exotic and bizarre; they are certainly not without inherent paradoxes for, as history tells us, the different goddess figures are profoundly ambivalent. There are not only the benign, protective, mothering figures associated with life-giving power, creative renewal and transformation which affirm the strong, dynamic and powerful energy of women, but there are also numerous goddesses of terrible demonic and destructive aspects representing the powers of darkness and death, horrible figures which are irrational, merciless and devouring. Much less has been said and written about these aspects than about the positive, life-giving and life-enhancing powers of female deities. Such an emphasis implies a choice which indicates that the contemporary rediscovery of the Goddess is not a simple historical reconstruction, but a new creation with the help of ancient materials. Thus it is perhaps less appropriate to speak of a return or rebirth of the Goddess than of her new birth and second coming.

Contemporary Goddess worship and feminist witchcraft

Many women feel in the depth of their being that they can identify much more closely with a female form and manifestation of divinity than with traditionally male metaphors of Godhead. Perceptions and constructs of the inexpressible, mysterious nature of Ultimate Reality are of profound significance for our own self-understanding and the way we shape our lives in society. A male writer who explored the female aspects of divinity in India under the title *God as Mother* (Brown, 1974) expressed these ramifications of feminine and masculine dimensions of Ultimate Reality in the following questions:

> What difference, we may ask ourselves, would it make to us person-ally if the Supreme Reality were a Woman, instead of a Man, or some union of the two? How would it affect our own faith, our attitudes and conduct towards men and women in our everyday lives, our ultimate fate? Would it alter our perception of the relationship of man and nature, spirit and matter, mind and body, intellect and feelings, sub-ject and object? (Brown, 1974, p. 1)

Worshippers of the Goddess feel that all these perceptions are altered, that they have found a new wholeness not found elsewhere. They are drawn to the Goddess because she accepts and affirms them and gives them new power. Meditating on the Goddess, celebrating and worship-ping her can take many different forms through individuals either work-ing out an approach of their own or joining small groups or newly developing cults which have spread throughout the USA and Britain.

The individual search is well articulated in a letter sent to me by an older woman who wrote:

> I am one of those women who, in my own and very individual way, worship the Goddess. (I *wish* we had some word to use which was not merely a male word, differentiated!) . . . I am using my study of the Goddess, in the past, and in myself and my own experience, as

a process, a method of consciousness-raising. I am very isolated here, both by my way of life and by my age, and I can't find any group I could reach, though I would join one if I could find one.

For 30 years, I was interested in all aspects of religion and philosophy, and in particular in the Goddess, but until the last few years, resisted the idea of worshipping her. It never entered my head, I suppose partly because I had always resisted the accepted religions, and had worked out my own private religion, devoid of rituals, for there were none I could inherit. I knew that all things are One, each individual thing not really separated from everything else, known and unknown. The One, I taught my four sons, is of all sexes and no sex, since all these exist.

A few years ago, after a traumatic experience, I woke up one morning, saying 'I know where my loyalty and duty and love are owed – to my Mother, the Earth, who births us, feeds us, protects us, and takes us back into herself when we die, to give new life to other life-forms'. I felt it was, philosophically speaking, a backward step, but one absolutely necessary AT THE PRESENT TIME. It's only since then that I have realised how difficult it must be to get rid of the God-in-the-head. . . . To me, the idea of the God is a false and forced idea, a lie. The idea of the Goddess (which I *deliberately* build up in my head) is nearer to the truth. It can never be an authoritarian religion or it changes into the God. If she ever takes on the definition of the god in patriarchal religions, she will, once again, bear the male child who will become first before her, again. She is something at the edges of one's vision, in between the salt sea and the sand, the night and the day, something wild which we need to make space in us to live alongside us, but which we can never imprison by too clear a vision.

This letter is a moving expression of the depth and sincerity of a personal search, a witness to a new sense of the divine which makes its all-encompassing presence and power felt within us and throughout all of life and nature. But beyond the perceptive insight of particular individuals, Goddess worship has by now gained considerable collective momentum. In 1978, American feminists organised a conference in Santa Cruz on 'The Great Goddess Reemerging' which was over-subscribed and attended by more than 500 people. By 1976 a regular publication devoted to the Goddess appeared under the title *Lady Unique*. Theological reflections about the Goddess are described as *thealogy* which is seen as fundamentally different from traditional male-oriented and male-dominated theology. Thealogy gives primacy to symbols rather than to rational explanations which are so prevalent in theological thought. So far however most writing on the Goddess, when not historical, is either inspirational or devotional, and a systematically ordered body of thought, even with reference to symbols, is only slowly coming into existence.

Much of contemporary Goddess thealogy, sometimes also described as 'coven theology', is produced by the feminist witchcraft movement with its characteristic covens. Organised cults of the Goddess can be found among such groups as the 'Church of the Goddess', the 'Sisterhood of Wicca' and the 'Covenant of the Goddess' which is officially recognised as a church in California. This witchcraft movement blends earlier beliefs and practices, said to stem from women's lore and ritual of medieval times or before, with modern views about the power of the Goddess. Contemporary witches' covens are not identical with the witchcraft practised in medieval times; they are a specifically new blend of the feminist movement. Their emergence is linked to a process of retraditionalisation using elements of the past, whilst they represent at the same time a religious innovation of the twentieth century.

Here again one must distinguish between the historical and contemporary phenomenon of witchcraft. A large literature exists on witchcraft and sorcery in pre-modern and non-literate societies which describes witchcraft as either beneficial or harmful. Some writers maintain that the term 'witchcraft' should be restricted to cases where it is believed that supernatural means are used for harmful, evil ends and that the term is erroneously used when adopted by self-styled witches of modern times who claim to be adherents of an ancient pagan religion which apparently predates Christianity, but was eventually displaced and driven underground where it survived until its re-emergence today. This claim, considered to be discredited by scholars, is often traced to the widespread influence of Margaret Murray's article on 'Witchcraft' in the *Encyclopaedia Britannica* (1929) and of her popular books on this subject (1970, 1971) which gave new respectability to witchcraft in the West.

This theory about witchcraft as an ancient religion, whether factually correct or not, must be considered separately from the accusations of witchcraft brought against countless women of the past who practised the wise craft of nursing and healing the sick (Ehrenreich and English, 1973) and from the explanations about the use of such accusations as a way of annihilating women's power and its challenges, as occurred in the frenzied witchhunts and past persecutions of western Europe (O'Faolain and Martines, 1979, pp. 219–30; Larner, 1983, 1984; Heinsohn and Steiger, 1986) or is manifest in the charges levelled against women in a situation of fast social change in contemporary Africa (Amoah, 1986).

Medieval witches may well have been linked to folk medicine and traditional healing practices, but this is quite different from seeing them as members of a pre-Christian matriarchal religion or as a dissident feminine movement organised against the medieval church. However, all these claims can be found among members of the modern feminist witchcraft's movement.

Apart from the historical, religious, socio-economic and political explanations which may be adduced, the persecution of witches must be seen as the epitome of misogynism in western culture which Rosemary Ruether (1975, pp. 89–114) has tried to explain by the development of paranoid patterns and the demonisation of female sexuality in Christianity. Several feminist writers look at medieval witches from a very positive perspective by exploring legends and rituals of witchcraft as part of women's spiritual heritage and by seeing the witch of the past as an inspiring image of female strength. But witchcraft has also emerged as a new syncretistic religion which combines the insights of ancient folk religions with Goddess worship and modern feminism.

The best known descriptions of feminist wicca or witchcraft come from Starhawk or Miriam Simos, one of the high priestesses of the American witchcraft movement, author of *The Spiral Dance: A Rebirth of the Ancient Religion of the Great Goddess* (1979a), and first national President of the 'Covenant of the Goddess' which has been characterised as 'a union of pagan and goddess traditions' (Christ, 1983, p. 247). 'Wicca' are the wise ones, the women priestesses, diviners, midwives, poets, healers and singers of power. Starhawk maintains that a woman-centred culture based on the worship of the Great Goddess underlies the beginnings of all civilisations. For her and her followers the old religion of witchcraft or 'the craft of the wise' was handed down in the covens of Europe where the mythology and rituals of ancient mother-centred times were preserved through the age of persecutions. This religion which existed before the advent of Christianity is said to have been an earth-centred, nature-oriented worship that venerated the Goddess, the source of all life, as well as her son-lover-consort who was seen as the 'Horned God' of the hunt and animal life.

Witchcraft covens within the contemporary feminist movement are extremely diverse. Some consist of hereditary witches who claim to practise rites unchanged for hundreds of years whilst others prefer to create new rituals. There are covens of so-called 'perfect couples' with an even number of women and men permanently paired, but there are also covens of lesbian feminists or of gay men, or covens of women only who prefer to explore women's spirituality in a space removed from men. The latter are sometimes described as the Dianic, the women-only tradition. To be a witch can be understood in many different ways, as can be seen from a statement of New York covens:

WITCH is an all-women Everything. . . .
WITCH lives and laughs in every woman. She is the free part of each of us, beneath the shy smiles, the acquiescence to absurd male domination, the make-up or flesh-suffocating clothing our sick society demands. There is no 'joining' WITCH. If you are a woman and dare to look within yourself, you are a Witch. You make your own rules. You are free and beautiful. You can be invisible or evident in how you choose to make your witch-self known. You can form our own Coven of sister Witches (thirteen is a cozy number for a group) and do your own actions.

Whatever is repressive, solely male-oriented, greedy, puritanical, authoritarian – those are your targets. Your weapons are theater satire, explosions, magic, herbs, music . . . your own boundless beautiful imagination. Your power comes from your own self as a woman, and it is activated by working in concert with your sisters. The power of the Coven is more than the sum of its individual members, because it is *together*.

You are pledged to free our brothers from oppression and stereo-typed sexual roles (whether they like it or not) as well as ourselves. You are a Witch by saying aloud, 'I am a Witch' three times, and *thinking about that*. You are a Witch by being female, untamed, angry, joyous, and immortal. (Quoted in Morgan, 1970, pp. 605–6)

This declaration emphasises the independence and power of the witch, her strong self-image which relates in a new way to others, whether sisters or brothers, without referring to the Goddess at all. But many witches worship the Goddess because they see in her the ground and source for a positive image of women in all stages of life. They teach that

the Goddess appears in three forms, as maiden, mother and crone, and
these are linked to both the stages of women's lives and the cycle of the
moon. To quote from Starhawk's article on 'Witchcraft and Women's
Culture':

> Our great symbol for the Goddess is the moon, whose three aspects
> reflect the three stages in women's lives and whose cycles of waxing
> and waning coincide with women's menstrual cycles . . .
>
> The Goddess is also the earth – Mother Earth, who sustains all
> growing things, who is the body, our bones and cells. She is the air –
> the winds that move in the trees and over the waves, breath. She is
> the fire of the hearth, or the blazing bonfire and the fuming vol-
> cano; the power of transformation and change. And she is water – the
> sea, the original source of life; the rivers, streams, lakes and wells;
> the blood that flows in the rivers of our veins. She is mare, cow, cat,
> owl, crane, flower, tree, apple, seed, lion, sow, stone, woman. She is
> found in the world around us, in the cycles and seasons of nature,
> and in mind, body, and spirit, and emotions within each of us. Thou
> art Goddess. I am Goddess. All that lives (and all that is, lives), all
> that serves life, is Goddess. (1979b, p. 263)

Starhawk encourages women to join together to explore a life-affirming,
Goddess-orientated spirituality. She considers all traditional patriarchal
religions as 'death cults' and maintains that the necessary transformation
of our culture towards love of life, of nature and of the female principle
will come from the cult of the Goddess which values independence,
personal strength, and the self, but has no set doctrines other than the law
of 'love unto all beings'. She candidly admits that her considerations
about the Goddess are limited to traditions from northern Europe. She
states that southern and eastern Europe, Asia, India, Africa and the
Americas all possess rich traditions of goddess religions and matricentric
cultures without giving attention to their individual differences. In any
case, historical details matter less than the 'inner' or 'mythic' history
of the Goddess which provides the touchstone for modern witches:
'Like the histories of all peoples, its truth is intuited in the meaning it
gives to life, even though it may be recognized that scholars might
dispute some facets of the story' (1979b, p. 268, n. 1).

The way into witchcraft is usually through initiation into a coven,
Organisation and beliefs are extremely diverse and so are the different
rituals celebrated by different covens. According to Starhawk, rituals

usually take place within a circle to allow for the free flow of energy.
Each ritual begins with the casting of a circle, whether it takes place on
a moonlit hillside or in a modern apartment. The circle is considered as
a space 'between the worlds', between the human world and the world
of the Goddess, and its casting as a transition into an expanded state
of consciousness. A particular witchcraft ritual may involve

> wild shouting and frenzied dancing, or silent meditation, or both. . . .
> The best rituals combine moments of intense ecstasy and spir-
> itual union, with moments of raucous humour and occasional silli-
> ness. . . .
> The Goddess, and if desired the Horned God (not all traditions of
> the craft relate to the male force) can be invoked once the circle is
> cast. An invocation may be set beforehand . . . but in our coven
> we find the most effective invocations are those that come to us
> spontaneously. . . . The power generated within the circle is built into
> a cone form, and at its peak is released – to the Goddess, to reenergize
> the members of the coven, or to do a specific work such as healing.
> . . .
> Energy is also shared in tangible form – wine, cakes, fruit, cheese-
> cake, brownies, or whatever people enjoy eating. The Goddess is
> invited to share with everyone, and a libation is poured to her
> first. . . .
> At the end, the Goddess is thanked and bid farewell, and the
> circle is formally opened. Ending serves as a transition back into
> ordinary space and time. Rituals finish with a kiss and a greeting
> of 'Merry meet, merry part, and merry meet again'. (Starhawk, 1979b,
> pp. 265–6)

It is impossible to describe in further detail the numerous feminist
rituals which have developed inside and outside the witchcraft movement (see Turner, 1978), but by far the most detailed account of the
celebration of the seasonal festivals of the old Celtic calendar of New
Year, Winter Solstice, Candlemas, Spring Equinox, Summer Solstice
and Autumn Equinox, as well as many other rituals, is found in Zsuzsanna
E. Budapest's two volumes of *The Holy Book of Women's Mysteries*
(1979 and 1980). An exile from Hungary and daughter of a woman artist,
Zsuzsanna Budapest is now a high priestess of the Susan B. Anthony
Coven Number One in Los Angeles and foundress of the 'Sisterhood
of Wicca' which combines insights of the Hungarian witch tradition

inherited from her mother with those of contemporary feminism. A major part of the work presents specifically created rites in answer to modern needs, whether they be a self-blessing, welcoming a new baby into a circle of mothers or freeing political prisoners.

How is the 'self-blessing ritual', said to come from an ancient oral tradition never written down, related to the Goddess and what is its meaning for women today? Zsuzsanna Budapest explains:

> It is a woman's own blessing on herself; her own divinity is honored in a ritual with herself. It is a self-affirmation, a very private, and a very powerful ritual.
>
> To do it, first take a shower or a bath to purify yourself. Have assembled on your altar some salt, in a nice container, and some wine and water. The altar is an important part of women's rituals, and a very female part of dwellings. Every house used to have an altar, for the house spirits, for the ancestors. Every women would do well to have one of her own. On it, you represent the Goddess in some symbolic manner – by a rose, for instance, or any flower. . . . Arrange your altar in a creative manner, for example, with a white cloth, two white candles on the two sides, and a rose in the middle. Put your chalice in front and fill it half with water and half with wine. Take the salt and put it down in front of your altar.

After explaining the symbolism of each element used and describing the ritual step by step, she points out its general significance:

> In self-blessing, you affirm the divine you. Self-blessing is very important for women, because too many of us have internalized our own oppression. . . . Self-blessing rituals are a way of exorcising the patriarchal policeman, cleansing the deep mind, and filling it with positive images of the strength and beauty of women. This is what the Goddess symbolizes – the divine within women and all that is female in the universe. (Budapest, 1979b, pp. 269 and 271ff.)

In her chapter on 'Feminist Witchcraft – The Goddess is Alive!' Naomi Goldenberg, (1979, pp. 85–114) argues that modern witches are using religion and ritual as psychological tools to build up individual strength. Many women can draw power and inspiration from the image of the Goddess in feminist witchcraft, so whatever the scholarly arguments about witches of the past, the witches of the present seem to be developing a religion for women which, according to its followers, is the only one in the west that recognises woman as divinity in her own right.

Feminist witchcraft and worship of the Goddess are not only present in America and Britain but also emerging elsewhere. For example Judith Jannberg (1983), drawing on similar sources and experiences, has described her newly found identity as a Goddess-worshipping witch for German readers in her book *I am a Witch* ('Ich bin eine Hexe') wherein she states the same ideas: 'We have the Goddess within us. Every woman can enter into contact with the Goddess through her inner Self. For our religion, for this relationship, we need no church, no building, no mission, no organisation, no covenant, no bible, no studies. The laws of the Goddess are effective within us and around us in nature' (1983, pp. 148ff.). Current statistics on different religious groups in Great Britain and Northern Ireland state that there are 'about 30 000 practising self-styled witches who practise occultism and black magic' in Britain (Barrett, 1982, p. 700) but unfortunately no mention is made of how many among these might be female witches worshipping the Goddess. In any case, not every Goddess-worshipping woman is necessarily a feminist witch nor would wish to be considered as such. There are other groups too, besides feminist covens, which practise and promote the modern cult of the Goddess.

Goddess worship in matriarchy groups and the debate about matriarchy

Several groups, whether consisting of a loose network of contacts or of a more formally organised structure, relate their worship of the Goddess to wide-ranging notions about matriarchy which are often not too clearly defined either. The most coherently formulated theology and community structure is represented by the small madrian group *Lux Madriana*. It claims to trace its ancestry back to a primordial matriarchal tradition and refers in its publications somewhat contemptuously to the 'self-styled witches' and other modern women cultists whose 'occult traditions' are nothing more than 'modern fabrications' with which its own worship has nothing in common. *Lux Madriana*, which began with a women's group in Oxford in the mid-seventies, but now seems to be centred in Burtonport on the west coast of Ireland with affiliated groups elsewhere, produces a regular magazine *The Coming Age* which first described itself as 'Magazine of the religion of the Goddess' and later as that 'of the British matriarchal tradition'.

Members of this group have created a small, self-sufficient community far removed from modern life, as they believe that we have fallen from a golden age to one of the worst possible materialism which has to be overcome by returning to a primordial tradition where all of life is governed by spiritual principles. According to their teaching, traditional society was first matriarchal and then patriarchal and is to be distinguished from modern patriarchal society which represents the worst of all possible worlds. The return to primordial tradition expresses itself in the group through a traditional way of life (without electricity or the television set), the wearing of traditional clothes and the pursuit of traditional crafts. Thus the madrians wish to bring in a new age, the coming age, linked to a new language, or at least new terms which they have created for the months of the year, their festival and rites. From within their own matriarchal perspective members of the group have developed ideas on cosmology, theology, ecclesiology, salvation history and liturgy with domestic and public rites, sacraments of initiation, and even religious education for the children in the community. The basic beliefs are stated in *The Catechism of the Children of the Goddess* whilst *The Creation and the Crystal Tablet* takes the place of scripture. Another brief work, *The Mythos of the Divine Maid*, relates the nativity, life, death and resurrection of the daughter of the Goddess. There could be no closer parallel to Christian theology, but in the reverse, from creation to redemption to the idea of the Trinity, all expressed from a female perspective. All souls are female too, whilst males embody the material principle; the spiritual principle is female and thus are men's souls.

In the section on 'Deity' the catechism of *Lux Madriana* deals with the question 'What is the Goddess?' in the following way: 'The Goddess is the one Spirit of the universe, complete in Herself, uncreated, and infinite in potency, perception and perfection.' The 'Mystery of the Divine Trinity' is described as 'one Goddess, yet she is three Persons' who are 'Our Celestial Mother, Her Divine Daughter and the Dark Mother who is Absolute Deity'. The Celestial Mother is 'the Creator of the world and Ground of all being' from whom all life, all action and all thought flow. Her Divine Daughter has a threefold nature as Princess of the World who governs all cycles of life and nature, as Priestess of the World who gives us Communion with Her Mother, and as Queen of Heaven who brings us to the Celestial Throne. The Dark

Mother is described as an Absolute Deity 'Who existed before the beginning of existence and is beyond being and unbeing. . . . She is outside space and time; She is all that is and all that is not'. It is also said that 'The exhaltation of Her breath or Spirit is our Mother, the Creator of the world', a function already associated with the aspect of the Celestial Mother. The Goddess has no beginning or end; she creates the world now and in every moment and she is in every place at all times. Though given many different names, there is only one Goddess and there are no other deities. From among the prayers to the Goddess listed in the catechism I would like to quote 'A Morning Offering':

> Celestial Mother, grant me this day that every work I do shall be as lovingly and well performed as though I were to give it into Your divine hands.
>
> Fill me with Your energy, that I may both give beauty to the world and perceive the beautiful in all of Your creation.
>
> Grant that this day shall add a stone to the temple of my soul.

Besides *Lux Madriana* in Ireland there are also groups in Britain devoted to the cult of the Goddess. They are as diverse as the Fellowship of Isis, the Earthforce, the Goddess of Maat, the Goddess of Truth and Love Centre, the Matriarchy Study Group, and the Matriarchy Research and Reclaim Network, to name only a few. In a study of matriarchy groups in contemporary Britain Kayoko Komatsu (1986) has examined the development, composition, activities and rituals of some of these groups. Matriarchy study groups were founded first and then the development of ritual came later. The 'Matriarchy Study Group' was founded in London in 1975; it published *Matriarchy News*, *Goddess Shrew* and *Politics of Matriarchy*. In 1981, a 'Matriarchy Research and Reclaim Network' was formed which has published a regular newsletter since then. In Sheffield a matriarchy group first appeared in 1977. The subscribers of the 'Matriarchy Research and Reclaim Network Newsletter' were found to be of varying ages, then largely in their late twenties and thirties, frequently of graduate background and with prior experience of political involvement, especially in the peace movement. Often disenchanted with political activity alone, these women were looking for an appropriate spirituality which can give meaning to their lives today. The worship of the Goddess is a self-affirmation of the strength and wholeness of women; it suggests immanence and encompasses a holistic understanding of nature as the earth is seen as body of the Goddess. As the manifestation and expression of divine energy and presence nature has to be reverently approached, not manipulated as an object which human beings can possess and exploit for the purpose of domination. Thus the Goddess religion connects the wholeness of self to the wholeness of nature and aims to overcome the dualism between nature and culture. The awareness that the Goddess is All and that all forms of being are One is expressed in the following invocation:

> All is one and one is all
> She is us and we are she
> Our will be done
> we shall be free. (Newsletter no. 7)

Although matriarchy groups are relatively small and insignificant in absolute numbers, their search for an alternative worldview connected to spiritual values has a great potential, not only for women but for men too, as it implies a profound transformation of religious consciousness and envisages a different attitude to both nature and the social order. Whilst the expression 'women's spirituality' used by these groups is understood in an exclusive sense by some members, it has a universal connotation for others and means a new spirituality for a new age.

The relationship between feminism and spirituality is much discussed in these groups, as is the meaning of Goddess worship which should not be seen as mere self-seeking or as a rejection of the world as it is, or as a simple replacement of the worship of the patriarchal Judaeo-Christian God with a matriarchal Goddess. Another important theme is the interconnection of spirituality and politics, for it is one of the symptoms of patriarchy that these two decisive aspects of human experience have been dangerously divorced from each other, much to the detriment of personal and communal development. Thus the Matriarchy Research and Reclaim Network stresses emphatically, in a cyclostyled statement about itself, that women's involvement with matriarchy and Goddess religion is 'most certainly NOT a cop-out or a withdrawal from the political struggles of feminism'. Not tied to specific creeds women are free to interpret their own feelings and experiences in a way that is personal and meaningful to them. Against the understanding of a male-centred creation, they affirm that the creative principle or energy is female rather than male and 'can be symbolised as the Great Mother or the Great Goddess'. The question 'Who we are' is answered by members of the Matriarchy Research and Reclaim Network in the following declaration:

> We are women who have been meeting to celebrate and exchange knowledge at the full and dark moons and at the eight festivals of the old religion. We have gathered information about women's past which has been lost until recently because of male cultural bias. . . .
>
> We are women who want to discover or rediscover our spirituality and to affirm and work with energies which are specifically female.
>
> Involvement in Matriarchy enables us to look back into the past, to Matriarchal religion and societies and to relate the concepts and images of women found there to our everyday lives. It is an opportunity to explore and interpret our female nature and strengths in positive ways, very different from patriarchal ideas of us. It is also a confirmation of the knowledge that we can and will overcome patriarchal domination. (Cyclostyled paper prepared by a group of women within the Matriarchy Network)

Whilst matriarchy groups propose a woman-centred worldview linked to Goddess religion, there is no general consensus as to their precise understanding of the meaning of matriarchy in historical or theoretical terms. An early discussion of matriarchy in relation to Christianity is found in the pioneering work of Matilda Joslyn Gage, *Woman, Church and State: A Historical Account of the Status of Woman through the Christian Ages: with Reminiscences of the Matriarchate*, first published in 1893 (and reprinted in 1982). Among scholars, including many women anthropologists, the question of the actual existence of matriarchies in the past is disputed since historical evidence is ambiguous. For the purpose of feminism the historical debate as such is perhaps less important than the need to construct a theory of matriarchy for contemporary women whose aim it is to create a new social order. The controversy is not new, however, and was originally not started by women. It has its roots in the nineteenth century, especially in Bachofen's *Das Mutterrecht* (1861). For Bachofen and his followers 'mother right' marked an earlier stage in the evolution of human cultures whilst Briffault's encyclopaedic work on *The Mothers* (1927) asserted the existence of a primitive matriarchy that universally preceded patriarchy. Much of Briffault's evidence was drawn from comparative religion and he maintained that the widespread existence of lunar deities in ancient cultures proved the early social dominance of women. These two earlier works, together with Neumann's treatment of Goddess worship in his psycho-analytic study *The Great Mother* (1955, repr. 1991), were an important influence on the contemporary feminist debate and are often quoted in feminist works.

Still more influential in the development of the matriarchy debate were the writings of contemporary women. Elizabeth Gould Davis's extremely popular book *The First Sex* (1971) interpreted myths literally and argued for the existence of a golden age of matriarchy in the past in a way which fired many women's imagination. The work has been praised as visionary and inspirational, but many of its details have been criticised and shown to be unsubstantiated. Also much read are Merlin Stone's publications *When God was a Woman* (1976) and *Ancient Mirrors of Womanhood: Our Goddess and Heroine Heritage* (1979, 1980). Critics, however, often refer to this and similar material as promulgating a modern 'myth of matriarchy'. Whilst the lively contro-versy about matriarchy has become a 'quasi-religious issue', anthropo-logists maintain that the data on goddess worship in ancient societies cannot be associated with a stage of matriarchy (Preston, 1982, 1987). In a brief critical article on 'Myths and Matriarchies' Sally Binford (1981) has argued that the belief in earlier matriarchies represents a 'new feminist fundamentalism' (for a reprint of her article with responses and counter-responses see 'Are Goddesses and Matriarchies Merely Figments of Feminist Imagination?' in Spretnak, 1982, pp. 541–62).

Many different arguments have been put forward against the theory of historical matriarchies. Feminists are accused of mistakenly assuming that the presence of goddesses is evidence of matriarchies and that goddess worship proves the rule of mothers in earlier stages of human history. Also the idea that matriarchal societies are survivals of an earlier matriarchal era or that matrilineality and matriarchy are directly related to each other cannot be taken for granted. The ancient symbolism asso-ciated with the worship of goddesses cannot give us incontrovertible evidence about the actual social position and roles of women in the past. This lack of equivalence between the symbolic and empirical realms of existence is also evident from the contemporary situation in such societies as Japan and India, for example, where the widespread venera-tion of goddesses has not enhanced that status of women. This shows how speculative our conclusions about these matters are and how tentative any parallels remain between the characteristics of sacred images, statues and symbols, the cult of female deities, and the life of actual women in society.

It has been argued that the myth of matriarchy is damaging to the cause of feminists and that women are not really freed by perpetuating this myth. Whilst matriarchy groups have tended to emphasise the historical existence of matriarchy and seen that stage of society as characterised by a communal life-style in which women enjoyed authority and respect as well as true social power, the lack of historical evidence and the critique of the myth of a matriarchal golden age has also led to a certain disenchantment. Some women now want to play down the importance of the historical issue about matriarchy and concentrate instead on the evidence of goddess-worshipping communities of ancient times without necessarily concluding that these were matriarchal. Certain writers, such as Starhawk, also argue that even the archaeological discovery of goddess worship is not essential for women's belief in the Goddess today. Present and future are not dependent on a hypostasised past. In other words, women do not really need history to justify their religion, for whether there was a religion of the Great Goddess in ancient times or not, there certainly exists one today.

We are thus faced with many contradictory arguments regarding the significance of both matriarchy and the Goddess in contemporary feminism. Whilst even enthusiastic feminists react to 'the unfortunate excesses and leaps' of Davis' popular publication (Spretnak, 1982, p. 129n) and accept that this and similar works discredit their cause, critical women scholars go on collecting data about goddesses which allow for the development of much more differentiated interpretations. The issue is by no means closed, and currently accepted academic views may well have to be revised in the future. For the present, Margot Adler (1982) has briefly summarised the multiple meanings of matriarchy in feminist debate clearly showing the uncertainties about whether women's power, associated with a possibly mythic matriarchal age, is predominantly understood as social, political, religious or psychological power. However, beyond the question of whether matriarchies ever existed or not, women can make creative use of the idea of matriarchy as a vision, an ideal which has considerable transformative potential for the contemporary lives and communities of women. Adler rightly points out that the critics of the matriarchy theory fail to deal with the central issue of the matriarchy argument among feminists, namely, 'that there have been ages and places where women held a much greater share of power than they do now and that, perhaps, women used power in a very different way from our common understanding of it' (1982, p. 128). Because of this, further research on earlier, prepatriarchal societies which were more egalitarian and gave more freedom to women is of great importance in feminist scholarship and self-understanding. Thus many women now define 'matriarchal' as

> a different kind of power, as a realm where female things are valued and where power is exerted in nonpossessive, noncontrolling, and organic ways that are harmonious with nature . . . a worldview that values feelings of connectedness and intuition, that seeks nonauthoritarian and nondestructive power relationships and attitudes towards the Earth. This is far different from the idea of matriarchy as simply rule by women. (Adler, 1982, p. 132).

Here matriarchal values are understood in almost the same way in which other writers speak about the rediscovery of feminine values or of the feminine dimension in all of us. For some women the word 'matriarchy' has come to mean mainly an age of universal Goddess worship, irrespective of questions of social and political power or control. (For important German studies on matriarchy dealing with historical and contemporary aspects and the relationship between matriarchy, aesthetics, and religion see Göttner-Abendroth, 1980, 1984; and Mulack, 1983.) The main issues in the current matriarchy debate thus lead back to the central figure of the Goddess whose meaning, like that of matriarchy itself, is controversial and can be considered at several different levels. To disentangle these we have to find an answer to the following questions: What are the different meanings assigned to the Goddess today? And what is their significance for the spirituality of contemporary women?

The many meanings of the Goddess

Does the Goddess assume the same place in women's worship as that assigned to God in traditional religion? Is the Goddess contemporary women's new way of naming what is ultimate for them because the term God has so many patriarchal associations which they must reject? Many women understand the meaning of the Goddess in this way, but this is not unproblematic since the Great Goddess is often associated or even equated with the Mother Goddess, or with an Earth Goddess, or with past goddess figures which represented fertility goddesses and functioned as such in ancient cultures. This is why some writers question whether the word 'Goddess' can ever become a truly monotheistic term for us.

The equation between the Great Goddess and Mother Goddess is expressed in the following statement as is the claim that the Goddess is not simply a reverse female image of the male God:

> The Goddess or Great Mother is NOT a female but otherwise mirror image of the male god; we do not think of a 'Big Mummy Out There' as the patriarchs think of a 'Big Daddy'. Neither were Matriarchal societies mirror images of our own but where women dominated men. The Goddess is not separate but is in everything. We are her and she is us. Her agency is our energy: it is in all of us at a deep personal level as a source of power and we have many choices as to how we may wish to express this power. The Goddess is also a symbol for our energy, for our being. We are all individual sources of energy but we are also all joined as one great pool of power, strength and creativity as are all things in the universe and beyond. (Cyclostyled paper prepared by a group of women within the Matriarchy Network)

Another source, a hymn about the Great Mother Goddess in *Womanspirit* (Spring, 1984, p. 2), equates the Goddess with the Earth Mother:

> I am the MOTHER. The GREAT MOTHER. The EARTH MOTHER. MOTHER SEA. The MOTHER of all. Your Mother.
> I have an abundance of energy. I have an abundance of love I AM abundance! I am the creative force of the Universe. Some call me LOVE. Some call me EMPRESS. They say that love rules the universe and that my laws are unalterable. But I do not desire to rule you. I would set you free. I would bear you and suckle you and set you free, for you will come back to me when your life is over; all come back to me.

With regard to historical data, however, there is the difficult question of how far ancient goddess figures may primarily be symbols of fertility and sexuality created and projected by men rather than signs of women's independence and power. The role of the Great Mother is often an ambiguous one too, as it raises the paradoxical issue already mentioned regarding the specific value assigned to women's experience of giving birth and mothering. Some feminists have celebrated this experience as liberating and enriching whilst others see childbearing and motherhood as oppressive because of the dependent and subordinate position in which it places women. To draw a parallel between the experience of human motherhood and the divine Mother Goddess is thus not unproblematic as a reviewer of *The Ancient Religion of the Great Cosmic Mother of All* pointed out:

> I must call in question . . . that women's spirituality and creativity are linked to motherhood, to parturition itself. [The authoress] has explained how the natural birth of her second child opened up for her these previously blocked off areas, but for many there is no connection. On the contrary, in our society, Motherhood cuts women off from the time and confidence to create anything personal, and motherhood is generally undervalued. Even if this were not so, I think that our creativity and our biological capacity are aspects of ourselves, no more specifically linked than other aspects. The goddess religions presented Isis as Mistress of Science, Nephtys as inventor of the arts of spinning and weaving, Demeter as bringing the art and science of agricultures to the world. Science . . . was part of the creativity associated with women's culture and religion and did not depend on reproduction. (Long, 1981, p. 18)

To interpret the meaning of the Goddess raises question in the realms of biology, history and theology. In his transpersonal account of human evolution Ken Wilber (1983) emphasises the difference between the Great Mother and the Great Goddess whose genesis and function must not be confused. He gives a naturalist explanation for the existence of the Mother Goddess whose image arose as a

> correlate of bodily existence, with such biological impacts as womb birth, breast feeding, separation anxieties, and so on – all of which necessarily centre on the *biological* mother. That simple biological dependence, amplified by the notion of the earth as the mother of farmed crops, accounted for the prevalence of the Mother Image in the basic mythologies. . . . All manifestation was seen to be *mother, maya, measure, menses, menstrual, metered* – which are all words stemming from the same Sanskrit root *ma* (or *matr*), which means essentially, 'production'. (pp.146–7).

Not unlike other writers who have looked at the Goddess from an evolutionary perspective, Wilber maintains that the Great Mother reflects the mythic-membership level of reality when human beings were still close to the body, instincts and nature, whereas the Great Goddess reflects a metaphysical truth, namely, that all is One. Many writers today make the mistake of either reducing the Great Goddess to the biological Great Mother, an image of bodily dependence and seduction, or they elevate the Great Mother to the status of the Great Goddess and then, according to Wilber, are forced to read deep metaphysical insights into all Great Mother rituals when they were in fact mostly nothing but primitive, magical attempts to coerce the fertility of the earth.

This distinction between the Great Mother and the Great Goddess is a valuable one. Whilst a symbol might integrate and reflect different aspects of experience and fuse them into one – in fact, this very capacity endows a symbol with a special power of attraction – from the perspective of critical reflection one must none the less ask how far the symbol of the Goddess is primarily biology-dependent (a symbol of fertility, birth and motherhood), or whether it can be truly biology-transcendent, i.e. express characteristics of beauty, power and independence as well as true ultimacy. The two aspects need not necessarily be completely separate; the first may well point beyond itself and lead to the second. The important point, however, is that whilst dimensions of immanence and transcendence can come close together, touch each other and be intertwined in the understanding of the Goddess, the human vision and conceptualisation of the Divine can never be solely grounded in women's experience of motherhood as exclusive starting point for reflection about ultimate reality. However rich and revelatory of dimensions beyond ourselves, human birth and motherhood are only one of the many possible expressions and manifestations of the Divine within and around us.

In her reflections on the power of the Goddess for women today Carol Christ (1979) has distinguished three major views. The first sees the Goddess as a personification, a divine female who can be invoked in prayer and is believed to really exist. The second considers the Goddess primarily as a symbol rather than a metaphysical reality; she symbolises above all life, death and rebirth energy in nature and culture, in personal and communal life. The third view also understands the Goddess as a symbol, but reads it differently as affirming above all the legitimacy and beauty of female power, made possible by the new becoming of women in the women's liberation movement. The powerful attraction and beauty of the Goddess as an important symbol for our time is evident from the richly illustrated volume of Elinor W. Gadon, *The Once and Future Goddess* (1989), which provides a very accessible introduction to the historical, contemporary and artistic diversity of Goddess worship past and present. More personal reflections on a journey to the Goddess are found in Carol Christ's *Laughter of Aphrodite* (1987).

The idea of the Goddess is often interiorised and psychologised, without being linked to any metaphysical claims about an absolute Godhead. This view is most prevalent among writers influenced by psychology and psychoanalysis. Edward Whitmont, in his *Return of the Goddess* (1983), describes the re-emergence of the ancient Goddess myth as the most important psychic event of our age, the recovery of the feminine aspects of the soul. Whilst modern society has been dominated by male-orientated concepts of power and aggression, he thinks that we are now entering a new period where the world may be fundamentally changed through greater emphasis on traditional feminine values such as instinct, feeling, intuition and emotion. But does this really require the return to an old myth or the creation of a new one about the Goddess?

Quite a few writers stress the significance of the emergence of the image of the Goddess in the psyche of modern women. This emergence can be seen as 'symbolic of women's sense that the power which they are claiming for themselves through the women's movement is rooted in the ground of being itself' (Christ, 1983, p. 247). However the main point, not sufficiently stressed by feminist writers, is the need for the values associated with the Goddess and her worship to emerge not only in the psyche of women, but in those of men too. Otherwise it will be impossible to bring about the necessary transformation of the social and political order of our world. For this reason the question arises whether Goddess worship can bring about a greater integration of the sexes or rather works towards their greater separation. The contributors to Alix Pirani's *The Absent Mother* (1991) have explored many different contexts and perspectives through which the power and presence of the Goddess can be restored to Judaism and Christianity. Naomi Goldenberg, in *Changing of the Gods* (1979), has argued that feminism spells the end of all traditional religions and that the religious future lies largely with Goddess worship whilst Carol Ochs, in *Behind the Sex of God* (1977), maintains that for a new religious consciousness to emerge, both the patriarchal God worship as well as matriarchal Goddess worship must ultimately be transcended. What is certain, a religion for women alone is not enough to change the social and political distribution of power in the contemporary world. As Angela Carter has sarcastically remarked:

> If women allow themselves to be consoled . . . by the invocation of hypothetical great goddesses, they are simply flattering themselves into submission (a technique often used on them by men). . . . Mother goddesses are just as silly a notion as father gods. If a revival of these cults gives women emotional satisfaction, it does so at the price of obscuring the real conditions of life. This is why they were invented in the first place. (Quoted in Spretnak, 1982, p. 559)

There is not only the serious objection of the social and political irrelevance of Goddess worship, or its description as 'neo-paganism' by Christian writers, but there is also the criticism that it may simply be a 'sanctified materialism'. In a pamphlet circulated by *Lux Madriana*, but not one of its official publications, it is pointed out that whilst feminist religion claims to hold no dogma, it is none the less very dogmatic in maintaining the right of every woman to define her own spirituality and sexuality. This new Goddess religion practised by women outside and unconnected to the ancient madrian tradition seems to reflect more the dark side of the Goddess for she 'becomes the mother of lust, the mother of drugs, the mother of self-indulgence, the mother of fearful minds' in the feminist spirituality movement. The same writer asserts that the principles of this movement stem from relativism, scientism, materialism and atheism. In short, it preaches some kind of hedonistic gospel to justify the self-indulgence of contemporary women without paying due attention to the soul, to prayer and worship as traditionally understood. Most of the criticisms in this pamphlet (Madrian Literature Circle: 'The Hollow Tree. Feminist Spirituality or Sanctified Materialism?' no date), however, seem to be directed against political involvement, especially the left-wing politics and Greenham Common demonstrations of women Goddess worshippers. Based on a special understanding of matriarchy, the author questions whether there can be a common ground between matriarchy and anarchy, as supposedly preached by the feminist spirituality movement whose supporters 'look to a destructured society' or 'matrianarchy' rather than work for a true transformation of the world.

Other critics, by contrast, maintain that the new Goddess spirituality must be criticised primarily because it represents an apolitical stance among women today and expresses a tendency towards irrationalism and occultism. Against these rather negative points of view one must consider Merlin Stone's (1978) balanced emphasis on three important aspects of contemporary Goddess spirituality whose rise in recent years has been a most unexpected occurrence within the feminist movement. Briefly these are, first, the emerging interest in the history and prehistory of ancient cultures that worshipped a female deity; second, a growing concern with a feminist perception of spirituality and theology; and third, an examination of the specific ways in which the organised male-worshipping, male-clergied religions of today have instituted and maintained a secondary status for women.

These are important developments, not only for women, since these insights have wider implications for religion and society, for theology and spirituality. Women today are redefining their spiritual heritage but in so doing, their vision often still remains too circumscribed, too much rooted in the western past. There is also the Goddess heritage of black women or that of Hindu, Buddhist, Japanese and Chinese women. Rita Gross (1978) has argued that in re-imagining the Goddess women can find an important resource, overlooked so far, in Hindu female deities in addition to the hidden tradition of western female God-language or the pre-biblical goddesses of the western world. Living religions with strong Goddess imagery can inspire feminist thought and worship although we must remember that this is not unproblematic. Whilst ancient goddesses are temporarily distant from us, contemporary goddesses in non-western religions are culturally distant and are susceptible to mis-interpretation, both positive and negative. Drawing primarily on Hindu iconography rather than textual materials, Gross examines several basic images of the Goddess in Hinduism. First there is the image of the divine couple and related to it the fact that every divine manifestation from insignificant spirits to the great Gods appears in both female and male form. An extension of this polarity is found in the images of God as bisexual and androgynous. More important still from the point of view of women are the independent manifestations of the Hindu Goddess. There is the image of the widely worshipped Bengali Goddess Durga, a com-bination of strength and beauty, of transcendence and dynamic creativ-ity, but also an image that points to universal significance. This image, like that of other Hindu deities, also demonstrates a symbolism of the coincidence of opposites, of both creation and destruction, as the God-dess has a dark, destructive side in the form of Kali. Another important feature is the emphasis placed on God as Mother (see Brown, 1974; Jayakar, 1990), understood in a metaphorical rather than a literal sense, though not unambiguous (King, 1989b). This image refers to the life-giving, creative motherhood of God, the creative potential of the God-dess in the absence of physical offspring, for there are few icons of the Goddess giving birth and none of the Mother and dependent child. Thus divine motherhood refers to the creative bestowing of life in general rather than literally to the physical act of birth. Related to this metaphorical use is the Hindu custom of calling rivers 'mothers', notice-ably 'Mother Ganges'.

Hindu Goddesses are involved in a broad range of culturally valued goals and activities. Lakshmi, for example, distributes wealth and good fortune whilst Sarasvati promotes learning and the arts. Another import-ant aspect concerns the pervasive sexuality in Hindu images of the Goddess and the importance of sexuality as a significant religious metaphor which can help women to overcome the body–spirit dichotomy and correlate sexuality and spirituality. Gross argues that whereas one cannot prove that goddesses, whether ancient or Indian, are a product of women's religious imagination one can none the less demonstrate that goddesses often present imagery that is significant to contemporary women seeking wholeness and self-respect. What is significant about the Goddess is 'Her sheer presence as *female*. By being there as female, She validates me as I am. Her limitlessness is exemplary for me. It is good to be in the image of the Goddess. That is the most important of Her many meanings' (1978, p. 288).

There is no doubt that the worship of the Goddess can provide deep personal affirmation, profound emotional satisfaction and spiritual sustenance for women as individuals and in small groups. But how far will these in the end always remain insignificant cult and fringe groups without any real social power, unable to change the position of women in society at large or to provide a viable spirituality for all? Can individuals define their spirituality in relative isolation, or do we need a more widely shared symbol system and generally accepted ciphers for ultimate meaning? Numerous women feel quite unable to identify with the Goddess and do not, in spite of all feminist claims, experience her as a ground for empowerment and affirmation. Some criticise the Goddess religion as 'neo-pagan' (whatever that may mean), whilst others see the insistence on matriarchal power as simply a substi-tute for patriarchal domination, a kind of sexism in reverse. We do not only need a religion for women, but a religion for both women and men. If the exclusive worship of a father God could not encourage a holistic spirituality, then replacing it with the worship of the Goddess cannot lead to this either. The Goddess may be *one* of the resources for spirituality and the affirmation of life today, but she is not the only one, nor is it true that life-hatred is inherent in all patriarchal social and religious systems, as some radical feminists maintain.

Where can a deeply longed-for spiritual balance be found which both integrates and transcends our polarities and divisions? Many women, as well as men, look to the ideal of the androgyny as the most comprehensive symbol to express new forms of wholeness and integration. But is this ideal always clearly understood or does it remain profoundly ambiguous too?

The ideal of the androgyny

What is the androgyny? The symbol of the androgyny has a long history in human thought and is found in widely different cultures. It expresses the unification of opposites or the integration of sexual polarities into one unity, and examples of it are found in ancient Chinese, Indian and Greek thought as well as in early Christianity (Meeks, 1974). At its simplest androgyny might be described as an integration of male and female, less at the physical than at a symbolic level, where androgyny has been used as a model of divine reality, especially in the experience of the mystics. In feminist literature the term 'androgynous' is given a psychological and symbolic meaning, and one can even occasionally come across its sociological usage.

From the perspective of spirituality both the psychological and symbolic meaning of the term are important. The OED makes no reference to these meanings at all, but simply describes 'androgyne' in three different ways as 'a being uniting the physical characteristics of both sexes; a hermaphrodite', 'an effeminate man: a eunuch' and in biology as referring to 'androgynous plant' (1989, I, p. 452). The 1974 edition of the *Encyclopaedia Britannica* states about 'androgyny': 'in mythology and other symbolic religious systems, sexual ambivalence of biformity in gods, mythical beings, heroes, and others (*Micropaedia*, I, 1987, p. 364). The *Encyclopedia of Religion* provides much more information and begins its long entry on 'Androgynes' as follows:

The androgyne (from the Greek *andros*, 'man', and *gune*, 'woman') is a creature that is half male and half female. In mythology, such a creature is usually a god and is sometimes called a hermaphrodite. . . . In religious parlance androgyny is a much more comprehensive and abstract concept than is implied by the literal image of a creature simultaneously male and female in physical form. To say that God is androgynous is very different from saying that God is an androgyne. (O'Flaherty and Eliade, 1987, p. 276)

There is no reference here either to the contemporary psychological or symbolic usage of the term where androgyny is primarily understood as an integrative psychological model which, by analogy, can be transferred to divine reality as encompassing all difference in unity. Feminists are obviously less interested in possible forms of mythological bisexuality than in androgyny as symbol of integration which can transcend sexual polarity. It comes as some surprise, though, that the term 'androgyny' has been taken over without criticism, as feminists might wish to emphasise more a woman–man integration than that of man–woman. The linguistic terms should accordingly be 'gynandry' rather than 'androgyny'. (I have only come across the term 'gynandrous' once; see Sjöö and Mor, 1981, p. 16.)

Many writers on androgyny maintain that both sexes possess feminine and masculine characteristics which each person must integrate within themselves to achieve inner harmony and maturity. Androgyny is not something external, but rather an ideal, a vision, a myth, as described in the following introduction to a working bibliography on androgyny:

Our androgynous vision can be informed by tradition and history, but it must be free of the misogyny and sexism which has pervaded much of what men have written about it heretofore. The continued use of the term androgyny is necessary if we are to transcend the dualistic culture and the sex roles we have inherited, but feminists must clarify that the androgynous society can exist only if women as well as men can live their lives in accord with the androgynous ideal. Moreover, many before us have demanded the 'feminization' of their male-dominated societies, but now feminists must clarify what they mean by 'feminization', how that will change economic and social structures. If we rout sexism from the idea of androgyny and enrich it with feminist ideas, we shall have a vision to guide us in the struggle ahead. (Bazin, 1974, p. 217)

References to androgyny in a psychological and sociological context relate closely to our understanding of sexuality and gender construction, i.e. what we mean when we speak of 'feminine' and 'masculine' (Kaplan and Bean, 1976; Singer, 1976; Vetterling-Braggin, 1982). Much current research tries to investigate the biological and psychological characteristics of women and men. Is the 'feminine', for example, a universal relating to definite characteristics present in all women and cultures (Dickason, 1982), or does its understanding depend on upbringing, and on different cultural and religious expectations? What are the feminine and masculine stereotypes in our culture? Does it help or lead to further conceptual confusion to see androgyny as an answer to sexual stereotyping (Warren, 1982)? What, if anything, can androgynous life consist of?

In her study *Toward a Recognition of Androgyny* (1973) Carolyn Heilbrunn expressed her vision in the following way:

> I believe that our future salvation lies in a movement away from sexual polarization and the prison of gender toward a world in which individual roles and the modes of personal behavior can be freely chosen. The ideal toward which I believe we should move is best described by the term 'androgyny'. This ... defines a condition under which the characteristics of the sexes, and the human impulses expressed by men and women, are not rigidly assigned. Androgyny seeks to liberate the individual from the confines of the appropriate.
> ... Androgyny suggests a spirit of reconciliation between the sexes; it suggests, further, a full range of experience open to individuals who may, as women, be aggressive, as men, tender; it suggests a spectrum upon which human beings choose their places without regard to propriety or custom. (Heilbrunn, 1973, Introduction)

Psychological androgyny, as widely advocated by some feminists, can then be seen as the combination in a single person, of either sex, of so-called feminine and masculine characteristics, a person 'who is able to be both rational and emotional, strong and nurturant, assertive and compassionate, depending on the demands of the situation. Her character, or his, defies the limitations imposed by the traditional stereotypes of femininity and masculinity' (Warren, 1982, p. 170).

It is an inherent paradox of feminism that feminists sharply criticise sexual stereotypes and argue against innate characteristics of the two sexes whilst they also launch a fundamental critique against the 'masculinity' of western culture or plead for 'freeing the feminine' within us (Strachan, 1985). Both these positions, as well as the ideal of androgyny, presuppose in some form the stereotypes they wish to reject. The analysis of masculinity has shown 'that the cultural ideal of the competent, aggressive, competitive and emotionally uncommunicative male is a psychological straightjacket which limits men both in their capacity for personal fulfillment and in their moral sensitivity' (Warren, 1980, p. 305). Feminists also reject a false idealisation and romanticisation of femininity, but does such false idealisation not come into play when so much emphasis is placed on the feminine as a desirable psychological trait?

Psychological models of femininity and masculinity, whether constructed on the basis of Freudian or Jungian theories, have attracted much criticism from contemporary feminists (Mitchell, 1974; Goldenberg, 1976, 1977, 1979, 1982, 1990; Weiler, 1985; for a cross-cultural discussion of femininity and masculinity see Gupta, 1987, *Sexual Archetypes East and West*). Many women feel particularly drawn to Jungian archetypes and Jung's theory about the integration of feminine and masculine traits in the psyche which each individual has to achieve to find wholeness and completion. Yet Jung still remains locked in a very androcentric perspective as he is much more explicit about the integration of the feminine *anima* in men than about the masculine *animus* in women. The whole ideal of androgyny is so often perceived from a predominantly male perspective for, as one perceptive male writer noted, 'men have rarely had the imagination sufficiently capacious to envisage a female androgyny, i.e., a woman entitled to the same self-completion that men require for themselves' (quoted in Warren, 1980, p. 22).

The American sociologist Philip E. Lampe (1981) has argued that a move towards androgyny in society may be expected to be accompanied by a change in religiosity. If the ideal of 'a genderless or androgynous lifestyle' became more common, it would result in an androgynous society defined by the *Encyclopedia of Sociology* (1974, p. 11) as a society 'whose members would have the social and personality characteristics of both sexes. In such a society roles, behaviours and personality traits would no longer be defined as either male or female, but each individual would incorporate characteristics of both, regardless of biological sex'. Lampe also points out that feminists, while on the whole less religious than non-feminists, can identify more easily with androgynous thinking regarding Ultimate Reality.

Much of this depends on what precisely one understands by androgyny.

Whilst it may be psychologically and spiritually enriching to meditate in a general way on the nature and worldview of an androgynous person and society (Nornengast, 1970), from a more critical perspective one must seriously consider the question whether the ideal of the androgyny remains too dependent on an oppositional mode of thought by implying a fundamental difference between male and female. If one does not agree with such differences and sees them primarily as culturally constructed sexual stereotypes, then the symbol of the androgyny is perhaps less satisfactory.

It certainly remains profoundly ambivalent as different authors consider androgyny as either tied to such polarisation, or as denying all differences, or as a symbol of truly transcending them. In their model of sex-role development Rebecca, Hefner and Oleshansky (1976) have proposed a first stage of undifferentiated sex roles, a second stage of polarised sex roles and a third stage of 'sex-role transcendence' which they see as sharply differentiated from what some authors discuss as androgyny. They write:

> For some, androgyny means a completely uni-sexual society, with no sex difference. . . . For others, androgyny is a stable psychological trait with equal balance of male and female characteristics, which allows the individual to conform to environmental demands to behave in either a masculine or feminine way. (1976, p. 95)

They see their concept of 'sex-role transcendence' as going beyond this, implying flexibility (over time, over situation, and over personal moods), plurality and personal choice for individuals and society:

> Given the diversity of situations a person encounters (some of which lend themselves to assertive, independent behaviors, and some of which lend themselves to expressive, nurturant, cooperative behaviors), that person will have to synchronize the particular situational expectations and personal inclinations and abilities. To a transcendent person, assigned gender is irrelevant to decision-making. (1976, p. 96)

Here the notion of transcendence is applied to personal behaviour, as going beyond the understanding of an androgynous model. Carol Ochs (1977) has similarly argued for the need to transcend an androgynous mode of thought with regard to our perception of ultimate reality. Matriarchal and patriarchal categories about the Divine remain in an oppositional mode whereas androgynous thought goes beyond, but still presupposes this opposition. Thus Ochs argues that the three modes of religious thought developed so far – matriarchal, patriarchal, and androgynous – all require transcending if we really wish to get 'behind the sex of God' and find the true meaning and centre of our lives. In her search for the Ultimate Ochs seeks for a God concept that transcends all previous models and maintains that the contemporary phase of androgynous thinking is only a transitional one. She maps out a monistic position which sees 'reality in one, undivided, with no unrelated aspects' and opts for a 'theistic monism' where 'God is not father, nor mother, nor even parent, because God is not other than, distinct from, or opposed to creation' (1977, pp. 135, 137).

This search for a more unitary or monistic way of thinking indicates again the need for integration, but it is not really a new alternative, as Ochs claims, nor is it clear from her discussion how this transcendent view can be translated into new religious and social structures. Many feminists simply do not realise that an integral concept of God is already available in the classical theologies of many religions with their profound reflection on the interdependent immanence and transcendence of Ultimate Reality. Whether particular authors advocate a spirituality of God, the Goddess, androgyny or transcendence may be due to a difference in personality, education, experience and overall perspective, but these are less important in the end than the question whether any particular vision is large and dynamic enough to ensure individual and social well-being by providing a path to true harmony and integration. That question is as important for feminist spirituality in general as it is for the spirituality growing out of Christian feminist theology. This new theology will be our concern in the next chapter.

6

Voices of a new theology

'Feminist spirituality has to grow out of a feminist theology as a critical theology of liberation. The task of such a theology is to uncover Christian theological traditions and myths that perpetuate sexist ideologies, violence, and alienation.

. . .

The Church has publicly to confess that it has wronged women. As the Christian community has officially rejected national and racial exploitation and publicly repented of its tradition of anti-Semitic theology, so it is still called to abandon all forms of sexism.

An analysis of Christian tradition and history, however, indicates that Church and theology will transcend their own sexist ideologies only when women are granted full spiritual, theological, and ecclesial equality. . . . Only if we, women and men, are able to live in non-sexist Christian communities, to celebrate nonsexist Christian liturgies, and to think in nonsexist theological terms and imagery will we be able to formulate a genuine Christian feminist spirituality.' – **Elisabeth Schüssler Fiorenza**, 'Feminist Spirituality, Christian Identity, and Catholic Vision', pp. 146, 147

Christian feminist spirituality is closely connected with feminist theology which has appeared as a new theology created and voiced by women, although men now also write about it occasionally. Characterised by strong commitment and fervour, this theology has been described as an 'advocacy theology', and as such it has attracted ardent supporters and vehement critics alike – largely from among men, but also from some women. The new subject of feminist theology is represented in many North American, but few European, universities and in Britain it is still being snubbed at or ignored by much of the official theological establishment. When I once mentioned to the editor of a widely read theological journal that I was interested in reviewing good books on feminist theology, he replied 'Do feminists ever write good theological books?' Such is the reputation of feminist theology among its despisers.

But what is feminist theology? How does it differ from theology as traditionally understood and practised? And in what way does it affect the practice of spirituality? Let us look at the meaning of feminist theology, its major positions and practitioners, the controversies they have created and, most importantly, let us consider the spirituality celebrated and advocated by feminist theologians and their followers.

The term 'feminist theology' is used in both a wider and more narrow sense among women who share a deep commitment and concern for both religion and feminism. Feminist theology is 'reflected in the sizable literature in the West that represents the women's movement in the synagogue, the Christian Church, and the feminist spirituality movement, and . . . has already developed into a tradition which is ecumenical, pluralist, and academically serious' (Carr, 1990, p. 94). The essential challenge for women interested in theological issues is summed up in questions such as: does traditional theology still speak to women's experience today or do women need to create a new religious and spiritual tradition? Do feminists need to reconstruct their religious tradition by reinterpreting its insights in the light of new experience? These issues are squarely faced in the essays edited by Carol Christ and Judith Plaskow, *Womanspirit Rising* (1979) and by Plaskow and Christ, *Weaving the Visions* (1989). From a Christian point of view they are more fully explored in the methodological and critical sections of Rosemary Radford Ruether's *Sexism and God-Talk* (1983), Elisabeth Schüssler Fiorenza's *In Memory of Her* (1983) and Anne E. Carr's *Transforming Grace* (1990).

In a wider sense, then, feminist theology can refer to the perspectives of Jewish and Christian feminists and to those practising new forms of feminist spirituality. In its narrower sense the term is often understood to relate to feminist writings closely connected with or at least arising out of Christian theological concerns, and I shall use the term from now on mainly in this more specific sense. In the previous chapter we explored some of the ways in which contemporary women try to create a new tradition by connecting elements and insights of earlier symbols, myths and stories with their experience and religious practice today. New we shall investigate how Christian feminists reconstruct and reinterpret the elements of their faith and thereby try to make theology meaningful for women today. But their vision is larger than that; it includes women and men and reaches out to the whole community. As its best and most dynamic feminist theology and spirituality contain a transformative potential for a profound restructuring of both church and society.

What is feminist theology?

Theology can simply be defined as the intellectual reflection on the experience of faith. Members of every religious tradition develop intellectual formulations and abstract concepts about their experience, whether it is personal or communal, original and new, or follows the established pattern of a historical tradition. In this general sense theology exists in every religion, but it can develop in very different ways. In monotheistic religions theology, as the original meaning of the word implies, concerns particularly ideas about God. But one can understand theology more universally as a quest for ultimate meaning and as a concern with transcendence, however thought of. The traditional subject matter of Christian theology is often summed up as consisting of an enquiry into 'God, man, and the world' or to put it differently, an enquiry into the nature of ultimate reality, of human life in its individual and collective forms, and of the natural world of which human beings form a part.

This brief description indicates that there can be different kinds of theology, different ways or models of understanding 'God, man, and the world'. Different religions can be seen as different symbolic maps or models of what ultimate reality and human life are understood to be about. These maps present us with visions of different countries which can be quite dissimilar although they also share many common features. Sara Maitland (1983) sees feminism as providing a map of a new country for Christianity and she emphasises that we need women as map-makers of the 'interior country', of that area of inwardness so important for spirituality which provides the matrix for much of our experience and action.

It is important to remember that all theology is originally grounded in experience, an experience of faith as a transforming vision, a revelatory experience that transcends ordinary common sense experience. Throughout history women and men have had such experiences, and have had them in abundance. But from a contemporary woman's point of view the question arises how far the experience of women has remained in the past an untapped source for traditional theology. Theological formulations which found official, institutional sanction and were handed down in the codified teachings of established theological schools were entirely the creation of men. This is true of the theologies of all religions. One must therefore ask how the creation and formulations of one sex alone can possibly be universally valid for all people, women and men? In the past it was always male theologians who wrote about the image, nature and place of woman in church and society, thus articulating and defining what a woman was to be. Today women write about themselves, about their own experience and interpretation of faith, their ministry in the churches, their self-understanding as women. In feminist theology women have become the subject of a new theological approach rather than simply being the object of theology, for feminist theology is rooted in the religious experience of women themselves. Thus feminist theology has an experiential as well as an experimental quality about it, and perceptive observers recognise in the feminist movement in the churches a new prophetic dimension of great importance for the future of Christianity.

It is perhaps too early yet to write a history of feminist theology although this new subject or, more correctly stated, this new critical theory and practice have been in the making for over twenty years now. Feminist theology developed in the USA before it came to Europe where it is found since about 1975. By now several North American colleges and universities have given some institutional backing to feminist theology whereas in Europe it has on the whole been given little official acknowledgement in educational institutions. It largely flourishes in loose networks in a non-institutional, non-hierarchical, informal way among women interested in theological ideas and research. A unique development occurred in the Netherlands where the Roman Catholic University of Nijmegen created a Chair in Feminism and Christianity in 1983 (first held by Catharina J. M. Halkes, then by Mary Grey). Holland is unique in that every theological faculty, whether Protestant or Catholic, has now some teaching on feminist theology. A two year research project has already produced a substantial report on ten years of feminist theology in the Netherlands (Bekkenkamp, Droes and Korte, 1986). However, feminist theology is by no means restricted to North America and western Europe but, like feminism itself, it possesses a global dimension. Feminist theological thinking can be found among women in Australia, Asia (Christian Conference of Asia 1985/86; Chatterji,

1979, 1982, 1986; Katoppo, 1979; Faria, Alexander and Tellis-Nayak, 1984; Fabella and Lee Park, 1989), South Africa (Vorster, 1984), and elsewhere around the world (Thompson, 1982; Webster and Webster, 1985; Fabella and Oduyoye, 1988; Russell, 1988). It is sometimes said that Valerie Saiving's article 'The Human Situation: A Feminine View', originally published in 1960 (reprinted in Christ and Plaskow, 1979, pp. 25–42), was the first landmark in feminist theology without being recognised as such at the time. As a student of theology, especially of the theological works of Niebuhr and Nygren, Valerie Saiving became aware that the universal human condition discussed by theologians did not take into account the difference between the experience of women and men. She had the courage to see that the sexual identity of a theologian has much to do with how the proper role of theology is perceived and thus makes a difference to the process of theologising. For example, such theological topics as sin and grace, much debated in the works of Niebuhr and Nygren, may well need to be approached differently when examined from the perspective of women (see also Plaskow, 1980).

Saiving did not use the term 'feminist' but called her analysis simply 'a feminine view' and argued that as our society is moving from a masculine to a feminine orientation, theology needs to reconsider its estimate of the human condition and redefine its categories. An explicitly feminist stance was articulated in Mary Daly's book *The Church and the Second Sex* (1968), a widely publicised work on the role of women in the church. Daly maintained that the church had encouraged the view of women as inferior, and that it had become a leading instrument of oppression. Following the publication of Daly's work a flood of books appeared on feminist theology, whether written from mainstream Christian or Jewish perspectives or whether representing mother goddess worship, witchcraft and the new spirituality movement. The names of Sheila Collins, Letty Russell, Rosemary Radford Ruether, Naomi Goldenberg, Judith Plaskow, Carol Christ, Starhawk and others became well known in America and abroad. Harvard Divinity School, after admitting its first women students only in 1955, saw the development of a Women's Caucus by 1970 (Hageman, 1974). Its work led to the foundation of the 'Women's Studies in Religion' programme in 1973, which now publishes 'The Harvard Women Studies in Religion Series' (Atkinson, Buchanan and Miles, 1985). The annual conference of the American Academy of Religion has organised a regular section on 'Women and Religion' since 1972. In Europe, feminist theology became first known through American publications, but now there are quite a few women writing and researching in this field. In May 1986, over 70 women from different parts of Europe met for a consultation in Switzerland and founded the 'European Society of Women in Theological Research' which publishes a regular newsletter and organises bi-annual conferences, most recently in Bristol, in September 1991, where over 150 women from 20 different European countries took part (for participants and contributions, see King, 1991a).

One of the earliest outlines of feminist theology was provided by Catharina Halkes' publication *Met Mirjam is het begonnen* (It all began with Miriam), available in German (Halkes, 1980a, *Gott hat nicht nur starke Söhne: Grundzüge einer feministischen Theologie*) but not in English. Major themes of feminist theology were widely publicised in England through Susan Dowell and Linda Hurcombe's *Dispossessed Daughters of Eve* (1981) and Sara Maitland's *A Map of the New Country* (1983). A substantial introduction to the sources and norms of feminist theology and its implications for different theological subjects is provided by Rosemary Ruether's *Sexism and God-Talk. Towards a Feminist Theology* (1983). More recently the work by the German theologian Elisabeth Moltmann-Wendel, *A Land Flowing with Milk and Honey. Perspectives on Feminist Theology* (1986) has also become available in English. It is particularly stimulating as it includes female images in religious art, both ancient and modern, on which the author draws in her discussion. Most helpful as a general introduction to the wide range of theological debates is the Reader on *Feminist Theology*, edited by Ann Loades (1990) and questions of method are explored in Pamela Dickey Young's book, *Feminist Theology/Christian Theology* (1990).

It has been said that the 'themes and perspectives of "feminist theology" are as broad as the women's movement itself. Furthermore, this theological genre has had no single organising theme, no obvious focus, no sharply identifiable set of objectives. To be sure, it is unified in its opposition to the maleness of God and tradition, and the consequent subordination of women. But it has lacked a clear-cut model for dealing with these issues' (Quebedeaux, 1987, pp. 132ff.). However, feminist theology should not be primarily characterised by what it is not, but rather by what it aims to achieve. It has both a negative and a positive task. Its negative task is the radical critique of all forms of sexism and androcentrism inherent in the language and thought forms of previous theologies (Ruether, 1987), a task calling into question and dismantling all exclusive, onesided presuppositions based on male norms and views alone. Its positive task is one of reform and reconstruction, of a reinterpretation of tradition in the light of women's experience, a reflection on faith in the light of feminism. The positive task of construction is always more difficult than criticism, and feminist theology has still got a long way to go before it has made its full contribution to theological thought and expression.

Susan Dowell and Linda Hurcombe have said: 'The overwhelming task of feminist theology is, in our view, to face the fact that Christian theology is guilty of sexism, as it has been guilty of racism and classism, but also to affirm that this faith, this theology, is not irredeemably sexist. This is a critical mission within all organized religion' (1981, p. 67). Basically, feminist theology is strongly holistic in intention. It criticises all dualistic separations, whether of body and spirit, heaven and earth, woman and man, man and God. It is born out of a certain women-togetherness, a community wherein women can ask their own questions about ultimate values, where they can work and think together to search for answers, for disclosure of meaning and for the divine presence within and around them. Feminist theology has been likened to process theology because it is about change and movement, about perceiving a new unfolding of God's revelation in time and history. Or it can be seen as liberation theology, for it was born out of women's historical experience of suffering, out of the subordination and oppression created by the structural violence of church and society. It embodies a new vision of reality founded on an ardent wish for liberation, for freedom and reconciliation, not only for women, but for people of all classes, races and nations.

Feminist theology can be described as inductive in its method, as 'pneumatological, utopian-prophetic, even Dionysian' in nature (Halkes, 1980b). Its experimental character is evident even in its language and style (Gerber, 1984). The traditional subjects of theology are mediated through new concepts, through a less abstract, more contextual language woven around stories, experiences and events set within a new perspective. And yet feminist theology is theology in the fullest and most fundamental sense of the word: it is centrally concerned with the encounter, experience and revelation of God or the Divine, and with human images and concepts relating to this ultimate mystery and to our abiding fascination with it. In its critical stance feminist theology highlights and makes explicit the pervasively androcentric and often misogynist character of much traditional Christian theology (Aubert, 1975).

Feminist theology is concerned with examining language about God and human beings, the language of the Bible and that used in the liturgy. It critically reflects on traditional topics such as the teaching about Christ and the Spirit as well as questions of Christian ethics, Christian ministry and community (Carr, 1980, 1982, 1990; Gerber, 1984; Sorge, 1985; Siegele-Wenschkewitz and Schottroff, 1986). Feminist theologians criticise the false abstractions and overly rationalistic conceptualisations of traditional theologies. Women, out of their experience of oppression, are suspicious of the suppression of experience in so much theological thinking with its abstract speculations. Whilst feminist theologians base themselves on scripture and the living tradition of the church as their primary sources, their thinking is at the same time deeply grounded in women's experience and consciousness as well as in feminist action for liberation. Thus action is closely linked to thought. Feminist theology does not develop in isolation, but grows out of interconnections, through bonds with other women which provide an important community dimension. Perhaps one of the most significant aspects of feminist theology is its non-hierarchical character as a non-clerical lay movement indicative of profound social changes. As such, it is capable of bringing much change into the church as community. One can truly speak of a 'feminist transformation of theology' (Plaskow, 1977) or more cautiously about a 'feminist reconsideration of Christian theology' which according to an outline produced by the British group 'Women in Theology' includes such questions as: Where we stand as women; The 'patriarchal system' and women's critique of it; What is theology and how can we do it? The way the Bible has been used; Wherein lies the Bible's authority? Women's approach to the text; How can we use God language today? God-language in the Old and New Testament, in the history of doctrine, in other religions; Women's participation in the history and literature of the people of Israel; Women's participation in New Testament times and in the early Christian communities; The discipleship and priesthood of women today; The community of the church and the feminist community; Mariology; Women's spirituality (see also the different themes in Weidmann, 1984, and Weaver, 1985).

Much of this is exploratory and breaking new ground. Feminist theology offers a new vision; it rediscovers and reinterprets old symbols and shapes new ones. It creates a new sense of community among women and gives them a new empowerment which many experience as a confirmation of the Spirit, the breath of life and creative source of all energy. Feminist theology also creates a new spirituality whose great themes are liberation, celebration and community. There is much life and positive strength in feminist theology, there is much that is shared through common characteristics and methods, but there is also much diversity and debate. The critical sifting of past inheritance is undertaken in very different and sometimes opposite ways. Far from speaking with one voice, feminist theology is profoundly pluralistic. It contains a number of different strands and orientations and has led to several controversies. Some maintain that this diversity within feminist theology and spirituality is its very strength. Let us explore these differences in some detail.

Basic orientations in feminist theology

The major orientations which have emerged in feminist theology so far are characterised by either a reformist or a radical, revolutionary stance. Profound disagreement reigns over the question of whether traditional religious beliefs and symbols can be reinterpreted and transformed in the light of new experience, or whether they have to be abandoned in order to be replaced by new ones. There is also the problem of experience. If one distinguishes between woman's traditional experience and feminist experience, what place is assigned to each of these in feminist theology? For the feminist theologian woman's experience in all its particularity becomes a source of theological insight and is used as a new theological norm. But how does this work in conjunction with other theological norms such as scripture, tradition and the Christian experience of faith?

The critical principle of feminist theology has been described by Rosemary Ruether as 'the promotion of the full humanity of women'. She writes:

> Whatever denies, diminishes, or distorts the full humanity of women is, therefore, appraised as not redemptive. Theologically speaking, whatever diminishes or denies the full humanity of women must be presumed not to reflect the divine or an authentic relation to the divine, or to reflect the authentic nature of things, or to be the message or work of an authentic redeemer or a community of redemption.
>
> This negative principle also implies the positive principle: what does promote the full humanity of women is of the Holy. . . . But the meaning of this positive principle – namely, the full humanity of

women – is not fully known. It has not existed in history. (1983, pp. 18ff.)

This is a much wider definition than the experience of women. Ultimately feminist theology must envisage the full humanity of all people, women and men. Applying a critical principle to feminist theology itself will mean the recognition that too often a particular dimension of women's experience is equated with women's experience as a whole and that the genuine diversity of women's experience is not sufficiently taken into account. Feminist theology must avoid the pitfall of universalising from particular experience.

It is difficult to group feminist theologians together for each has her own definite emphasis and individual approach, but the basic division between either a reformist or a radical stance cuts across denominational differences. One of the best known and most radical feminist theologians is the American Mary Daly, a former Roman Catholic. She was not only the first to fully articulate a feminist stance in theology, but she also repudiated her earlier reformist position taken in *The Church and the Second Sex* (1968) by developing an extreme radicalism in her subsequent publications. In her 'New Feminist Postchristian Introduction' to the 1975 edition of her book *Beyond God the Father* (1974a, first published in 1973) she argues that it is not sexism alone which makes Christianity oppressive, but its very core symbolism of God the Father and the male Christ. Whilst her earlier work manifested some anger, she later greatly shifted her focus and radicalised her perspective, succinctly summarised in such articles as 'Theology after the Demise of God the Father: A Call for the Castration of Sexist Religion' (1974b) and 'After the Death of God the Father: Women's Liberation and the Transformation of Christian Consciousness' (1979b). Her radical, separatist stance is writ large in her fierce, highly original books full of new word creations, *Gyn/Ecology* (1979a), *Pure Lust* (1984) and *Outercourse* (1992).

The first radical step was already taken in 1971. Daly was then invited to be the first woman preacher in Harvard Memorial Church and chose as the theme of her sermon 'The Women's Movement: An Exodus Community' (reprinted in Clark and Richardson, 1977, pp. 265–71). The sermon concluded with the symbolic act of women leaving the church together, an event of profound significance for many participants. Daly described the feminist community of sisterhood as a community with a mission whose first priority is the liberation of women and the positive refusal to be co-opted any more. For her the sisterhood of women opens out to universal horizons pointing toward the sisterhood of man. She concluded with the words:

> The sisterhood of man cannot happen without a real exodus. We have to go out from the land of our fathers into an unknown place. We can this morning demonstrate our exodus from sexist religion – a break which for many of us has already taken place spiritually. We can give physical expression to our exodus community, to the fact that we must go away.
>
> We cannot really belong to institutional religion as it exists. It isn't good enough to be token preachers. It isn't good enough to have our energies drained and co-opted. Singing sexist hymns, praying to a male god breaks our spirit, makes us less than human. The crushing weight of this tradition, of this power structure, tells us that *we do not even exist.*
>
> . . .
>
> Let us affirm our faith in ourselves and our will to transcendence by rising and walking out together. (Clark and Richardson, 1977, pp. 270ff.)

Daly's early theological thought was much influenced by Paul Tillich (Stenger, 1982). In her later works she identifies woman's experience with religious meaning itself, but the two are not identical and she does not pay sufficient attention to the ambiguity of experience. Sometimes she even equates experience with the Ultimate and one can criticise her for having made the experience of woman becoming into a new absolute which carries with it an affirmation, especially in *Gyn/Ecology*, which can justifiably be described as 'idolatrous' (Stenger).

Daly has consciously moved out of the church and found a new community in the feminist movement which, in radical separation, constitutes for her a new messianic community alone able to challenge the oppressive tendencies of traditional religion. She identifies with the radical strand of feminism and recasts religion in a radical mode. In fact, her thought does not belong to feminist theology in the narrow understanding of that term any more but has become 'post-Christian'.

This term, now widely used in the United States, is sometimes also found among religious feminists in Britain, yet its meaning remains undefined and is far from clear. Does it imply moving beyond Christianity in the sense of developing it further or simply going outside it? Does it imply the tacit claim of having reached a more inclusive universal position or is it, on the contrary, far more exclusive than Christianity itself? Is the term equivalent to being 'non-Christian' or does it mean being religious in a new sense? If the latter, why not drop the 'Christian' altogether? Or do particular women still have a continuing need to refer back to Christianity in order to maintain their identity, an identity so tied to a past framework that they have not really moved beyond it and therefore they cannot conceive of theologising in an altogether new intellectual and existential context?

Some of these issues were explored from almost opposite standpoints in a public discussion 'Is there a Place for Feminists in a Christian Church?' held in London in May 1986 between Daphne Hampson and Rosemary Ruether. Hampson argued for 'the ultimate incompatibility between feminism and Christianity', a position not much different from that of many secular and non-Christian religious feminists. Hampson maintained 'that in feminism Christianity has met with a challenge to which it cannot accommodate itself' (Hampson and Ruether, 1987, p. 14). But why then hold on to being a 'post-Christian'? Ruether criticised Hampson for seeing Christianity as statically enclosed in a past revelation whereas, according to her, it is open to development and thus open to feminist restatement. Christianity is not simply a culture of domination but it 'is also deeply rooted in a culture of liberation. . . . Prophetic faith included the critique of religion'. The past contains many partial insights which can spark the imagination so that Ruether could affirm 'As a Christian, I am engaged in restating the insights of Christianity in feminist terms because I am concerned that the churches become vehicles of hope, rather than of oppression, for women' (1987, pp. 20 and 21). Hampson's post-Christian position is more fully developed in *Theology and Feminism* (1990), yet many reviewers disagree with her radical assertion that feminism is the deathknell of Christianity (see Elwes, 1992).

A sound measure of radicalism may be required in many areas of Christian life, especially when one thinks of the inflexibility of the male bureaucracy of the churches, but it does not necessarily mean abandoning Christianity altogether. There are still many Christian women who believe with Ruether that we can move further within the church, transforming it from within without having to adopt the radical stance of Daly, Hampson and other 'post-Christians'. If extreme feminist radicalism, whether of the theological, cultural or socio-political variety, became the general norm – which seems unlikely at present – it would be a source for a potentially vaster conflict between the sexes than any other racial, cultural or social tension. But perhaps it is necessary at our present stage of development to experience the extreme limits of possible female being-in-the-world to achieve a truly new breakthrough. To create new structures for church and society, harmonious integration may have to be won by passing temporarily through a stage of separation.

Compared with Mary Daly's extremism, Rosemary Ruether's voice is one of balance and moderation. Its strength lies in blending the best of Christian tradition with feminist vision and restating Christian insights in the context of women's experience today. Whilst Daly has been called a 'revolutionary', Ruether is often seen as a 'radical reformist'. However, Daly's 'revolution' is mainly grounded in the power of her ideas which in the end remain based in philosophical idealism. In some ways Ruether is 'revolutionary' in a more realistic sense as she links her ideas much more closely to social praxis as is also the case with South American liberation theologians and other Christian feminists such as Sheila Collins, Letty Russell and Dorothee Sölle. It has been said that Daly and Ruether represent 'two kinds of prophecy' which in a way complement each other:

> Daly's perception of the depth of the historical problem of patriarchy and sexism is more unequivocal than Ruether's. She names the systemic demon, not as a theological construct, but rather as a *human agent – i.e., men*, creators and rulers of the patriarchal world. But she then flees inward, for a personal exorcism of the mind. Ruether does not name the demon with the same unmistakable clarity; she suggests that it is a theological concept (e.g., 'dualism'). Ruether, however, does not flee inward; rather she joins her sisters and brothers in the world for the corporate task of exorcising a historic, systemic demon whose human name and face remain elusive.
>
> . . .
>
> It may be that Ruether's strong and valuable sense of commitment to her people, her community – especially Christian women – is militating against her assumption of a more revolutionary *prophetic* role within the community – the role of one who speaks *as an individual to the community instead of as a member of the community for the community*. Daly's voice is prophetic, but she has chosen to stand outside the very community (Christianity) to whom she could most forcefully speak prophetically. . . . Ruether stands within the community that needs the prophecy, but she is not 'sparking' quite

the same terrifying and devastating warning. (Heyward, 1979, pp. 71ff.)

Ruether's early work was concerned with *Liberation Theology* (1972) and the theological roots of anti-semitism (*Faith and Fratricide*, 1974a). This was followed by two collections of essays – *Religion and Sexism* (1974b) and *New Woman, New Earth* (1975) dealing with sexist ideologies and human liberation. After a brief study on *Mary – The Feminine Face of the Church* (1979a) she edited with Eleanor McLaughlin *Women of Spirit* (1979) which explores the lives and insights of several women leaders in Judaism and Christianity. Ruether's important introduction to feminist theology, *Sexism and God-Talk* (1983), has already been mentioned. This has been supplemented by *Womanguides. Readings Toward a Feminist Theology* (1985) and *Women-Church. The Theology and Practice of Feminist Liturgical Communities* (1986a), and *Gaia and God* (1992).

Ruether's feminist theology is based on a vision of a world without sexism, a world truly transformed by divine redemption. Over the years, her perspective has widened considerably and she now lists among the sources of her theologising not only the Bible and the dominant theological tradition of the major Christian churches, but also countercultural movements in early Christianity and church history, pagan veneration of nature and the Goddess, and modern resources found in liberalism, Marxism and romanticism. In order to express a fuller, more comprehensive meaning of the Divine than that conveyed by the traditional word 'God' or by the new 'Goddess' of the feminist movement, Ruether has developed a new written symbol 'God/ess'. It combines words of male and female linguistic form whilst preserving the fundamental affirmation that divinity is One. But she concedes that this term 'is unpronounceable and inadequate. It is not intended as language for worship, where one might prefer a more evocative term, such as Holy One or Holy Wisdom. Rather it serves here as an analytic sign to point toward that yet unnameable understanding of the divine that would transcend patriarchal limitations and signal redemptive experience for women as well as men' (Ruether, 1983, p. 46).

The readings in *Womanguides* take up the same themes by providing historical source material with commentaries and reflections which open with a chapter on 'Gender Imagery for God/ess'. Other themes explored are the Divine Pleroma, male and female saviour figures, foremothers of the womanchurch, and visions of a new earth in terms of a redeemed society and nature, and a new understanding of heaven. (For a critical discussion of Ruether's christology see Snyder, 1988.)

Feminist theologians, whether sharing the radical orientation of Mary Daly or the reformist one of Rosemary Ruether and such writers as Collins, Halkes, Moltmann-Wendel, Russell, Sölle and Schüssler Fiorenza, have had a wide influence across Christian denominational boundaries. Feminist theology is truly ecumenical in that it brings together Christian women from different churches. It is also ecumenical in a wider sense since both Jewish and Christian feminists are engaged in challenging the patriarchal language and culture of their traditions which hold many symbols and stories in common. Well known Jewish feminists writers on theological issues are Naomi Goldenberg, Carol Ochs and Judith Plaskow. Rita Gross, now deeply committed to Tibetan Buddhism, was at one time also connected with Judaism and devoted some earlier work to Jewish theological issues.

Each feminist theologian has a somewhat different perspective and approach by bringing her own insight, courage and vision to bear on theology. Feminism has even taken root in Christian evangelicalism, especially among graduate women in the United States. The evangelical bi-monthly *Daughters of Sarah* has been published since 1974 and the Evangelical Women's Caucus (EWC) has had its own newsletter since 1977 which has since grown into a full-scale quarterly journal called *EWC Update*. Virginia Ramey Mollenkott and Letha Scanzoni are among the best known evangelical writers on feminism in the United States. The rise and significance of feminism among American evangelicals has been discussed by Richard Quebedeaux who writes:

Evangelical feminism as a movement has distinguished itself from secular feminism . . . and even from mainstream Christian feminism, by its insistence on the centrality of biblical authority on the issue of women in church and society. Its adherents often call themselves 'biblical feminists'. (The movement can also be distinguished from the more radical feminist sentiments, secular and Christian, by its conciliatory attitude toward men – stressing the *mutual* submission of all Christians to each other.) Yet despite their commitment to the full authority of the Bible, evangelical feminists share a traditional 'liberal' methodology in dealing with that authority. (1987, p. 141)

This brings us to some of the theological controversies in feminist theology, of which that surrounding the Bible is especially important but by no means the only one.

Controversies in feminist theology

Feminist theology challenges the customary understanding of Bible and tradition in Christianity and calls for a radical re-examination of the presuppositions and expressions of Christian faith. Members of different Christian denominations respond differently to the challenge of feminist thinking, but there is little doubt that feminist thought has by now influenced individual people in all Christian churches. However, the emergence and growth of feminist theology has created considerable controversy relating to both internal and external aspects. Debate about matters internal to Christian theology concern such issues as the understanding of God, the teaching and role of the Bible in the Christian community, the nature of the ministry and the sacraments, and the place of Mary in the church. Other controversies concern the relationship between feminist theology and external matters such as ecumenical dialogue between different Christian churches, Christian attitudes to Judaism, and the link between feminist and black theology.

We can only briefly touch upon these issues, some of which are discussed in detail by Dowell and Hurcombe (1981), Maitland (1983), and in the essays edited by Monica Furlong on the *Feminine in the Church* (1984a). The controversies surrounding the interpretation of biblical texts and the understanding of divine reality described as 'God' have already been mentioned when we discussed the place of women in religious language and thought in Chapter 2. The image of God the father has been so dominant in Christianity that it has been absolutised and become an almost exclusive model for our perception of God (McFague, 1983, 1987). Yet at the same time there exist many resources for alternative models of God drawing on matriarchal and feminine elements in the Judaeo-Christian tradition (Mulack, 1983; Plaskow, 1990; Pirani, 1991; Long, 1992).

The reformist wing of feminist theology seeks new models through which to express the always newly experienced encounter with the divine and the nature of divine–human relationships, whilst revolutionary feminist theology breaks the traditional models completely and rejects them as idolatrous. Mary Daly cannot use the word 'God' any more because she thinks there is no way in which we can remove the male imagery traditionally associated with 'God', a term which represents for her 'the necrophilia of patriarchy, whereas *Goddess* affirms the life-loving be-ing of women and nature' (1979a, p. xi). Others might argue that the term 'Goddess' absolutises female imagery to the exclusion of male models and thus leads to a dominance in reverse rather than to a harmonious balance.

The symbols of God and Goddess have been widely explored in feminist theology (Christ, 1983; for a critique see Heine, 1989) and Rosemary Ruether's decision to use 'God/ess', at least in written form, has already been mentioned. Whether God symbolism needs to be expressed in both female and male linguistic terms or whether one should transcend both and find other forms, as Ochs (1977) has argued, is difficult to decide. It may well be that different people feel the need to settle this issue for themselves in different ways. Whilst a large measure of consensus is necessary to create and maintain community life, we none the less come to realise that here as elsewhere a pluralism of views can exist side by side. Rosemary Ruether has suggested that it is not the maleness of God and Christ as such which gave rise to sexist attitudes, but rather their association with our patriachal models of maleness as dominance and of femaleness as subjugation. But how to disentangle the two until we have acquired new modes of thinking and being? The feminist attempt to introduce or recover female God symbolism in Christianity and Judaism (Ochshorn, 1981; Gross, 1981; Long, 1992) is of great importance, not only for women, but for the vitality and comprehensiveness of theological thinking. Considerable resources exist in both religious traditions which can be drawn upon for inspiration. In early Christianity a greater pluralism of symbols prevailed than was later officially acknowledged once the church became institutionalised (Schüssler Fiorenza, 1979b, 1983). Evidence exists that both father and mother symbolism were used, but the latter was particularly associated with gnostic groups who were soon declared heretical by the mainstream church (Pagels, 1979).

The relativisation of the absolutised symbol of the fatherhood of God is the least contemporary feminists can ask for. However, whilst the image of God's motherhood may provide a corrective balance, one must not absolutise it either, for we must not forget that the mother image can be ambivalent and misleading too (King, 1989b). Besides the image of the wrathful, overbearing father we all know of the image of the stern, reproaching and oppressive mother who never allows her children to grow into true independence. Thus the mother image is not necessarily always all good and comforting but can be negative too, whereas the father image need not always be negative either. We must in fact ask ourselves which are the elements in the fatherhood symbolism used for God we cannot do without (Sölle, 1981b).

It is interesting to reflect on some research findings in the psychology of religion published in Belgium in 1968 (quoted in Wulff, 1982) which investigated the correlation between parental images and the image of God found in a group of men and women. The investigations showed that concepts about the deity were often more closely related to mother than father images. This could be more reliably predicted for males than females, but for both sexes the image of God was likely to be more strongly associated with the image of one's preferred parent, whether mother or father. The study indicated that the God image found among a group of western Christians appeared on the whole to be more maternal than paternal – something not widely known.

It is clear that feminist theology contains strong themes of protest against God the father (Halkes, 1981, 1985), but discerning feminist theologians know that speaking about the female nature of God presents numerous problems too (Ruether, 1981b). Yet the debate about God symbolism has considerable importance for both theology and spirituality. Theologically it highlights the relative nature of any symbol for expressing the Ultimate which remains ultimately inexpressible. At the spiritual level it shows that the psychological perception of divine reality within each individual can take many different forms and that symbols used in prayer and worship may vary widely according to personal and group preferences. Feminist thinking profoundly affects and reshapes spirituality, but its challenge is initially perhaps more provocative towards public language and symbolism because the dominant God model has influenced our institutions in terms of hierarchy, inequality and submission. If one wishes to maintain these institutions in their traditional form, one can easily feel threatened by the force of the feminist challenge. A concerned conservative critic of feminism such as William Oddie (1984) sees the church as threatened by the 'revolt against God the father' and seems profoundly disturbed when he asks 'What will happen to God?' (as he does in the title of his critical study on feminist theology which carries the subtitle 'Feminism and the Reconstruction of Christian Belief'). Is this reconstruction too bold, too imaginative, or simply too fanciful? Is feminism really bent on destroying the Christian church and putting a matriarchal religion in its place, or is this only the wish of some feminists but not of others? In her countercritique Monica Furlong (1984b) rightly asked 'What is Dr Oddie afraid of?'. She sees his anger and stern criticism of feminist theological concerns as basically grounded in a male sense of fear, the fear of being consumed, emasculated and destroyed, the sense of losing the long established grasp of power. 'It is this fear which women are now asking men to examine, in or out of the Church, if we are to get on to a more realistic understanding of the complementary roles of the sexes within the Church' (1984b, p. 1046).

It may be neither wise nor desirable to abandon the image of God the father nor any of the other biblical images deeply rooted in the Judaeo-Christian tradition. But the challenge of a living faith also demands not to merely hand down symbols which do not speak easily to us any more. We have to respond creatively to the images and symbols of the past and ask what they mean for us today. Thus we can see the horizon of their meaning expanded in new ways rarely suspected before. This has been shown again and again in the feminist interpretation of the Bible which attempts to reinterpret the androcentric passages of the Bible and thus liberate the text from the sexist interpretations which continue to dominate Christian and Jewish teachings (Trible, 1978a, 1978b). Many women and also men seek to liberate the word of the Bible so that it can become truly liberating for people today. Feminist and liberation theologians are working on this process but, as in other fields of enquiry, women scholars in biblical studies have long been marginalised and the exegesis of feminist scholars is only slowly beginning to make an impact. We certainly have come a long way since Elizabeth Cady Stanton first published *The Woman's Bible* in the late 1890s. Letty Russell has edited a book of papers by Christian and Jewish feminist scholars on the *Feminist Interpretation of the Bible* (1985) wherein she argues that

> the Bible needs to be liberated from its captivity to one-sided white, middle-class, male interpretation. It needs liberation from privatized and spiritualized interpretations that avoid God's concern for justice, human wholeness, and ecological responsibility; it needs liberation from abstract, doctrinal interpretations that remove biblical narrative from its concrete social and political context in order to change it into timeless truth. (1985, p. 12)

Fresh insights derived from feminist consciousness and experience have produced substantial scholarly studies on particular biblical passages and books (Trible, 1984), as well as popular works for use in women's groups (Chatterji, 1979, 1982, 1986; WCC, 1985). What a feminist reinterpretation of biblical passages can yield in terms of understanding the growth of the early Christian community from within Judaism has been shown with much sensitivity in Elisabeth Schüssler Fiorenza's study *In Memory of Her* (1983), a most stimulating book which has raised much discussion but has not remained without criticism from other feminists (Setta, 1984).

Reading the Bible makes us aware of the need to reinterpret its passages in the light of women's experience (Robins, 1986). It is not only a question of *what* the Bible says, but *how* its message has been translated from an androcentric perspective into an androcentric language. The revolt against a patriarchal image of God extends also to much of the traditional presentation of Jesus and his message. Christology, the theological teaching about Jesus Christ and his redemptive work, has often been presented through symbols that have made it an instrument of patriarchal domination (Ruether, 1981a). Here again we have to look for alternative models, for different expression of christology which liberate it from its encapsulation in patriarchal structures and androcentric modes of thought (Brock, 1988; Grey, 1989). If Jesus is seen as the redeemer of all of humanity in whom 'there is neither male nor female' (Gal. 3.28), then his person and work must be inclusive of all people, of women and men, to have truly universal significance (Wilson-Kastner, 1983). In her discussion of feminist theology Catherina Halkes speaks of the 'Menschwerdung' of woman which means literally the 'becoming human' or full hominisation of woman. However, in theological language the German term 'Menschwerdung' is traditionally applied to Jesus Christ; it is the word by which we express that 'he became man' in the sense of becoming human. This has an inclusive meaning as the word 'Mensch' is applied to both sexes and carries no exclusively male connotation with it.

For God to have become human – rather than simply male – is the profoundest truth about the Christian belief in the incarnation. From a contemporary feminist point of view it seems important to speak and think about a female Christ or the female part of Christ which must be an integral part of the incarnation. But one might also speak about a female Christ in the sense that Christ's suffering stands for all the suffering, all the oppression, all the silent surrender and sacrifice that women as victims have undergone through the ages. Christian feminists have both drawn and sculpted the cross with a naked female body hanging on it, a female 'Christa' which has outraged many traditionalists (an image of such a sculpture of a crucified woman is found on the cover of Oddie's book, 1984, and in Ruether, 1985, p. 104). But such an image of a female Christ is not just the fancy or figment of an aberrant feminist imagination, as some might think, but it is the recovery of an ancient insight which recognises the divine in both male and female form. It expresses at a symbolic level what we can all deeply feel within us, the need for a visualisation, for a form and shape with which we can identify because it expresses something of ourselves.

It is important to draw here on the rich resources of the religious imagination as expressed in art and iconography. Popular piety and imaginative artists through the ages have often envisaged alternatives to the dominant tradition of their time and held a vision of the divine and holy far larger and more accommodating than our own. This is evident from the diversity of their symbols and images whose rediscovery can be a source of profound surprise. In an exhibition on romanesque art I found a small gold cross from the early eleventh century, the 'Herimannkreuz' from Cologne, on which the body of Christ is crowned with the lapislazuli head of a woman. This head has been identified as a carved Roman gem, the head of empress Livia, wife of Augustus – perhaps the most precious thing the artist could find to complete his creation of Christ in gold. Here male and female are fused into one to express the unity and completeness found in Christ.

Another extraordinary example is found in the expression of popular piety which often depicts various aspects of faith quite differently from the way they are treated in the doctrinal manuals of theological literature. One such example is the medieval legend of St Uncumber or Wilgefortis (St Kümmernis in German – she who frees from sorrow) which, like the widely popular legend of St Ursula, has no historical basis. The legend of St Uncumber tells of a Portuguese Christian princess who refused to marry the pagan king of Sicily because she had undertaken a vow of virginity and was betrothed to Christ. To be freed from her suitor she prayed to become unattractive and as a result a beard and moustache grew on her face. In punishment her father had her crucified and while on the cross, she prayed that all who remembered her passion should be liberated from all encumbrances and troubles. St Uncumber is depicted as a fully clothed woman hanging on the cross. Her image was widely venerated from the fourteenth century onwards, first perhaps in Flanders, but it is found in many place in South Germany, Italy and Switzerland and examples of it exist even in Sweden, England and Spain. It is thought that this extraordinary icon, particularly venerated by women who wanted to be freed from their husbands, may have originated from twelfth century crucifixes on which Christ was fully clothed, the most famous being at Lucca (Italy). The cult of St Wilgefortis was particularly popular during the Baroque period but it is extinct today, although examples of her painting still exist in some churches on the Continent and apparently there survives a statue of her in Henry VII Chapel, Westminster Abbey. Although the cult as such may not appeal to us today, the encounter with a large Baroque painting of a fully dressed woman hanging on the cross can be quite a discovery which makes one reflect on the extraordinary richness of the religious imagination of the past. Far from being all male, the divine and the realms of the holy, of saintly perfection, were visualised in both male and female form, particularly in the rich cult of the saints in catholicism.

Elisabeth Moltmann-Wendel (1986, p. 104) includes another example showing a female image of the Trinity. A painting for an altar-piece executed according to the wishes of a German Protestant princess in 1673 shows three women as Father, Son and Holy Spirit arranged in triangular form. The painting forms part of a large altar whose pictures are a provocation to traditional conceptions of the Christian faith, presenting a non-patriarchal view of salvation. Inspired by Jewish Kabbalah mysticism, the princess had the courage to express her own experience of God pictorially in the church of her spa. Elisabeth Moltmann-Wendel comments:

> It is not just the case that here a female person has been added to the male Trinity – a development that one can often find. Here there has been a matriarchal transformation of an experience of God which was tolerated and kept intact.
>
> If we are to discover the history of women it is not enough to point to female elements in a religion which has been taken over by patriarchy.... Nor is it enough just to discover the counter-culture.... It seems to me that in addition there is a tendency to overlook the matriarchal sub-culture that has been preserved, reflecting women's

own independent experience of freedom which was neither integrated and thus absorbed, nor destroyed, and which found expression in images and symbols – silently but eloquently. (1985, p. 114)

Mary

Much of the experience of the divine feminine in Christianity has been projected on the figure of Mary and it is no surprise that both secular and religious feminists have shown an interest in the thought and cult associated with her. Mary has also been described as 'the feminine face of the church' (Ruether, 1979a) and is often seen as the theological counterimage to Eve, as a 'new Eve'. Both Mary and Eve have often performed an oppressive function in the lives of Christian women, although this may not always have been realised. The cult of the Virgin Mary became widely popular in the West from the twelfth century onwards, but it has a long history before that. It provided a feminising element in an otherwise wholly masculine religion, and yet one must ask in what way the veneration of Mary was actually related to the real status of women in church and society. Here, as in other religions, the function of the symbolic realm of myth and image may well have been to provide a compensation for women's lack of influence and position in the real world. The intensification of interest in Mary in the medieval church is not necessarily a proof of a more positive evaluation of women. Writing on 'Woman in Medieval Theology' Eleanor McLaughlin has suggested that

the medieval cult of the Virgin at every level, theological and popular, displayed an androcentric bias that, rather than deepening an appreciation of the bipolarity of God's creation or female equivalence, underlined the weakness, inferiority, and subordination of real females. The reasons for this suggestion are in essence two. The first is Mary's theological isolation from human femaleness, which by implication, degrades the real woman and which often prevented Mary from functioning psychologically as a model for female personhood even in the medieval context. The second lies in the roles given to Mary in the divine plan by theologians and popular myth: her actions, reactions, her personality, all of which can be seen to reflect the theologically supported popular misogynism of the medieval period. (1974, p. 246)

Given this ambivalent heritage Mary is a controversial figure today. Even people with a strong religious commitment often find her unattractive. The rich symbolism and contradictions of the figure of Mary in Christian art and worship have been profusely documented by Marina Warner's study *Alone of all her Sex. The Myth and Cult of the Virgin Mary* (1985), but for a theological elucidation one has to look elsewhere. Warner's judgement that as 'an acknowledged creation of Christian mythology, the Virgin's legend will endure in its splendour and lyricism, but it will be emptied of moral significance, and thus lose its present real power to heal and to harm' (1985, p. 339) is a harsh conclusion which needs to be questioned. For Warner, Mary cannot be a model for the new woman today; she is merely an instrument in the hands of the Catholic Church to perpetuate an unequal, unjust structure of society. Whilst there is some truth in Warner's assessment and critique, she none the less underrates the real significance of Mary in the lives of millions of Christians, not only in the lives of women, but of whole countries. One only has to think of Poland or Latin America, or of the intense Marian devotion associated with many pilgrimages and the apparitions of Mary which have occurred in several countries, most recently in Yugoslavia.

Mary's power in the contemporary world cannot easily be denied, and much of it is positive rather than negative, relating to much more than the image of woman. But Mary presents a problem for feminists with which feminist theology has not yet come to terms. Many women who have lost their faith can no longer relate to Mary except in protest. Others who remain Christian also object to her because of the false sentimentality and infantilism associated with much of her cult (Halkes, 1980a). Their anger is directed at the stereotype of a serving, passive woman associated with Mary, 'the servant of the Lord'. Her exaltation has so often enforced the subordination of Christian women. This is what feminist theologians criticise, but they also attempt to develop new perspectives on Mary, especially as we meet her in the New Testament in her association with the mission of Jesus. From a feminist perspective Mary can be seen as the first among the faithful, actively responding to Jesus and showing courage in doing so. Mary is also presented in a challenging, prophetic role linked to the theme of liberation, especially as expressed in the Magnificat. It is not the traditional role of comfort and solace which is stressed, but one of challenge and independence, an image of autonomy rather than subjection.

The reduction of Marian devotion, first brought about by the Protestant Reformation, diminished the role of the feminine in the church and led to a marked loss of the place of affectivity in religious life, a loss which has grown larger still in our own time. Rosemary Ruether has argued that the disappearance of an independent female image in Protestantism was compensated for by a feminisation of Christ, especially in the pietistic strands of Protestantism. Mary, as traditionally understood, presents a problem for contemporary women if she continues to be unduly exalted and distanced from the life of ordinary women or if she is solely identified with self-negation and a subservient role characterised by receptivity and passivity. But Mary can also become a new model which may help to humanise the church if her example is reciprocally related to both men and women. If activity and receptivity are interdependent and characteristic of each person, then a ministry of service which comprises both active and passive moments can be equally undertaken by both sexes. Thus Rosemary Ruether thinks that Mary may help to develop the church as a true community of equals responsive to the message of Jesus concerning the freely given gift of God and the freeing power of the spirit. Whilst a new interest in Mary is developing in some Protestant churches today, such an understanding also raises further questions about the nature of Christian ministry. This is one of the most widely debated subjects among Christian feminists and their opponents, as an appropriate understanding of the ministry is central to the struggle for the ordination of women. This is the most contentious issue of all which divides the Christian churches and has assumed much importance in Christian ecumenical dialogue. For feminists it is the very test case of the churches' attitude to women. But what is the debate and struggle all about?

The ordination of women, ecumenism and dialogue

Ever since the General Synod of the Church of England put the ordination of women on its agenda, there was rarely a week when there was no reference to this issue somewhere in the British press or media. For many years the worldwide Anglican Communion ordained women ministers in other parts of the world, but not in England, and for decades such groups as the Society for the Ministry of Women in the Church and the Movement for the Ordination of Women mounted campaigns to get women ordained in the Church of England. Although the ordination of women, at long last accepted by the Church of England in November 1992, is emphatically rejected by official authorities in the Vatican, there has been a considerable public debate about this issue in the Roman

Catholic Church worldwide ever since Vatican Council II (see the many articles listed in Asen, 1981), and even the Catholic press in England has considered this issue from every possible angle (Kennally, 1986). A Catholic women's group, St Joan's International Alliance, with roots in the earlier suffragette movement, has worked for the ordination of women for about thirty years now and found support among several well-known male theologians.

The arguments in the wide-ranging debates concern the nature of ministry and priesthood, the nature of woman, and the many stereotypes related to the role of the two sexes as traditionally understood. Historical and theological arguments from scripture and tradition, right from the beginning of the early Christian communities, can be mustered to back positions for or against the ordination of women (see Carr, 1990, ch. 3). In her study *The New Eve in Christ* Mary Hayter (1987) has carefully examined the use and abuse of biblical passages in this debate and comes to the conclusion that the Bible, contrary to many opinions, does not provide a manual for or against the issue of women's ministry. For one thing, biblical writers were not concerned with this question in the form in which it needs to be considered today. The Bible has to be discovered as a truly life-giving word which sets people free and makes Eve a new creation. In Hayter's view 'The liberty of the new Eve in Christ is a freedom which is neither self-assertive nor careless of others' needs. . . . It is a freedom which facilitates the priestly service of all God's people – to his greater glory' (1987, p. 171).

Historical arguments against the ordination of women are based on evidence drawn from the tradition of the Christian church, but refined historical-critical methods have revealed much of this evidence as onesided. One must also remember that the hierarchically structured Christian priesthood evolved as an institution through several centuries, and its later understanding was projected back onto early scriptural texts born out of a very different and much more pluralistic situation.

Theological arguments against the ordination of women are based on the interpretation of the nature of woman as created by God, the nature of ministry and offices in the church, the role and symbolic function of Christ in relation to the ministry, and even the nature of God. The irrationality of many arguments against the ordination of women can be shown through examining points of detail in this debate (Badham, 1984). It is also worth pointing out, as Daphne Hampson (1986a) has done, that the debate about the ordination of women is really misnamed, for at the heart of the issue lies the ordination of persons without respect to sex and gender. Many writers have explored the rich dimensions of and need for a grater participation of the 'feminine in the church' (Furlong, 1984a). The need for the ministry of women has even been argued by a woman rabbi who wrote in *The Times*:

> It is not adequate to argue that the current campaign for the ordination of women has not properly comprehended the role of the minister of God. The argument seems, to this outsider at least, to be both about fear of women's advancement and about stereotyped roles for both sexes.
>
> Let it be understood that women will no longer be silent. We wish to minister, alongside men, to the needs of Jews and Christians irrespective of sex. In the non-conformist churches it has happened for years. In progressive Judaism we have been around for 15 years. The earth has not opened up nor the heavens caved in. Our congregations have not diminished nor have those in our care perished. Perhaps we have something of value to offer, which the Church of England would do well to use. (Neuberger, 1987)

The diversity of ministries and women's crucial participation in the life of the early Christian communities is evident from New Testament studies and early church history (Schüssler Fiorenza, 1983; Portefaix, 1988). New archaeological evidence about the role of women as leaders of synagogues (Brooten, 1982) and of church gatherings in the first century CE has increasingly come to light (Irvin, 1980). There is much debate about the various forms of service and the distinctions which developed subsequently between charismatic and cultic ministry. How is the priestly office, as practised today, related to the priesthood of the whole people of God and to the priestly office of Christ himself? Distinguished scholars of the early church, such as the Anglican Canon G. W. H. Lampe (1974) and the Roman Catholic Fr Jean Daniélou SJ (1974) wrote long ago supportively on the question of the ordination of women in relation to the development of the historic ministry. Daniélou concluded a brief essay by saying 'We have thus three possible ways of ordering the Ministry of Women: lay, clerical, religious. It can be said that all three are equally traditional' (1974, p. 31). Lampe emphasised the great movement of the spirit giving us guidance

> in a new understanding of the relation between the sexes and of the place of women in the priesthood of the whole people of God. What

God is saying to the Church today through this radical change in the human situation and the greatly altered nature of our society demands a change in this part of the Church's tradition. (1974, p. 6)

This is not so unlike what is stated in one of the brochures of the Movement for the Ordination of Women (MOW):

> Many people believe that the Holy Spirit is leading the Church towards a fuller understanding of the relationship between men and women, and their relationship to God who created them, male and female in His image. This understanding needs to be expressed in a whole shared priesthood of men and women.
>
> . . .
>
> MOW believes itself to be part of a movement towards a reunited ecumenical Church. In such a reunited Church, women priests and ministers, those already ordained and many of those, in all denominations, who are experiencing the call to ordination, will be able to share fully with men in the joys and sufferings of Christian ministry.

Many arguments depend on whether the Christian ministry is primarily seen as that of preacher or priest (Ruether, 1980b). Many women taught and preached in the early Christian communities, but when the priesthood emerged as a hierarchical office, much influenced by the old Roman model of priesthood, then women were excluded. During medieval times there existed more polemic against women as preachers than priests, perhaps because teaching was more of a live option than being a priest. However, when one looks at iconographic evidence, one is again surprised to find paintings such as 'The Preaching of Mary Magdalene' in the Marseilles Museum. There is of course a long tradition of Mary Magdalene coming to the South of France and being buried there. But the fifteenth century painting showing Mary Magdalene preaching in the harbour of Marseilles depicts her as speaking with authority to a crowd of medieval men and women present in about equal numbers. What did Mary Magdalene's preaching express to the medieval mind? Was she as a woman, especially as a privileged woman disciple of Jesus, able to speak out in public and proclaim the gospel in a way later women were not, with the authority of her experience and witness recognised in a way which women today are trying to recover?

Preaching is linked with prophecy, with the gift of the spirit to speak to the community, a gift which the church cannot bestow on individuals, but which it has to recognise as given by the spirit. Ruether thinks that the charismatic view of the preaching office was of central importance in opening the pulpit to women from the time of the Reformation onwards (for examples of female preaching in England see Valenze, 1985; Trevett, 1991). Later the development of liberal Protestant theology and a more liberal interpretation of the Bible opened up the possibility of the ordination of women. During the nineteenth century women occupied pulpits in liberal churches such as those of the Congregationalists (who ordained the first women minister, the Reverend Antoinette Brown, in 1853) and Unitarians as well as among Evangelical and Pentecostal revivalists where the charisma of the spirit was more important than institutional office. At that time Evangelical revivalism was close to reform and to such movements as abolitionism and feminism, whereas today it has espoused an anti-liberal theology and insists on male headship of society. Ruether thinks that the acceptance or rejection of liberal theology and exegesis are ultimately more important in deciding whether one supports or rejects the ordination of women today than the fact whether one views the ministry primarily in terms of preacher or priest. The Roman Catholic and Orthodox churches still reject the ordination of women and so do the fundamentalist churches. However, those theologians who accept a more liberal interpretation of the Bible and historical criticism tend to support the arguments in favour of women's ordination, and no institutional church has formally ordained women unless it has also adopted the arguments of liberal theology in some form.

Throughout the history of the church, but especially during the Middle Ages, women have held powers of jurisdiction and of certain high offices in the church (Morris, 1974; Pernoud, 1980). Yet the opponents of women's ordination are fond of using again and again arguments from medieval theologians stressing woman's subordination and defective nature without looking at other statements expressing the equivalence between women and men. Critical women scholars have not only re-examined the history of canon law relating to women's exclusion from priestly office (Raming, 1976), but their detailed studies of theological sources also indicate that medieval theologians often argued with greater subtlety than some of their contemporary heirs. Duns Scotus, for example, argued that the ordination of women might have considerable pastoral benefits and could not possibly be ignored by the church, except on the explicit instruction of Christ himself (Cardman, 1978).

Whilst considerable differences of opinion exist today regarding Christ's instruction about the ministry, the argument about pastoral needs and benefits is certainly an important one too. Women have long wished to be ordained to care for people's spiritual needs in a ministerial and sacramental way, and a considerable number of women in different churches have experienced a vocation to the ministerial priesthood. In the Church of England arguments about the ministry of women first centred from the mid-nineteenth century onwards around the female diaconate (Canham, 1983; Prelinger, 1986). In 1862 an Anglican bishop ordained a woman as deaconess and the Anglican Deaconess Community of St Andrew emerged, but the debate continued. Women have only been admitted to the full order of deacon since 1987, and by 1992 there were 1300 women deacons.

The member churches of the worldwide Anglican Communion are autonomous. Although progress is extraordinarily slow in the Church of England itself, other Anglican churches have ordained women as priests. The very first was a Chinese Christian, the deaconess Florence Tim Oi Li, made an Anglican priest when the Bishop of Hong Kong ordained her in 1944. The fortieth anniversary of her ordination was celebrated in 1984 in a service at Westminster Abbey and her story has been told in detail in the book *Much Beloved Daughter* (Li and Harrison, 1985). However, it took another thirty years before women were ordained elsewhere. In 1974, three bishops of the Episcopal Church in the USA irregularly ordained eleven women as priests in Philadelphia, followed by four more ordinations in Washington D.C. These irregular ordinations were regularised in 1976 when the ordination of women to the priesthood was voted for and accepted by the General Convention of the Episcopal Church. The Anglican Church in Canada ordains women since 1976; the Church in New Zealand since 1977; and the Anglican Church in Kenya as well as in Uganda since 1983. Several other Churches or Provinces of the Anglican Communion have agreed in principle to the ordination of women, and so has the Church of England, without having put this into practice so far. Some British women have gone for ordination abroad, for example Elizabeth Canham, who in *Pilgrimage to Priesthood* (1983) has described her personal journey from teaching and lecturing to ordination in the USA. A most detailed documentation of the long history of institutional resistance to the ordination of women in the Methodist Church (which ordains women since 1974), the Church of England and the Roman Catholic Church is found in *Women Towards Priesthood* by Jacqueline Field-Bibb (1991). The most comprehensive survey on the subject, it discusses questions of institutionalisation, power relations, sexual identity, and symbolism whereas Monica Furlong's briefer *A Dangerous Delight* (1991) entertainingly relates the delaying tactics in the Church of England over recent years revealing how much issues of power are central to the debate. The Australian situation is described by Barbara Field (1989) in *Fit For This Office.*

Whilst the debate about the ordination of women seems to be essentially settled in much of Protestantism, it is almost new in the international ecumenical movement (Bührig, 1985). How often is the ordination of women to full priestly ministry still presented as an obstacle to a greater unity among different Christian churches! Yet about half the member churches of the World Council of Churches now ordain women. The difficulty is that in terms of sheer numbers these do not balance the three major church bodies that do not ordain, namely the Orthodox Church, several churches of the Anglican Communion, and the Roman Catholic Church. Are women merely pawns in the ecumenical debate? Are their legitimate aspirations and hopes to live the Christian life to the full and bear witness to the spirit in all ministries of the church simply ignored in order to achieve the unity of men and of male-dominated institutions?

The ecumenical movement of the Christian churches represents perhaps one of the most dynamic developments of institutionalised religion, but where are the women? The spokesmen of Christian ecumenism – and of global, interfaith ecumenism – are quite literally only men, mostly white and middle-aged. Women rightly question the marginality and invisibility of women in official Christian ecumenism knowing full well that in a less obvious and visible way women at the grassroots level make a most important contribution to ecumenical and interfaith dialogue (King, 1985a; Mollenkott, 1988; O'Neill, 1990). The great exception to this generally depressing situation is the World Council of Churches (WCC) itself which since its inception in 1948, through the inspiring vision and leadership of several women, has actively promoted the fuller participation of women in the life of the churches, especially through what is called its Subunit on Women in Church and Society (for the fascinating history of this unit see Susannah Herzel, *A Voice for Women*, 1981). Not only was the question of sexism in the churches examined at an early date (WCC, 1975), but the question of the ordination of women and their wider participation in the life of the churches came up again and again. This is evident from such consultations as the *Ordination of Women in Ecumenical Perspective* (Parvey, 1980) or on *Orthodox Women: Their Role and Participation in the Orthodox Church* (WCC, 1977) or the important Sheffield Report on *The Community of Women and Men in the Church* (Parvey, 1983).

In the World Council of Churches at least women are now plainly visible. During the 1968 WCC General Assembly only 9 per cent of delegates were women, whereas at the 1983 Assembly in Vancouver this number had risen to almost 30 per cent. The aim to elect on all committees one-third of women was not fully reached. But at least there were then 26.1 per cent women committee members (Bührig, 1985, p. 96). Women are visible in the Presidium of the WCC where, since the Canberra Assembly (1991), three women now share office with five men and the Executive Committee counts six women among its fifteen members. As a matter of equality and justice women should ideally be represented by 50 per cent on all committees and institutions in the world, but this is rarely ever the case at present. The WCC has perhaps gone further in taking practical steps towards realising this ideal than most other religious, political, educational or industrial institutions except for the Norwegian government which aims at a representation of 40 per cent women. Looking ahead in 1983, at the WCC Assembly in Vancouver, the Subunit on Woman in Church and Society stated that its work needed to be continued and intensified. The process of developing women's participation involves:

(1) developing the *female voice of the church* further, to enable women to speak out on the issues of theology and doctrine and to bring their new experiences in spirituality and action into the church life. . . .

(2) strengthening the *global sisterhood*, giving further emphasis to mutual support and enablement of women. . . .

(3) continuing to pursue the concerns of the *community of women and men in the church* study, securing a fuller participation of men in this dialogue, and helping the churches to appropriate the insights of the study. (WCC, 1983, p. 209)

Much remains to be done, even in the WCC where the participation of women has developed far ahead of situations in ecumenical dialogue elsewhere. Numbers alone are not important, whether they concern the number of women ordained or the number of churches which ordain women. What is important is the growing participation of women themselves – that their presence has become visible and that their impact is felt, that their voices are expressed and heard and their experiences shared with others.

Now that women are speaking out in ever growing numbers the question of the ordination of women will not go away again, but assumes an ever greater urgency. The churches which have remained hostile to the participation of women must learn to recognise that the ordination of women does not only raise obstacles in ecumenical negotiations but, as stated in another WCC document, that this development requires not hostility but openness to each other which 'holds the possibility that the Spirit may well speak to one church through the insights of another. Ecumenical considerations, therefore, should encourage, not restrain the facing of this question' (quoted in Bührig, 1985, p. 93).

The ordination of women certainly provides a focal point in the debates of Christian feminists. Feminists are in full support of this issue whilst opposition comes largely from elsewhere, from official church institutions and their spokesmen, and sometimes from other Christian women who are still shaped by traditional role models and teachings which remain unaffected by the new consciousness of women. They are more likely to be found among older rather than younger women who have already internalised much of the new consciousness even if they do not see themselves explicitly as feminists.

Other controversies arising out of feminist theology concern its relationship to black theology and to Judaism. Critical voices have asked whether feminist theology is perhaps too elitist or even anti-female by not including the experience of black women. But it is not only feminist theology which is criticised, but also black theology. Whilst the latter developed as a form of liberation theology in the USA to overcome the oppression of blacks, the experience of black women has not been integrated into this theology, as both black and white feminists have pointed out (see 'Black Theology and Black Women' in Wilmore and Cone, 1979, pp. 363–443; also Ruether, 1979c). To be black and female is a double jeopardy, but black women in the churches labour under an even greater jeopardy (Hoover, 1974) yet so many black women make important contributions to the life of the churches.

There are certain historical similarities between the subjugation of blacks and women, and there are certain themes common to black theology and feminist theology. Both are strongly critical of the churches, both are committed to radical political and social change. Both offer critical reflections on the Christian faith in the light of suffering and oppression. Both seek clearer self-definition, try to recover their own history and traditions, and search for alternatives to culture-bound theological images which have supported oppressive attitudes and institutions. The dialogue between feminist theology and black theology can be mutually enriching and broaden out the concerns of both (Murray, 1978). More material on nineteenth-century black women preachers is coming to light (see Andrews, 1986) and a distinct theology of black women – womanist rather than feminist – is developing (see Jacquelyn Grant, *White Women's Christ and Black Women's Jesus*, 1989).

Quite different issues are raised in the debate between Christian feminists and Judaism. A whole number of the journal *Christian Jewish Relations* (June 1986, Institute of Jewish Affairs, London) explored the relationship between Christian-Jewish dialogue and the women's movement. Several contributors pointed to the anti-Judaism and implicit anti-semitism of some statements made by Christian feminists (see Eckardt, 1986: Heschel, 1986; von Kellenbach, 1986; see also the debate on feminist anti-Judaism in the *Journal of Feminist Studies in Religion*, 1991), and this charge has also been made by Jewish writers elsewhere. Judith Plaskow said in a debate

> that one of the obstacles to dialogue between Jewish and Christian feminists is a tendency on the part of some Christian feminists to try to isolate a pure, non-patriarchal core to Christianity by blaming patriarchal elements in Christianity on Judaism. For example, the argument that Jesus was a feminist often depends on contrasting Jesus' openness to women with the supposed misogyny of ancient Judaism, a misogyny which reasserts itself in Paul and in later New Testament epistles. (Quoted in Setta, 1984, p. 98)

Another example concerns the effort to re-establish the worship of the Goddess which, from a Jewish perspective, leaves some troubling implications, as Susannah Heschel has pointed out:

> Whether or not an ancient matriarchy which worshipped the Goddess actually existed, the myth raises the question of what happened to this society. Who killed the Goddess and why did she allow herself to be dethroned and forgotten and replaced by an evil patriarchy? While the Goddess myth may promote women's power, her dethronement bears with it a myth of women's loss of power. The motif repeats the theme of an original state of Eden, followed by a fall after

which human beings live in a state of sin, waiting for a redemption. In this case, it is not a woman but the Jews, who often function as similar perpetrators of evil in such myths, who are responsible. Moreover, the suggestion that Israelite religion dethroned the Goddess and introduced a patriarchal society worshipping a male deity reminds us of similar charge of deicide levelled against the Jews. (Heschel, 1986, pp. 30ff.)

The debate between Christian feminist theology and Judaism has only just begun and will require a great many further clarifications. A. Roy Eckhardt has offered the daring thesis 'that in the long run today's women's movement may prove to have as much significance for the Christian-Jewish relation as the Holocaust and the refounding of the State of Israel – or larger significance' (Eckhardt, 1986, p. 13). Whether this can be the case will also depend on the further development of Jewish feminist theology which has its own possibilities and problems (Umansky, 1984; Plaskow, 1990). But it also shares a number of similar topics with Christian feminist theology, especially with regard to a critical examination of God language and the search for feminine imagery of the Divine (Gross, 1979, 1981).

We have surveyed the main orientations and controversies in feminist theology and must now turn to the question of spirituality. If Christian feminists seek to liberate the church from sexism and androcentrism, if they seek to celebrate non-sexist liturgies, to create non-sexist Christian communities in the churches, and help to develop a new kind of ecumenal and interfaith dialogue, this will lead to a new kind of spirituality, to a different vision of world and self and different connections between inner and outer life. Let us now look more closely at this connection between feminist theology and spirituality.

Feminist theology and the quest for spirituality

For religiously committed feminists faith and feminism are two important parts of their experience. But how relate the two? Christian women around the world experience a change in consciousness, choices and life-styles; they understand their newly experienced sense of self and the togetherness of women as a 'chance to change' (Thompson, 1982) for women and men in the churches. As faith is a challenge for secular feminism, feminism is a strong challenge for the communities of faith. 'Feminists of faith do provide something of a bridge between alienated women and the sexist religious structures from which they are alienated – the churches and the synagogues that have blessed women's repression through history and called it God's will' (Papa, 1981, p. 123).

All feminists share the recognition of the sexist structures of religion, but they hold widely different views on what to do about this. Christian feminists are holding out in the hope that a church they love will listen to their voices, share their experiences and become more open, understanding and compassionate, as well as more just and truthful to its own calling. Christian, and Jewish feminists for that matter, do not support a radical woman-centred religion but are committed to discovering and developing their own spirituality from within the root-experience of their faith. The general dilemma of the feminist movement whether to emphasise the otherness of women and build autonomous women's institutions, or whether to work for absolute equality between women and men and seek women's integration into existing structures and institutions is also a profound dilemma for Christian feminists. Should they leave the church or radically reform it? Can women find their own space in existing church institutions so that their spiritual development can flower to the full and be under their own control? These questions are urgent ones and recur again and again in discussion. More and more women voice them and thus express their deep malaise, their un-ease with existing churches as structured at present. Women's spirituality must be developed as a deep inner resource which shapes and sustains outward action – first for women themselves, then for others, for community-building. The question of spirituality has not only come to the fore in feminism in general, but it is also explicitly expressed and implicitly present in many works on feminist theology. Feminist reflections on spirituality from a perspective of faith, both Christian and Jewish, are found in the collections *Walking on the Water: Women talk about spirituality* (Jo Garcia and Sara Maitland, 1983), *The Feminist Mystic and Other Essays on Women and Spirituality* (Mary E. Giles, 1982), in the books by Carol Ochs, *Women and Spirituality* (1983), *An Ascent to Joy* (1986), by Maria Harris, *Dance of the Spirit* (1991) and Katherine Zappone, *The Hope for Wholeness* (1991). Examples of women theologians who have explicitly addressed the question of spirituality are Elga Sorge, *Religion und Frau. Weibliche Spiritualität im Christentum* (1985) and Catherina J. M. Halkes, *Feminisme en Spiritualiteit* (1986). As was pointed out in an earlier chapter, spirituality expresses itself in many different ways, not as something separate and apart from life, but as deeper, more richly lived and reflected experience, what is often called insight – insight into the meaning of our experience and its illumination from within through something greater and deeper than ourselves. Feminist theology is not only about controversies and issues, not primarily about subtle conceptual distinctions (although it has a powerful intellectual dimension to it), but it is ultimately about the life of the spirit, experienced as a gracious gift of transformation and renewal, celebrated, shared and communicated to others. Here experience, thought and action come together.

The experience of spirituality is contained and cradled, rooted and wrapped in our experience of God, a reality which centres and focuses our life both within and without. But this reality is not something abstract and separate set over against and apart from us, but it breathes and pulsates in everything we experience, encounter, suffer and do – it transcends every boundary and defies all definition. It is the Divine as power within human beings in all of creation. Alice Walker has described this all-embracing God-experience through one of her woman characters in *The Color Purple*:

> I believe God is everything. . . . Everything that is or ever was or ever will be. And when you can feel that, and be happy to feel that, you've found It.
> . . . My first step from the old white man was trees. Then air. Then birds. Then other people. But one day when I was sitting quiet and feeling like a motherless child, which I was, it come to me: that feeling of being part of everything, not separate at all. I knew that if I cut a tree, my arm would bleed. And I laughed and I cried and I run all round the house. I knew just what it was. In fact, when it happen, you can't miss it. (1983, p. 167)

Women seek and find the Ultimate within the midst of life. They also experience a profound desire to discover something of what is most precious in their own experience in that great Reality we call by many names. Women thus long to find God as 'immanent Mother'. As Meinrad Craighead has written in a reflection on this theme:

> A woman's spiritual quest in God the Mother awakens her to forces of energy within herself, yet larger than self, transcending self, deeply connecting her with the cyclic movements of creating and per-

sonally with her foremothers whose energies still surge through her body. . . .

In solitude our deepest intuitions of an indwelling personal God Spirit are confirmed, the Mothergod who never withdraws from us and whose presence is our existence and the life of all that is. Her unveiled glory is too great for us to behold; she hides her face. But we find her face in reflection, in sacred guises, mediated through the natural elemental symbols.

. . .

And apart from the multifarious marvels of natural creation there is sufficient poetry in any well-made article of human craftmanship to engage our attention for a lifetime. Or in the innocent presentations of human traditions – a handful of grain, a basket of blackberries, a vase of flowers, a clutch of hen's eggs, a board of cheese, a family photograph, a table laid for a meal.

These are the symbols for a woman's spirituality and their importance cannot be overestimated. . . . Each is but a fragment of the 'world' body (as each of us is), yet through it we may apprehend the incarnate presence of the holy in all creation. Through the God our Mother communicates with us through her body, within her own mysterious creation. (1982, pp. 78–81)

Such a spirituality is life-affirming and in love with all created life; it is a sense a true 'creation spirituality'. It leads to self-acceptance and self-affirmation, to being grounded in the self as centre, a self that opens up and radiates outwards in love, and a self that feels connected and responsibly linked to all else. This process of growth and maturation can be seen as different dimensions of women's spirituality (Koppers, 1986) – in fact of all genuine spirituality in human beings – but women especially have to learn true self-love and self-affirmation as they are so often maimed and moulded by subjection, self-effacement and rejection. Empowered by divine love, they have to learn to love themselves and come to say: 'I am good. I am whole. I am beautiful' (Moltmann-Wendel, 1986, p. 151).

This also includes the full affirmation of the body, of the goodness and beauty of sexuality. As Dody H. Donnelly has said, we have to love with a radical love, with a love rooted in cosmos, nature and body, ultimately grounded in the experience of God's loving touch:

Radical love . . . is a profound way to live our sexual spirituality by mutual sharing of our lives. Love has to do with a feeling response, with self-giving, and with presence. Love is actually *being* in the loved one; it is also the gift of self, for the lover is in the beloved as a gift.

. . .

No matter how we name God, She operates deeply, constantly within us. All that's true, beautiful, loving, and good in us is the shining out of our innate desire for God. This radar yearning for God, the homeland of our souls, was installed long ago in the journey of our spirit. When we hear the good news that God has *first* loved us, the spark of yearning within us bursts into flame. We now have permission to respond, to expand that love forever, because we are loved and by such a One! (Donnelly, 1984, pp. 31 and 40)

The passages quoted in this and previous sections demonstrate perhaps that feminist theologians may best be characterised as 'affective existentialist thinkers', to use one of Karl Rahner's terms. They reflect from the depth of their existence as concretely lived through their experiences and feelings, as do all women, and men for that matter, who are attuned to inner realities and the dynamic of the spirit. The passages also show that the whole God-debate so central to feminist theology – and the consequent battle for inclusive, gender-free language in worship and prayer – is of great importance for the understanding and practice of spirituality and is itself an important expression of the search for a life-affirming and life-sustaining spirituality appropriate to our time.

There are other important themes too in feminist theology which relate to the spiritual quest, though more indirectly. These are especially the themes of liberation, community, and celebration. In the churches the struggle for the liberation of women is linked to the removal of sexist practices present in church life, language and organisation. In exploring a theology of human liberation from a feminist perspective Letty M. Russell (1974) has shown that this struggle for women's liberation is rooted in experience and fraught with risk and peril. It is also a discovery and journey towards freedom, towards the full humanisation of all people, women and men.

Liberation is then an ongoing process to find greater freedom. But freedom from what and for what? Feminists give different answers to these questions which are as old as humanity itself, but have assumed a new meaning for us today. For Russell 'Freedom is a journey with others and for others towards God's future . . . liberation helps us to think of a process, a struggle with ourselves and others towards a more open future for humanity. The exact description of that struggle varies for each women, and for each human being in each situation' (Russell, 1979, pp. 234ff.). She speaks of the ferment of freedom in the women's liberation movement, and of the cost of freedom as freedom is not given without struggle and pain. Women have to pay this cost in order to discover what it means to be fully human, to risk the responsibility and share the task of building a better world for all women and men. Ultimately each woman must liberate herself, and yet raising our own consciousness is not enough: 'We must learn to act together with others to transform the societies in which we live . . . to work for the revealing of what real live children of God might look like. . . . The horizon of freedom is hope: hope that God's promised future will become reality' (1979, p. 240).

This hope is an impulse to change the world in the perspective of God's promise, to create a new community, a 'different heaven and earth' (Collins, 1974). This requires mutual dialogue in a relationship of equality and trust. Women who seek liberation have as their goal

first to become feminists themselves, second to help men become feminists; and last to carry on genuine dialogue so that the world will be transformed to the point where no feminists (male or female) are needed because there *is* social, economic, and political equality of the sexes who become equally human.
. . .
Women form the vast majority of those who find themselves oppressed in Christian communities. Yet hope for change and renewal of the church for the world can come only as new forms of human community, new life-styles are developed which eliminate domination and submission and express cooperation. As this begins to happen, women will be set free to use their God-given gifts in the service of ministry for others. (Russell, 1974, p. 70)

Is this a vain hope, or a hope unfulfilled or even betrayed? Do women need their own communities within the church, an *ekklēsia* of women', as Elisabeth Schüssler Fiorenza has called it? Women's religious communities have of course always existed in the Catholic tradition, but they were practically all under male hierarchical control. The continued existence of nuns raises some interesting questions (Bernstein, 1976),

[handwritten: declare communities of nuns]

[margin handwritten: Vatican II]

but under the impact of feminism and other forces of social change, not least the influence of Vatican II, these communities are experiencing serious problems of identity, coherence and decline. In the USA, where this trend has gone furthest, 55 000 women left congregations of sisters between 1965 and 1980, and many congregations have no or few new entrants. However, it is among the women religious that some of the strongest supporters for feminist demands regarding fundamental structural and spiritual changes in the church are found. It comes as no surprise that male church authorities and traditional faithful declare the radically innovative stance of some religious sisters as 'counter-cultural'.

Elisabeth Schüssler Fiorenza argues, as others have done before her, that by abolishing the religious communities of women the Protestant Reformation strengthened patriarchal church structures. She writes:

> A Christian feminist spirituality claims these communities of women and their history as our heritage and history and seeks to transform them into the *ekklēsia* of women by claiming our own spiritual powers and gifts, by deciding our own welfare, by standing accountable for our decisions, in short, by rejecting the patriarchal structures of laywomen and nun-women, of lay-women and clergywomen, which deeply divide us along patriarchal lines. (Schüssler Fiorenza, 1983, pp. 346ff.)

Schüssler Fiorenza applies the term '*ekklēsia* of women' or 'women-church', as she subsequently called it, to early Christian beginnings as a discipleship community of equals. By moving from a reading of the androcentric texts of the New Testament to a reconstruction of the history of women in early Christianity, we discover the 'vision and praxis of our foresisters who heard the call to coequal discipleship and who acted in the power of the Spirit'. This vision must 'become a transformative power that can open up a feminist future for women in biblical religion' (Schüssler Fiorenza, 1983, p. 343).

[margin handwritten: women's church]

This vision of a 'women-church' has become a focus for action now and for a new experience and celebration of community within the church. In November 1983, 1400 Catholic women from the USA, Mexico, Canada, Central America and Latin America declared themselves to be a 'Woman Church' (later renamed 'Women-Church') and refused 'to return to the land of slavery to serve as altar girls in the temples of patriarchy' (quoted in Bührig, 1985, p. 97; for women-church and

Roman Catholic feminist spirituality see also Weaver, 1985). This is not an exodus from the existing church, as practised by Mary Daly and her followers, but it is the development of sub-communities within the church, where women can create their own liturgies and ritual to nourish their spirit, heal their wounds and celebrate the joy of divine life within and around them.

This is a growing movement as more and more Christian women seek 'bread not stone' (Schüssler Fiorenza, 1984) to nourish their inner and outer life. Fiorenza insists that 'to speak of the church of women does not mean to advocate a separatist strategy but to underline the visibility of women in biblical religion and to safeguard our freedom from spiritual male control' (1984, p. 7). Women are becoming more radical as their patience has been eroded. As current church authorities will only rarely listen to their voices, women have to initiate action themselves. They cannot wait for the Christian churches to reform themselves sufficiently to provide the life of faith and worship women need today. For Rosemary Ruether, who has published a book on the theology and practice of the *Women-Church* (1986a), the women-church movement encompasses nothing less than the shaping of an entirely new symbolic universe of meaning:

> Women in contemporary churches are suffering from linguistic deprivation and eucharistic famine. They can no longer nurture their souls in alienating words that ignore or systematically deny their existence. . . . The call for new communities of faith and ritual assumes that existing institutional churches do not have a monopoly on the words of truth or the power of salvation, indeed that their words for women are so ambivalent, their power so negative, that attendance at their fonts poisons our souls. (Ruether, 1986a, pp. 4, 5)

Christian women across the different churches are seeing more and more clearly that the struggle for change within their present church must be supplemented by an autonomous feminist movement in order to retain a critical perspective on patriarchy. Women who have gained a foothold in the ministry and are struggling to change the churches from within need to join together with those who press for radical changes from outside the existing power structures. Women are trusting their inner spirit and are acting on this inspiration from within. As a Catholic laywoman who conducts retreats for women wrote to me:

I develop . . . the concept of creative ministry, which means that we do not wait for ministries to be formed and opened to us but we discern our gifts, be attentive to the moment, and create our own ministries. I believe that this kind of creative moving is more promising, more exciting, more challenging, and more life-giving than trying to squeeze into existent models – or pleading with structures to let us come in. Why waste our energy on old models when each of us is called to create our own mode of loving God?

Women are experiencing community in a new form, as an exodus-community within the churches. Half of Rosemary Ruether's book on *Women-Church* is devoted to new liturgies and rituals for celebration by women. Women everywhere are creating their own materials for worship to celebrate in a way that recognises and voices their experience instead of making them invisible, silent and hidden, as is often the case in both churches and synagogues. Women need 'sister-celebrations' to express their own community and togetherness, their shared experience of suffering from which they seek liberation, their own joy and affirmation of life. (For texts see *Celebrating Women* by Janet Morley and Hannah Ward, 1986; *Psalms of a Laywoman* by Edwina Gateley, 1986; also Janet Morley, *All Desires Known*, 1988; the Book of Services and Prayers used by the St Hilda Community in London, *Women Included*, 1991, and the two collections by Miriam Therese Winter, *Woman Prayer, Woman Song*, 1987, and *WomanWisdom*, 1991; for Jewish rituals see *The Jewish Woman* by Elizabeth Koltun, 1978). The 'women-church' movement expresses women's need for meaningful, spiritually empowering community. Their growing support is evident from the 3200 participants who came to the women–church conference in Cincinnati (Ohio) in October 1987. Women in their spiritual struggle for wholeness, for interconnections, for change, renewal and affirmation experience risk and isolation. They experience being in the wilderness from which they seek the promised land – a community where non-sexist liturgies are celebrated and where women and men will eventually come to share in giving and taking the bread of life.

Rosemary Ruether has described feminism as the most important prophetic movement in contemporary culture and society. The new dynamic movement of the 'women-church' speaks prophetic words from within the church to the whole Christian community. Ruether (1986a) explains that the separation of women is not absolute; rather, it is a temporary stage in a process which seeks the full liberation of women and a new community of equality through which the church can be seen as the true people of God.

Will the prophetic promise come true? Will feminist theology and spirituality have a future in the church? An increasing number of women in the churches experience Christian feminism as a source of transformation, regeneration and hope, a voice of prophecy which bears witness to the working of the spirit in our midst. The feminist vision proclaims the full humanity of women, their freedom and liberation from all forms of oppression. This vision has its roots deep in history and in the message of the gospel itself. Women through the ages have perceived the outline of this vision and have worked, hoped and prayed for its realisation. Women's continued search, suffering and longing may be linked to a vision quest which, as in the vision quest of the North American Indians, is inseparable from initiation and ordeal which eventually lead to profound transformation and new life. This vision has only become fully visible in our own time and women around the globe now strive and struggle to give it full embodiment. It is a powerful and inspiring vision of great spiritual significance in the global process of hominisation, of the growth of all of humankind to greater maturity, responsibility, critical self-awareness and unifying love. In religious terms one can see in this process the further revelation of the face of the Divine in and through history and human life.

We have no way of knowing whether this promise will fail or succeed, but the more women everywhere work for its realisation, the more the transformation will become real. The future of the churches may much depend on the radical vision and compassionate outreach of Christian women moved by a new spirit, just as the future of the world will much depend on the strongly voiced self-determination and active participation of women in all areas of public life.

If the best of women's experience and insight – care, concern, compassion for others and reverence for life – enter all spheres of human activity, then the world will become truly transformed in both a spiritual and political sense. The previous chapters have indicated several times how the themes of spirituality and politics are often interwoven in contemporary feminist thought and action. To conclude this study, the next chapter will especially examine some feminist political concerns and consider how feminism, though beset by many dilemmas, powerfully transforms the consciousness of contemporary women and men, thereby pointing the way to an integral, holistic spirituality so much needed in our deeply divided world.

7

Voices of prophecy and integration

'We all want a better world. We are all political. We all understand long-range struggle. As we break down the systems that oppress us, we must begin to form the future. Right now. Already the connection has been made between transformative ritual and political mobilization: At anti-nuclear demonstrations and at conferences on violence against women, women have led rituals that involve the transformation of rage and depression into constructive, activist energy. . . . What will political meetings, organizations, strategies be like once we acknowledge spiritual power? Spirituality enables us to feel a deep connection between one another. It heals and avoids the fragmented sense that often plagues political movements, in both personal and collective terms. Our bonding is profound. Do we know that yet?

Like feminist goals in education, law, health care, etc., feminist goals in spirituality are ultimately humanist. Some of our brothers want to work with us; can we recognize them? What divides us from a humanist future? We must expand our vision and propose options for restructuring. Floods of them.' – **Charlene Spretnak**, *The Politics of Women's Spirituality*, pp. 397ff.

Women are profoundly dissatisfied with the world as it is, and much of that dissatisfaction is directed at our contemporary political world and its structures. From the perspective of spirituality the often quoted feminist statement 'The personal is political' can be extended into 'The spiritual is personal and political'. That is to say spiritual concerns, orientations and choices do not only affect a person's own inner life, but have social and community dimensions: they shape social structures, political behaviour and public ethos.

Many feminists, perhaps the majority, are committed activists who devote much of their energy to political and social campaigns focused on numerous issues of urgent concern. Some women may not at all see these as connected with questions of spirituality often perceived as quite separate from active politics. Feminists who have become disenchanted with purely outward activism explore new paths of spirituality which sometimes can be excessively inwardly orientated and too much focused on the individual, especially when the spiritual quest is inspired by psychological and psychoanalytic theories. The journey inwards, the search for the true self, is pursued by many today, not only by women, but it must not be a journey without return to the outside. The health of social and political life is only possible if connections are made between the inner and outer, personal and social worlds. A life-affirming and action-orientated spirituality needs to animate personal and political life if we are to create a just and peaceful world. Whilst a few secular feminists criticise the growing interest of women in spirituality, especially when centred on the individual, as escapist, anti-political and dangerous, there is no doubt that the spiritual power of the women's movement finds direct expression in decisive political concerns on which more and more voices speak out – in meetings, demonstrations, publications and political action. What are some of these concerns which imply definite spiritual options?

Power, peace, non-violence and ecology

Women's protest and political action has been specially expressed through the peace movement. This is certainly the case in Britain, but numerous women's peace groups have come into existence all over the world, whether in the USA, Japan, Scandinavia, Germany, France, Italy, Austria, Switzerland, the Middle East, Mexico, Central America, the Philippines, South East Asia or elsewhere. The international dimension of women's work for peace was made highly visible through the presence of numerous women's peace groups at the 1985 International Women's Conference in Nairobi devoted to 'Equality, Development and Peace'. Everywhere women have come together to express their non-violent protest against the destructive power of militarism and the proliferation of nuclear arms and policies. Contrary to some critics who regard women's quest for spirituality as opting out of political action, many women consider the unity of politics and spirituality an important, central aspect of contemporary feminism. In their understanding, both spirituality and politics are concerned with power, power which is both personal and social. Today women have discovered a new sense of power within themselves, the power of shaping their own consciousness, of trusting their own experience, and of creating a new, powerful web of connections between people. The evolution of a new female self linked to images of strength and a sense of identity rooted in the power of experience is central to feminist spirituality, and so is the theme of interlinking and networking.

The deep change in women's psyche also affects society and politics. Spirituality can act as a political force by helping to channel the energy of womanpower, the power within us, towards power without. Charlene Spretnak reflected on this in her essay on 'The Unity of Politics and Spirituality':

> Politics, by its very nature, is partisan; spirituality affirms the inter-relatedness of all things. An awareness of this inter-relatedness must inform our sense of revolutionary urgency, as expressed in political ideologies, strategies and lifestyles. Our spirituality – the awareness of oneness and openness to new sources of power – should help us to deal with the inevitable tensions between goals and process, com-promise and ideology, survival and revolutionary integrity.
>
> It is the recognition of this intimate relationship between spiritual-ity and politics that makes the women's movement different from other movements. . . . We are in the process of re-evaluating power, recognizing the many kinds of power that exist.
>
> Concern for spirituality does not mean false innocence, fear of power, or the avoidance of compromise often necessary for life. The attainment of power is necessary to change the position of women. What we are calling for is a new perspective on power, an effort to use power differently, and an openness to new sources of power and energy. (1982, p. 370)

Feminists sharply criticise and object to the existing politics of separa-tion whereby international power politics and economics are kept sep-arate from other areas of human activity so that politics fail to integrate a spiritual vision of life's goals and meaning, the nature of human community and the sacredness of the earth. Nowhere is this more evident than with the issue of peace. Governments pay lip service to it whilst stockpiling arms and spending unimaginable sums on the military, thereby creating a mega-war-machine threatening to devour us all. Within the context of international capitalism the sale of arms is lucrative business, second only to that of oil, and the economies of many nations directly depend on it. But this is shortsighted opportunism and utter irresponsibility which cannot hide the haunting spectre of a universal dance of death moving in on us from the horizon.

But why should peace be a feminist issue? Some radical feminists have claimed that women's involvement with the peace movement means losing sight of some more immediate feminist goals, of being coopted into a male struggle. It is true that peace has always been a perennial concern for humankind, but today it must take priority of place. The goal of peace has been a central theme in all religious thought, yet traditionally this has focused more on inner than outer social and political peace and, given certain circumstances, religious leaders have been able to argue persuasively for the justification of violence and war (Ferguson, 1977). Most of these arguments now strike us as utterly untenable and completely unethical considering we are living under the cloud of the atom bomb. It also seems a tragic contradiction that western civilisation has created and continues to promote such an aggressive and destructive military industrialisation when one considers that one of the major forces which shaped the West – Christianity – has as its central figure the unaggressive man Jesus whom the church calls the 'Prince of Peace', a figure of love and reconciliation in stark contrast to western power politics of domination and exploitation.

Peace has become an urgent survival issue for the contemporary world, an issue of extraordinary magnitude ever since Hiroshima. In a way we are all survivors of that event which changed the face of history. The possibility of the self-extinction of the human species could now be so likely that some think we may not be a viable species any more. Radical alternatives in thinking and action are required to save life on earth and make a future possible. An appeal from Hiroshima and Nagasaki for a total ban and elimination of nuclear weapons states quite categorically: 'The use of nuclear weapons will destroy the whole human race and civilisation. It is therefore illegal, immoral and a crime against the human community. Humans must not coexist with nuclear arms. . . . There must never be another Hiroshima anywhere on earth. There must never be another Nagasaki anywhere on earth'.

Peace is truly *the* major issue today. Not peace as merely the absence of war and conflict – a peace under the tension of fear – but as something greater and more positive: the vision of a world community of justice and equality for all, a life worth living on planet earth. This vision is born from an ancient dream of humanity which calls today for new thinking, a new sense of responsibility for our togetherness, a sense of wholeness based on new linkage skills among humans – a revolutionary turning point in politics and spirituality. The consciousness of this need for change is rising fast, as is evident from numerous action groups and peace centres around the world. 1986 was the International Year of Peace and many institutions promote peace studies and peace education programmes. There exists a World Conference on Religion and Peace based on interreligious cooperation, and since 1974 we have an annual multifaith week of prayers for peace. It is in the same spirit that the Archbishop of Canterbury and Cardinal Hume have published a fine selection of *Prayers for Peace* (1987) drawn from different religious traditions. Given all these developments, what is the link between pacifism and feminism?

Women's work for peace did not begin with contemporary feminism, but has a long history (Oldfield, 1989). The first Women's Peace League in Europe was founded in 1854 (Jones, 1983, p. 1), but it is less well known than the Women's International League for Peace and Freedom (WILPF). Started by the American feminist Jane Addams in 1915, this still exists today as the oldest peace organisation of women. Over the last decade there has been a proliferation of autonomous women's peace groups whose work is documented by a wealth of literature showing the extraordinary richness and diversity of women's way of acting for peace (see Lynne Jones, 1983, *Keeping the Peace* for many helpful resources and contact addresses; Cambridge Women's Peace Collective, 1983, *My Country is My Whole World*; ISIS, 1983, *Women for Peace*; Brown, 1984, *Black Women and the Peace Movement*; also Brock-Utne, 1987 and Pierson, 1987). To name a few, there are such diverse groups as the Women's Peace Alliance, Women for Life on Earth, Women Opposed to Nuclear Technology, Women's Party for Survival, Women's Pentagon Action, Feminists against Nuclear Power, Women Oppose the Nuclear Threat (WONT), Women Strike for Peace, and various Women for Peace groups in Germany, the Netherlands and Norway (Burmeister, 1982). There also exist numerous women's peace camps of which that at Greenham in Britain is perhaps the best known as it caught the imagination of people everywhere (see Cook and Kirk, 1983, *Greenham Women Everywhere*; also *You Can't Kill the Spirit: Yorkshire Women Go To Greenham*, 1983).

Women have shown themselves to be imaginative, resourceful campaigners. Traditionally, they have often been peacemakers in the private sphere of the family, but now many women have decided to leave their homes to work publicly for peace, just as men for centuries left their families to fight in wars. Today, at a crucial turning point in history, women feel a very special responsibility for the continuity of life of earth, for the lives of their children and all future generations to come. It is a central part of women's experience to conceive new life, give birth, nurture and sustain the newly born. Thus they are most clearly in touch with the utter vulnerability and fragility of living beings. In the past, individual women writers have repeatedly expressed their protest against military masculine might which has created war and crushed human beings into death – lives which had been borne and cared for by women's toilsome labours, bodies which Olive Schreiner called 'women's works of art'. Today women's protest is no longer individual, but has become corporate and global. Women have raised their voices everywhere, not so much against the death of individuals as against the death of the entire species.

The rise of a separate women's peace movement is directly rooted in women's commitment to the values of life, in their capacity for compassion and care. Men as a group have shown an extraordinary insensitivity to the suffering of others. Perhaps women as a group use their imagination more vividly in visualising more concretely what war and destruction can do to their loved ones. Perhaps they acknowledge more honestly to themselves the utter fear, pain and agony they feel when contemplating human mass death in a world without a future.

Whenever I remember my experience of the bombing and conflagration of Cologne which I witnessed as a small child during World War II and which gave me nightmares for years to come, I think of this experience writ large a million times around the world in the minds of the children of Vietnam, Africa, South America, India, Pakistan, and the Middle East. I know the dreams of those children have been singed by the fire of destruction, by hatred and aggression, and their imagination and hope has been maimed for life. Perhaps it is more difficult to survive with such memories than to be dead.

Life is the most precious gift we have, and we must treasure it as a life worth living, a truly human life. Must we not all, women and men, strongly object and protest when we hear the American bombing of Tripoli/Libya (April 1986) described in a news report as a 'mission accomplished with perfect professional competence and accuracy'? What a horrendous way of referring to the deliberate killing of others, what a cold, objectifying turn of phrase to camouflage the immorality of war! Similarly, a British politician argued in a radio interview that women are not programmed to be in the military because, unlike men, they do not experience 'the joy of killing'. How can any human being have such joy in committing such acts of horror? Is men's nature perhaps programmed wrongly? Similar questions could be raised about the language used in the Gulf war. We must seriously deconstruct our habitual thought and language in matters of peace and war so as to define more clearly, that is to say more holistically, what it means to be human today.

Although not necessarily true of every individual woman, women as a group often tend to emphasise cooperation more than competition. They work with consensus and compromise rather than through conflict and confrontation; they are more inclined to settle differences by nego-tiation than by aggression. Perhaps the development of these qualities has had much to do with women's traditional position of powerlessness and vulnerability. Used in a position of strength, these qualities can bring about a fundamental change of values which will enable us to build a world of tolerance and mutual help rather than persecution.

Women feel strong and proud in acknowledging their feelings, in linking up with others in gestures and action of love. 'A woman of power walks the path of the heart' proclaims a contemporary magazine of feminism, spirituality and politics (see *Woman of Power*, published since 1984). The path of the heart is the path of love in which all being and thinking ultimately find their origin. Women also realise the importance and power of dreams, of imagination and symbols in shaping human life and action. In their demonstrations for peace women have often used innovative visionary action (such as threading webs, lighting can-dles, planting tombstones, making puppets of mourning and rage) – symbolic gestures indicating a change of orientation and values. These are prophetic acts based on hope and faith, but how effective will they be in solving the world's troubles? Will they merely remain the dreams of powerless dreamers at the edge of the real world of power politics? Or are they the potent signs of prophets whose vision will shape a different world for tomorrow?

Perhaps peacefulness has been rejected as too passive, too unmasculine for too long. Today women look at the power of peace differently. Fiona Cooper wrote on 'Women in the Peace Movement':

> It seems to many women that the way men have been running things for centuries has come to its own end. The patriarchs are trying now

to out-threaten each other; and the protection they are promising us only increases our fear.

The visions that women evolve are very different. There are as many visions as there are women. Some of the common features are an absence of strife, a harmony with nature, an awareness of the seasons and cycles of the earth, an acknowledgement of each person's worth. The symbols of these visions are also new. At Greenham we use the sign of the tree of life: in one badge it can be seen splitting a rock with its own natural growth force. There is the rainbow, which expresses the variety and colour and hope of our lives. Above all there is the web: the sign of the ancient women's skills of spinning and weaving, a spider's web that grows stronger as it is tested. The web also symbolises our linking and joining together. . . .

The feeling that 'we may not be here tomorrow' has sparked many women into action. Why follow the role of the home-maker and provider when the whole lifestyle is under threat? (1983, pp. 135, 136)

One of the strongest messages of the women's peace movement is that education towards peace requires personal and social transformation, that it is linked to moral, spiritual and political changes. Peace will only become a realistic possibility when we learn to resolve our conflicts without resorting to violence. Peace does not come from above, but from below, through women and men working for peace. How can we encourage peace-making? The Catholic Women's Network in Britain has begun to sponsor 'peace preaching' as a new venture to develop preaching skills among Christian women in the peace movement. Particularly well known are the long-established efforts of the Quakers to work for peace and encourage peace education. Elise Boulding has argued that peace-making is an evolutionary capacity in the human species, that we possess the capacity to develop a peaceful social order, but that it will only be created with great effort. We are now beginning to pay more attention to the linking of knowledge and competence with spiritual maturity and to the sharing of strengths across cultures:

If there is an evolutionary transformation going on in this time of troubles, it consists of a growing awareness that we live on a tiny planet, and that technology and power alone cannot ensure peace or justice on that planet, nor control or eliminate violence and war. The dimensions of human caring has entered the public domain, and the

need to understand the Other, the different, is beginning to be acknowledge as a condition for human problem-solving. (Boulding,
1981)

Women's work for peace is not only concerned with getting rid of
nuclear weapons, but with abolishing the very structures which created
these weapons in the first place. Currently half the world's expenditure
on research and development is devoted to military purposes whilst
millions of people go hungry. It is a desperate situation of overkill and
undernourishment which women recognise as due to completely wrong
priorities bordering on madness and insanity. We need new alternatives
and new dreams to heal our divisions and create the wholeness the world
desperately needs. Women's faith in the possibility of peace is deeply
grounded in a faith in the strength and greatness of the spirit. One of the
songs of the Greenham women expressed this succinctly:

> You can't kill the spirit
> she is like a mountain
> old and strong
> she goes on and on
> and on.

Whilst the women in the peace movement are not necessarily all committed feminists, there is no doubt that many active feminists are deeply
involved with peace issues, opposing not only nuclear weapons and war,
but all form of violence. Global warmongery is the strongest expression
of corporate male violence, inextricably rooted in patriarchal structures
of domination and oppression. Our present political, social and economic institutions are linked to structural violence under which all
people suffer, women most of all. Yet at a personal level many women
also experience violence in a much more direct form through sexual
abuse, rape, battering, assault, pornography, and the widespread use of
women as sex-objects in advertising. Many feminists work for the abolition of particular forms of oppression and violence, but some explicitly
link the whole philosophy of feminism with that of non-violence. Non-
violence is seen in both practical and spiritual terms. At a practical level,
women use non-violent forms of opposition in their demonstrations
whilst spiritually they link the idea of non-violence to the web of life, to
healing and to a new source of power which comes from within:

Nonviolence holds life to be the highest value – life in its full wonder. Thus, hunger, poverty, ignorance, psychological manipulation, the lack of meaningful work, the denial of people – these are all alike violent. They are also signs of patriarchal, capitalist society. Nonviolence is organized, and goes out to confront the violence of society. . . .

Nonviolence entails a different understanding of power than that which predominates today. Usually power is understood as the *power-to-do-to*. In practice, such an understanding of power leads people to dominate, to want to control, to belittle, to deny the existence of the other, or to consider the existence of the other only in terms of one's own self-interest. In the extreme, such an understanding of power leads people to seek the utter extinction of other people. The power of nonviolence, on the other hand, is the power to simply do, or the *power-to-be*. Talk about power from a nonviolent perspective is expressed in terms of empowerment of ourselves, of others, communication, sharing, creating an alternative social order which draws boundless strength from having incorporated the energy of everyone's reality. (Michalowski, 1976, p. 43)

The connection between the women's movement and non-violence is again not new. It goes back to the early nineteenth century when, inspired by the Christian faith, the non-resistance movement grew out of the American abolitionist movement, just as the early women's movement did. Lucretia Mott, a radical Quaker activist, was one of the women pioneers advocating and practising non-violence. More recently, women's thought on non-violence has also been much inspired by the example of Mahatma Gandhi and Martin Luther King. In 1965, the American folk singer Joan Baez, together with another woman, established the Institute for the Study of Nonviolence in the United States. For many women today the issues of feminism, pacifism and non-violence are intimately interconnected (see the numerous testimonies by women edited by Pam McAllister 1982, *Reweaving The Web of Life. Feminism and Nonviolence*).

Feminists maintain that there are spiritual imperatives for non-violent action if we want to transform our warring world which goes on using organised violence to solve national and international problems. Women want to change the world through their commitment to life, joy, creativity, love and truth. Women believe in the power of non-violent discipline as an inner, spiritual energy which can make us experience the essential harmony between ourselves and the world around us, and lead to human reconciliation. Margaret Bishop ends her reflections on 'Feminist Spirituality and Non-violence' with an expression of the belief that we not only can, but must change:

> If we love ourselves, then we also love the changes that we must, as living beings, go through, as well as the changes that make life around us possible: changing seasons, changing vision, and the changing states of one's body. We hold to the faith that as we have found positive ways to change and grow, others can change as we have changed . . . truth does not come to us from books or any authority, but from careful exploration of ourselves, tempered by a love that embraces our world. This exploration involves not only our intellect, but all those less verbal aspects of our consciousness as well. I believe that those of us who have embraced feminist thinking have already begun to use this process. We must continue in this, and begin to bring deep reflection, 'cosmic spinning', into our lives not only as a reaction to crisis, but daily. As we deepen our commitment to ourselves and the world, we will build a spirituality which will speak to us so deeply and seriously that we will never compromise with violence again. We will be moved to speak actively against the pervasive and deadly cultural passivity that surrounds us and isolates us from each other. (1982, p. 161)

Feminist commitment to a new spirituality finds expression through campaigning for peace and non-violence, or rather campaigning non-violently for peace, as well as in its strong support for ecology. There exists such a fertile cross-connection between feminist and ecological ideas that some writers speak of 'ecofeminism' inspired by a vision of the interrelationship and unity of all life on earth. Ynestra King (1984a) has described ecofeminism as a movement where the spiritual and political come together. She said at a meeting of Women for Life on Earth:

> We here are part of a growing movement of women for life on earth, we come from the feminist movement, the anti-nuclear movement, the disarmament movement, the holistic health movement. We have come because life on earth and the earth itself is in terrible danger. . . . We're here to say the word ecology and to announce that for us as feminists it's a political word. . . . It's a way of being which

understands there are connections between all living things and indeed we women are the fact and flesh of connectedness . . . feminism and ecology are where politics come face to face with biology, and where the spiritual and the political come together. These movements come together in the way that they understand the world. . . . This is something that the left and socialism in general has not been able to come to terms with, that the crisis of this civilisation which has led us to the brink of nuclear annihilation, is spiritual as much as it is economic. And that it has to do with a world divided against itself on many different fronts. . . . Both (the feminist and the ecology movement) are deeply cultural and even spiritual movements, whose principles explode the categories of the political to include the biological on the one hand and the spiritual on the other. (1984a, pp. 4, 5, 6)

Traditionally, the semitic religions have taught that the human being is lord and steward of creation rather than its servant and beneficiary. A hierarchical worldview has proclaimed the human right of power and control over nature and, used irresponsibly, this had led to a domination and exploitation of natural and animal resources (Ruether, 1979b). It has been argued that men, in their objectifying distancing from nature, particularly since the development of modern science, have oppressed, exploited and raped her in the same way they have dominated and oppressed women (Merchant, 1982; Griffin, 1984). As Ynestra King has written elsewhere, from a feminist perspective it is important 'to understand the connection between the misogyny and violence against women in our culture and the contempt for nonhuman nature that has resulted in the rape of the earth by men, especially white men. Women and nature are the original "others" in patriarchy – those who are feared, the reminders of mortality, those who must be objectified and dominated' (1984b, p. 56).

Rather than being set apart, humanity is an integral part of the larger non-human nature on whose power of generation and self-renewal it is wholly dependent. The scientific revolution with its exclusive, onesided use of analytical reason, combined with uncontrolled human greed, have so endangered natural life that we might be faced with an imminent death of nature if we do not radically change our attitudes and behaviour. Increasingly, more and more women are raising their voices to save life on earth and protect the resources of our natural environment (see the testimonies in Caldecott and Leland, 1983, *Reclaim the Earth. Women speak out for Life on Earth*). Women fight to preserve the land, save trees, undertake planting and growing, campaign for natural foods, global 'Green Politics' (Capra and Spretnak, 1984; Spretnak, 1986), and many other goals to restore a harmonious balance between human beings and nature (Shiva, 1988).

Global militarism is inextricably bound up with considerable violence against the land. In Japan the Shibokusa women have put up a strong fight of non-violent resistance against the Japanese army to defend the right to their land at the foot of Mount Fuji (Caldecott, 1983) whilst elsewhere in the world many small women's groups combine their strength to preserve the renewable resources of their environment and encourage 'good housekeeping' through the balanced, non-exploitative use of the powers of nature. This also involves a non-hierarchical, non-anthropocentric view of nature which respects the rights of other species. Feminists refer to the interstructuring of four forms of oppression in contemporary civilisation to which they are equally opposed: racism, sexism, class exploitation, and biological destruction which derives from human domination over nature and 'speciesism' – the belief that the human species is superior to animals rather than part of the same natural world. To restore ecological justice and balance, our attitude needs to be biocentric rather than anthropocentric, life- rather than human-centred. The emergence of ecofeminism and its promise for reconnecting nature and culture, politics and ethics is documented in *Reweaving the World* (Diamond and Orenstein, 1990). We need an ecofeminist spirituality to heal our wounds and shape human community anew (see Plant, *Healing the Wounds. The Promise of Ecofeminism*, 1989).

Women strongly affirm the celebration of life and a new spirituality of the earth which praises the ever new wonder of creation, the beauty and splendour of nature in its myriad forms. In the last few years ecological thinking has opened up into a new 'Gaia spirituality', a spirituality of the earth, with which some feminists strongly identify. For the ancient Greeks Gaia was the personification of the earth – Mother Earth who watches over human and animal fertility. This spirituality is being enhanced through a new scientific approach to the study of the earth which sees the totality of life on earth as a single, self-regulating organism, a biosphere or sphere of life in which all living is interrelated with the earth which provides the sustenance for all of us (Lovelock, 1979). This ecological perspective has produced new theological insights among contemporary feminists (Primavesi, 1991; Halkes, 1991; Ruether,

1989, 1992) linked to an integral vision of the sacredness of life which sees all living things bound up together in one single interdependent web without any boundaries and suffused with the divine spirit. It is a vision of an unbroken bond and continuum, a vision more akin to eastern religions than to the western tradition, and to the primal vision of humankind of which we still find traces in archaic and tribal cultures. Adapting a saying from the Indian Chief Settle recorded in 1854 we can say:

> Whatever befalls the earth
> befalls the daughters and sons of the earth.
> We did not weave the web of life:
> We are merely a strand in it.
> Whatever we do to the web, we do to ourselves.

Women's voices speak out powerfully for peace, non-violence and re-spect for nature – for a new spiritual and religious attitude towards life on the planet. However different these voices are, taken together they strongly affirm the unity of the personal, spiritual and political and thereby provide an inspiring new paradigm for our culture, a radical alternative based on the strength of insight, experience and feeling, a sense of kinship and bonding, a mode of thinking and acting which makes more use of integrative than analytical skills by stressing the interplay and connectedness of all polarities rather than their separation, opposition and conflict. These are voices of prophecy and integration which proclaim the strength of the spirit and the vision of a new world.

But are feminists strong enough to move beyond the power of ex-perience and vision so that they do not only live in harmony with nature, but shape the world of culture, history, and politics and thereby give their vision concrete expression? The answer to this will probably not depend on feminism alone, but also on the vision of others to which feminists must learn to relate. I have indicated that the very strength of feminism lies in its diversity and the encouragement of pluralistic models. Given this pluralism, one must ask what are the unresolved paradoxes, the dilemmas and choices inherent in present-day feminism? The critical principle of feminism must also be applied to the ideas and actions of feminists themselves if the internal difficulties and contradictions of feminism are to be resolved.

Feminist dilemmas and choices

Any social, political or spiritual movement, if it is truly dynamic and alive, will include a wide range of different views and options, some of which may well be incompatible. Feminism is no different in this. Yet it is a sign of its coming of age that the tensions and contradictions inherent in feminist views are increasingly criticised and clarified from inside and outside the movement. Women philosophers have carefully examined and highlighted the philosophical and ethical problems facing feminism (McMillan, 1982; Midgley and Hughes, 1983; Welch, 1990). These relate to the understanding of biology, the different meanings of nature, the place of both reason and experience in human knowledge, the definition of what it means to be a woman as distinct from a man, and the symbolic value assigned to 'feminine' and 'masculine'.

Some dilemmas and choices, existing in feminism as a whole, but recurring in the lives of individual women, are particularly significant from a spiritual point of view. Looked at critically, there can be little doubt that feminist experience and consciousness, in spite of their vision of integration, are in practice a source of profound conflict. These conflicts arise first of all within the individual woman regarding her identity and role, her self-determination and choices for action. The conflicts also arise in families when women are no longer willing to take up traditional roles without questioning. And they arise in society and all its institutions, not least religious institutions, with their traditional chains of authority which always relegate women to the bottom of the ladder. What space do women need? Which roles do they want to perform in public and private life? Which parts of their identity do they recognise as pregiven (through biology, inheritance, or education) and which aspects are they truly free to create and shape?

Have individual women the inner resources – a sufficient awareness for critical self-examination, the conscious power to choose, and the determined will to act – to face and resolve these conflicts? Have religious institutions made any efforts to help women to cope with situations of conflict requiring decision? To overcome the ambiguities within feminism and within themselves, women have to become increasingly more aware of the great significance of the choices now open before them: the choice of gender role, the choice of work, of experience, of relationships, of motherhood, of an authentic existence and of reaching out to transcendence. For the individual woman the question of what kind of choice, what kind of identity, and what kind of self are central and closely interwoven with her way of relating to others, whether through bonding with other women or with men and children. How each woman will resolve the difficulties posed by these choices will in turn influence and shape her spiritual outlook and options.

The right kind of choice – a choice which is personal, spiritual and political – is the central issue for feminists as persons and for feminism as a movement. Agonising questions as to what is the ethically right choice arise with regard to many issues facing women today (and men too). How to resolve the paradox between advocating and guarding the sacred powers of life, of nature, of the earth, and yet campaign at the same time for the right to abortion? How to defend sexual freedom and a pluralism of sexual lifestyles and yet prevent powerful male groups from exploiting female sexuality as a marketable product?

There also exist many obstacles within the feminist movement itself which prevent women from coming more closely together. Most important are perhaps the great differences in historical consciousness and contemporary experience among different groups of women. These can lead to deep misunderstandings and tensions between black and white women, between women from the West and women from the third world. There exists an 'unacknowledged misogynism' in the women's movement itself (Morgan, 1982) which has to be fully faced and dealt with.

Criticising patriarchy as a system which is 'normative, exclusive, hierarchical, impersonal, alienating', women in a workshop on 'Women's Spirit Bonding' described the features of the feminist alternative as 'pluralistic, inclusive, egalitarian, personal, integrating': 'The feminist vision is pluralistic. Because it strives for unity rather than uniformity, it affirms diversity. To this end it works to build coalitions with constituencies that reflect the diversity of the human race and human concerns' (Kalven and Buckley, 1984, pp. 234, 235). The future of feminism and its power to transform the world will depend first on whether this pluralistic vision can be maintained within the feminist movement itself without one position developing into a dominant ideology, and secondly, whether the strength and adaptability of the feminist web is great enough to relate to and integrate other plural visions into itself.

The newly discovered power of women's experience is a major resource for shaping our human future. But its potential must not be marred by women's own politics of separation. If feminists oversimplify the burning issues of our times, their large vision will become parochial and sectarian, and thus lose its power of transforming the world. If women's experience is understood as an exclusive, separate norm, set over and above all else, then feminism will grow into a deforming ideology leading women not into the liberation it promises, but into another kind of bondage. This also relates to what is perhaps the major dilemma in contemporary feminism, the emphasis on women's newly defined otherness versus their equality with men. Sometimes this is seen as a difference between the women's movement in the USA and in Europe, a difference in campaigning either for autonomous women's institutions or for women's full integration into existing institutions and structures.

But is this alternative really necessary? At the present time of transition one can argue that both developments are needed. Women need to create space for themselves to nurture their own growth and test their strength. Thus they need to develop separate groups and structures, and yet women – perhaps not always the same individuals – also need to take an equal part in existing institutions so that these are restructured and changed. This does not necessarily always mean being coopted into a male-dominated world as women, if present in sufficient numbers, can create a revolutionary transformation from within existing institutions, as well as from without. This is true of religious institutions too. In order to gain their equal share in the shaping of society, politics, religion and spirituality, women must actively participate in all decision-making processes – and change those very processes by making them more personal, more holistic, more life- and community-centred, more truly spiritual.

Another feminist dilemma concerns the value assigned to time. Feminists are primarily interested in changing the conditions of women and of the world in the present, and in decisively influencing its shape in the future. It therefore seems almost contradictory that some feminists assign such a normative status to women's experience in the past, to the existence of matriarchy for example, or the worship of the goddess in ages gone by. Why should the past have such special significance? Why should it provide a model for the future? The past may be an important source of inspiration and strength, but feminists need to be clear in their own mind that their vision points to the creation of a new world, not to a revival of the old.

Feminist ideas now circulate so widely that they affect most women in one way or another, even when they do not fully understand or when they reject them. Young women now growing up have already internalised many feminist ideals. They have to make a conscious choice who they want to be and which aspects of women's traditional experience they wish to affirm, reject or transform. The radical challenge of feminism does not only create personal problems for individual women, but for men too, and it affects the relationship between women and men. Seen in its widest dimension, feminism is ultimately a challenge to reflect on what it means to be human today in quite new ways and under new conditions. Do feminists primarily wish to underline differences between women and men and thereby emphasise polarities and tensions? Or is the feminist vision large enough to heighten our sense of personhood and common humanity, not in the way it was one-sidedly defined in the past, but in a new holistic way where women's voice is fully articulated and integrated into a larger vision of the human? This is the vision of a life of human dignity and worth for all, a life sustained by the hope that wholeness and peace are possible and that the miracle of life on earth will retain all its gracious, gratuitous wonder and beauty. Seen not from within, but from a wider context outside, feminism is a process of conscientisation whereby the significance of what it means to be human – human as female and male – is being transformed and redefined. This seems to me the most crucial contribution of feminism which relates to a profound transformation of consciousness marking a new era in the history of humankind.

Transformation of human consciousness

It is possible to see the rise of feminism as part of the modern process of secularisation, and yet it also points to new religious and spiritual developments which affirm the resacralisation of nature, the earth, the body, sexuality, and the celebration of the bonds of community. But above all feminism articulates a new stage of critical reflection concerning the meaning of sexual differentiation for individuals and society.

Sexuality is constitutive of being human, whether one is sexually active or not. Sexual differences are basic to human beings and undergird all other differences, whether racial, cultural, social, political or educational. But through most of human history this basic human bi-polarity has been so taken for granted that few attempts have been made to elucidate its meaning at the level of critical reflection, and they have been made by men alone rather than by women and men together. The critical examination of the social nature of the human being begun by

Marx, and of the depth-dimension of the human psyche pioneered by Freud and Jung have opened up for us entirely new areas in understanding human-being-in-the-world. Similarly, the great awakening of women which is now taking place can be seen as yet another threshold in the history of human consciousness. Ultimately, it may transform the depth structures of self and society more radically than previous developments have done.

It is possible to discern within the history of human consciousness a threefold movement of conscientisation regarding the existence of sexual differences. Initially, one might speak of a 'presexual' or 'asexual' phase of consciousness when sexual differences were not explicitly acknowledged or accounted for in human reflection. This stage has characterised most of human history whilst now a second, explicitly 'sexual' phase has begun where sexual differences are fully explored and emphasised. Sexuality and sexual differences are now critically examined and reflected upon in all areas of human activity, including the area of spirituality. Initially, this may heighten differences and be a source of tension. Yet we can already perceive a further development consisting of a 'postsexual' or rather 'trans-sexual' phase of human consciousness. This does not mean a denial or exclusion of sexuality and sexual differences, but their recognition, affirmation and integration into a newly found wholeness. This phase represents a new kind of holistic consciousness which fully incorporates the meaning of sexual differentiation and relates to it in an integral manner. It is also an affirmation of the primacy of human personhood irrespective of gender, but in a way which is profoundly different from the past.

An integral, holistic consciousness allows for the growth of an integral spirituality beyond all dualisms. This can lead to true spiritual freedom and wholeness, not only to liberation from oppression. Such freedom is positively, not negatively, defined as unity arising out of the experience of complexity, a unifying wholeness relating to and integrating differences rather than denying them. Such a spirituality has the integrative strength of a truly interconnecting web, and when such connections are made, the split self and all separations are healed and made one, all life possesses new significance, meaning, and value.

To find an integral spirituality it is not only women who have to be liberated and made whole, but men too. There is also a need for 'liberated work' and 'liberated marriages' (Clinebell, 1973), for a new reciprocity in relationships so that women and men live and work out together the meaning of being human. Writing about the masculine and feminine in the human psyche Sukie Colegrave has said:

The emergence of a feminine consciousness whose salient characteristics are those of recognising and helping to create relationships, of
being receptive and recognising harmony, depends on a prior differentiation by the masculine principle of human awareness; we cannot
receive, integrate and harmonise before discovering the separate parts
both in the outside world and within our own psyches. (1979, p. 98)

We need a new, holistic self-understanding of both women and men
based not on a 'politics of separation' advocated by some feminists, but
on a 'politics of integration' to develop a truly humanistic civilisation. If
the so-called 'feminine' values are recognised and pursued as truly
human values by all, then the world will be transformed. What I have
described as an integral consciousness and spirituality Patricia Doyle
(1974) refers to as a call 'for a new, "androgynous" or "bisexual" unity
in religious, secular and psychological capacities, skills and consciousness'. She quotes an earlier study by Erik Erikson in which he appeals
to women to transfer to the public realm the values they have developed
in private life:

Maybe if women would only gain the determination to represent
publicly what they have always stood for privately in evolution and in
history (realism in householding, responsibility of upbringing, re-
sourcefulness in peacekeeping, and devotion to healing), they might
well add an ethically restraining, because truly supranational, power
to politics in the widest sense. (Quoted in Doyle, 1974, p. 35)

The global rise of feminist consciousness makes women around the
world articulate similar views and address challenging questions to long
established religious institutions. Yet at the same time, through their
actions and words, women affirm the need to face the important religious
issues of our times – the issues of peace, justice, equality, and freedom,
the meaning of human life on earth and the urgent call for a world
community. The themes of feminist spirituality explored in this book
relate to the creation of several new paradigms: that of a new self and a
new identity, that of new relationships, of a new social order, of a new
culture and civilisation, of peace, ecological harmony and non-violence.
Beyond the stridency of feminist debate and the clamour of protest
one can discern the promise of a new world, not only for women but for
the entire human community.

But will the powerful transformative potential of the feminist promise
come true?

At its strongest, deepest and largest the feminist vision is a spiritual one linked to the strength of faith and the dedication of spirit. It is a vision which ultimately calls for a new kind of sanctity and holiness. But other faiths too, traditional religions and their secular substitutes, possess a transformative potential which is part of their continuing attraction. And yet how often has their promise remained unfulfilled and even been contradicted in the institutions they have created? Will this happen to the new vision of women too? Or will feminism remain faithful to its prophetic vision and change the face of the world as we know it? Looking back on the late twentieth century, will people in the future judge the rise of feminism as of the same decisive influence in shaping the twenty-first century as the thoughts of Marx, Freud and Jung were in shaping the twentieth?

These questions can only be answered in the future as it is still far too early to assess the full significance of feminism. One thing is certain, however. The protest and promise of the women's movement opens up a new horizon for human development which touches the horizon of transcendence. Women's voices of protest and challenge have spiritual implications and much in contemporary feminist experience has religious significance, though not necessarily in a traditionally understood sense. Feminists speak of a 'post-patriarchal' spirituality, but this term is too circumscribed by one idea, as if patriarchy alone represented all evil and oppression, so that once this particular evil were overcome, all evil would be done with and we would be whole. I prefer to speak of an integral, holistic spirituality which I see not so much defined by that which needs to be negated than by being linked to the central feminist theme of making connections, of weaving a new pattern. Feminist wholeness affirms pluralistic ways of being. It is part of this larger vision of pluralism to be able to perceive parallel searches and intentions in the attempts of others to create transformative, holistic spiritualities elsewhere. There also exists a pluralism of the spiritual quest. The search for a viable spirituality is not only found in feminism, but in many other movements today.

Feminism and spirituality: an integration of perspectives

Feminism is concerned with constructing a new order which has social, political and spiritual implications for all peoples, not only for women.

Feminists challenge traditional spiritualities because they see them as profoundly dualistic and divisive, and they seek instead a new unitary and holistic approach to life. Women often experience traditional religious teachings as alienating, and yet women's new consciousness is creating new connections to age-old spiritual concerns. Thus the wider significance of feminism for our culture relates as much to the understanding and practice of spirituality as it does to that of politics, even though some feminists may be too shortsighted and dogmatic to perceive this. Examining the psychological and cultural implications of the relationship between women and religion Patricia Doyle has written:

> The debate on women and religion is the single most important and radical question for our time and the foreseeable future precisely because it concerns religion and because it affects all possible people and peoples. . . . Feminist analysis of culture and society stops prematurely if it does not dare to tackle religion. When feminists take on religion they oppose the most deeply held motivations, beliefs and life orientations. It is this dimension of religion that makes the debate the most radical of all feminist encounters with cultural and individual thought and feeling. We should not be surprised if the dispute thus results in radical resistance within the churches and individual men and women, as well as in the possibility of radical cultural, psychological and religious transformations for others. Nonetheless religious consciousness cannot help but be changed by the impact of the question, and even those who resist change will have to struggle with the issue if and when they decide to repudiate women and the feminist challenges to religion, culture and individual orientations. (1974, pp. 15, 16)

Over the last few years the interest in questions of religion and spirituality has grown considerably among women in the feminist movement, although this has as yet found little recognition in women's studies courses. Not only do women write on women's spirituality (Washbourn, 1979; Giles, 1982; Spretnak, 1982; Coghill and Redmond, 1983; Garcia and Maitland, 1983; Iglehart, 1983; Ochs, 1983; Yates, 1983; Krattiger, 1984; Sorge, 1985; Conn, 1986; Hurcombe, 1987; Harris, 1991; Zappone, 1991); they organise spirituality meetings, new rituals, prayer and meditation groups, and retreat houses for women. In a way these activities are all signs of faith growing in new forms, of a new religious consciousness which re-examines spirituality as a dimension which seems to have been lost and needs recovering in our present world (King, 1985b).

These developments are paralleled elsewhere. For example, there is at present a lively debate in Britain about the place of spirituality in religious education in state schools. Some time ago the *British Journal of Religious Education* devoted a special issue to the theme 'Spirituality across the Curriculum' (summer 1985) and the topic is often discussed at meetings and conferences. This is only one expression of a much wider attempt to reappraise spirituality in our technological world. Much of this reappraisal is also apparent in the various experiments of New Age thinking and in the attempts to foster a new creation and Gaia spirituality mentioned earlier. Then there is also the widespread holistic movement in science away from an outdated mechanistic model of energy, nature and life to a more organic perspective which sometimes brings together the unifying insights of mysticism and science. Some scientists even go so far as to assert that the current more holistic scientific analysis points to a profound paradigm shift which indicates the need for a quasi-religious transformation of contemporary culture. One of the few women writers who weaves these larger perspectives into her feminist reflections is Robin Morgan who in her book *The Anatomy of Freedom* (1982) connects current developments in feminism with those in the new physics and in global politics. Some of these convergent perspectives, especially in relation to ecology and spirituality, are pursued in the courses run by the Schumacher College at Dartington/Devon.

Robert Muller, former Assistant Secretary-General of the United Nations and now Chancellor of the UN Peace University in Costa Rica, has argued that at the present stage of technological development we need to combine the powers of science with those of love in order to create a more humane world. Does that not express in another way what women's voices are saying when they plead for the transformation of our scientific–technological civilisation? Out of his wide secular experience of working for global economic and political development Muller has reflected on the contemporary need for interiority and spirituality. In his book *New Genesis – Shaping a Global Spirituality* (1982) he pleads for giving urgent attention to questions of spirituality, even in the work of the United Nations, as efforts for global physical, mental and moral wellbeing alone are not enough to meet all the needs of humanity. What is, according to him, most required today is a sense of direction, an education towards interiority (the dimension concerned with the self), in morality (concerned with the self, others, and the world) and in spirituality (concerned with dimensions of transcendence). Only then can we hope to bring about a greater unification of the human family rather than its disintegration and destruction (see also Muller, 1991).

A similar idea has been expressed by Barbara Hubbard in her book *The Evolutionary Journey* (1983) which is concerned with an exploration of how the collective potential of the human species can be realised to transform the nature and destiny of our society:

> When we fuse as a group, our consciousness begins to rise to a new kind of spirituality. We crave to stay connected. This deepening togetherness stimulates a form of consciousness that does not yet have a name. Evolutionary consciousness, co-creative consciousness, may be appropriate. It is a synthesis of mystical and secular awareness emerging in this super-rich information environment under the pressure of convergence and growing responsibility. (1983, p. 62)

These few examples show how the search for a viable spirituality commensurate to the needs of our world exists among many people, not only feminists. Whilst some women understand feminist spirituality in an exclusive manner, others define spirituality in much more general terms so that it is easier to make connections between women's interest in spirituality and that of others. Writing about spirituality and feminist experience Gayle Yates maintains that the definition of spirituality 'includes collective and institutional attitudes, expressions, and experiences, as well as those of individuals', but she believes that 'the word is most easily understood as the core of a person, the center from which meaning, self, and life understanding are generated' (1983, p. 60). Charlene Spretnak in her introduction to *The Politics of Women's Spirituality* gives a still more wide-ranging description of spirituality:

> In truth, there is nothing 'mystical' or 'other worldly' about spirituality. The life of the spirit, or soul, refers merely to functions of the mind. Hence spirituality is an intrinsic dimension of human consciousness and is not separate from the body. . . . From one perspective, we realize that we need food, shelter, and clothing; from another that some sort of relationship among people, animals and the Earth is necessary; from another that we must determine our identity as creatures not only of our immediate habitat but of the world and the

universe; from another that the subtle, suprarational reaches of mind can reveal the true nature of being. (1982, p. xv)

Spirituality so understood is not the privilege of a few, but it grows in all of us as a horizon of transcendence in the midst of life. Feminist spirituality, too, is not just a fringe interest, but it lives in the lives of all women as they learn to be attentive to what is spirituality significant in their experience. Among religious experts, too, spirituality is much debated, but this debate is often far too past-orientated as spirituality is approached more from a historical than from a contemporary point of view. The practical applications of traditional spiritualities may be many (Jones, Wainwright and Yarnold, 1986), yet male writers on spirituality are unfortunately little aware of the implications and importance of feminist thinking on spirituality.

Spirituality must relate to the burning issues of our times. For this it needs to be crosscultural and interreligious. But spiritual awareness must also be attentive to gender differences and the new consciousness among women which calls them to wholeness, unity, and a larger community. It has been said that we are entering an era of civilisational mutation with a change from a material-centred to a life-centred civilisation which requires new theological and spiritual reflection. We need a change in orientation and perspective, we need to see with mind and heart, and care with passion for the future of our world. We have to find new visions and call on all the powers of our imagination, feeling and will to link up together in a larger human and cosmic web.

As women see it, the old androcentric way of viewing the world has to give way to a new integral vision. But women's vision has to expand to include other visions too. What is often a monologue of feminist voices has to become a dialogue so that women's voices are heard and listened to. Only then will the world be awakened to the powers of radical change, of true liberation, and of spiritual transformation. Only then will it recognise that feminist awareness is the source of an authentic religious vision and a witness to the life of the spirit.

Epilogue

The preceding chapters have presented different women's voices expressing protest, anger, agony and oppression, but also promise and hope, freedom, justice and peace. They speak of a quest for wholeness and point to a challenging vision of a world made new.

Is it a vision which can come true, or is it utopian? A mere fringe phenomenon without an impact on the world as a whole? As has been said long ago, a people without vision will perish. Given the magnitude of our problems, the world today is more in need of a transformative vision of hope, and the will to act upon it, than anything else. Contemporary women possess such a vision, a vision which can give us new hope and strength and encourage us to change the world as we know it.

Since the book was first written, many more voices have joined the chorus of women who spelled out a new vision earlier on. The themes of feminist writing have become both more global and more particular at the same time. Contrary to some western critics who decry the feminist movement as a middle class, white, western phenomenon, it is clear that more and more women from all social and religious backgrounds around the world are speaking up and making their voices heard. This is also true in the field of theology and spirituality. A growing number of publications are appearing in different countries (and languages) and whilst debates about religion were once dominated by developments in the USA, new indigenous developments have occurred in Europe, Asia, Africa and Latin America. Feminist theology has grown into an independent field large enough to produce a substantial dictionary surveying central concepts, debates and literature (Gössmann *et al.*, 1991). But more important than that are the exciting and challenging developments among women of the third world where we now hear more voices than ever before.

223

Feminist thinking has taken off among Christian women of various dominations but as mentioned in an earlier chapter, such thought is also developing among women of many different faiths, whether Hindus, Buddhists, Muslims, Sikhs or others. Looking at the Christian women who are publishing on feminist theology and spirituality in the third world (often through Orbis Books, Maryknoll, New York or the World Council of Churches in Geneva), they are from different denominations and work together in an ecumenical spirit. Quite a number are teaching in theological faculties or seminaries in Asia, Latin America or Africa, and several are women religious. They mostly have had a conventional theological training, often in the West, where they have first met with feminist ideas which have radically transformed their thinking and enabled them to rethink their own position back at home. Other developments have been nurtured by the work of the World Council of Churches (WCC) which has long been committed to achieving equality for women in church and society. Through its programme and conferences it has brought women from different churches and continents together, facilitated an exchange of ideas and created a network of Christian women around the globe which helps to nurture and empower new dreams and foster the developments of the necessary organisational, practical and intellectual skills to put them into practice as development projects which are particularly valuable and needed in rural areas.

Dreams provide new visions. Dreams are central to this groundbreaking transformation at grassroots level, to the new spirit and life bursting forth in base communities around the world. In sketching out their new theology Asian women have affirmed with confidence '*We dare to dream*' (see Fabella and Lee Park, 1989). Yet as some of the women associated with several of the 230 development projects among rural women funded by the WCC between 1976 and 1988 have emphasised, '*We cannot dream alone*' (see Rebera, 1990), thus pointing to the web of interconnections and the spirit of solidarity which has arisen among women around the globe.

Much of the energy of Christian women, in England at least, was given to struggling for the access to ordination (see the detailed documentation on the history of this struggle in Field-Bibb, 1991 and Furlong, 1991), a struggle which has much to do with the issue of power in the church. The analysis of power is central to feminist thought – what power is, how it functions, who wields it and whether women should have it in the same measure as men. But secular feminist writing has not fully fathomed the deep ramifications of all power in religion. Here power is sacralised and given its strongest locus of legitimation. To understand the subtle nuances and uses of power as well as its abuses, its creative and exploitative faces, one has to fathom the heart of religion where power has its deepest roots and gains its greatest strength. The challenge of feminism to religion involves a fundamental battle over power between the sexes, power as equally shared in harmony and collaboration rather than power as domination and control. Reconceiving power as enabling, as empowerment, is linked to a spiritual perspective, a transformation which comes from within and affects everything without.

Ordination is a particular issue which affects different churches differently, but when looking at women globally, acknowledging in particular the plight of women in the third world, other issues attract more attention. Christian women in the third world are of course a very small minority, but their voices speak out loud. They speak about economic, political and social issues, but they also speak about new ways of living in community, of understanding the church differently, of new approaches to God and the spirit, of a new, emerging spirituality born out of the context of their own suffering and oppression. They read the Bible with new eyes (Pobee and von Wartenberg-Potter, 1986; Robins, 1986) and challenge the dominance of western theology from the vantage point of their own context and experience (Fabella and Oduyoye, 1988; Tamez, 1989). A particularly exciting development is the feminist awareness among the women theologians of the Ecumenical Association of Third World Theologians (EATWOT). The latter, founded in 1976, had women members since its inception but did not pay particular attention to their voices and experience. Whilst the male theologians described their challenge to traditional Christian theology as the 'irruption of the third world', the women members developed their own bonding and affirmed their own, different perspective as 'the irruption within the irruption', a position where third world women did not want to be controlled by either first world women or third world men. In other words, they had to take their own stance against white, western feminist theologians and also against third world male theologians. In 1983 the women created the EATWOT Women's Commission, which has organised conferences in different countries and continents, resulting in a number of substantial publications on third world feminist theology and spirituality.

The vitality and concrete approach of this new thinking rooted in the experience of third world women is vividly felt in Chung Hyun Kyung's book *Struggle To be the Sun Again. Introducing Asian Women's Theol-*

ogy (Chung, 1991a). The title takes up a Japanese woman's poem which claims that woman originally was the sun; she was an authentic person. But now woman is the moon; she is dependent and defined by men. Asian women struggle to become self-defining, independent, 'to be the sun again'. The rich material of this book is well worth close study. It includes an inspiring chapter on 'Emerging Asian Women's Spirituality' whose characteristics are described as being concrete and total, creative and flexible, prophetic and historical, community oriented, pro-life, ecumenical, all embracing, cosmic and creation-centred. Chung Hyun Kung, who teaches theology in a Women's University in Seoul, Korea, created a stir at the 1991 World Council of Churches Assembly in Canberra with her presentation 'Come, Holy Spirit – Renew the Whole Creation' (Chung, 1991b). This was one of the two keynote addresses of the Assembly which vividly expressed the experience of Christianity within an Asian context seen from the perspective of women, drawing on biblical material, Korean spirit heritage (especially shamanism) and the cries of suffering from around the world. It was a powerful and truly empowering speech which bears witness to the creative contribution of women in the field of spirituality. (These developments can only be mentioned here but not discussed in full; I am in the process of collecting material for a Reader on Feminist Theology from the Third World, to be published by SPCK.)

Feminist theology has taken off in the third world but it has also become further sub-divided and diversified in the United States through the separate development of *womanist* theology by black Afro-Caribbean women and *mujerista* theology by Hispanic women, especially those from Cuba, Mexico and Puerto Rico. Whilst there is a growing interest in universal themes of spirituality, attention is also being paid to the spirituality of particular groups, to the recovery of women's spiritual heritage in the North American Indian tradition for example.

Other writers are concerned with women in interfaith dialogue (Mollenkott, 1988; O'Neill, 1990) where again questions about the universality or particularity of feminist insights come to the fore. The particular position of individual women depends much more on particular social, cultural, economic and religious conditions than on abstract religious beliefs; thus there exists not only a wide range of different situations among women of different faiths, but also between women of the same faith. On the one hand feminism is a universal movement based on new experiences and insights, yet on the other hand ideas developed by western feminists cannot always be applied globally. If they are imposed from the outside they can in fact help to foster a spirit of cultural neo-colonialism. Thus another tension arises in women's attitudes towards the traditional heritage of their faith. More and more women around the globe – women belonging to very different cultural and religious traditions – are affected by the process of consciousness-raising. They experience a new awareness and are determined to act with autonomy, shaping their own destiny. In the course of this they experience the ambivalence of religion in that it can be both an oppressive as well as a liberating force in their lives. Much depends on how particular women and groups of women react to their religious heritage, how far they can critique and excise the oppressive elements and emphasise the empowering, liberating spirit of their faith. Women from the third world and from underprivileged groups of society, whatever their religious background, in their active struggle for liberation and the transformation of their communities show clearly that the pursuit of justice, of concrete political and social aims, need not be separate from that of spirituality.

Much new networking and exchanging of ideas between women is going on all around the globe. In Europe this can be seen in the ongoing work of the European Society of Women in Theological Research founded in 1985 and in the practical outreach, especially into eastern Europe, of the Ecumenical Forum of European Christian Women founded in 1982. At an intellectual level much searching is going on to find a language for transcendence and for speaking about God which makes sense to women and men today (Chopp, 1989; McFague, 1987; Wren, 1989). Nowhere is this more movingly expressed than in the publications of ecofeminists. To be alive, to stay alive, means to revere life. To heal the wounds of our planet means to heal ourselves and see the deep connection between Gaia and God. Vandana Shiva has movingly written on *Staying Alive. Women, Ecology and Development in India* (1988); Judith Plant has edited a collection on *Healing the Wounds: The Promise of Ecofeminism* (1989); Irene Diamond and Gloria Feman Orenstein have brought together contributions on *Reweaving the World: The Emergence of Ecofeminism* (1990). Coming from diverse and multicultural backgrounds they all share a global vision of healing for life on earth and stress the need to bring together politics and spirituality, activism and vision (see also Spretnak, 1986, 1991; Ruether, 1992).

This integral approach also characterises Anne Primavesi's study on ecology, feminism and Christianity entitled *From Apocalypse to Genesis*

(1991) which spells out how we need to move from a hierarchical paradigm of domination and subordination to a new ecological paradigm grounded in a new sense of connectedness, an experience of belonging to a larger organic system of life which functions as a whole. Seen from this perspective, traditional attitudes to nature and oppressive patriarchal attitudes to women come under critical scrutiny when Anne Primavesi examines their theological foundations and also the possibility of their transformation. Ecofeminist insights can lead us to re-imagine transcendence by reintegrating it with the whole of creation, and out of this a new creation spirituality is born which celebrates the interconnectedness of spirit and all created being. Here the spirit of God embraces and breathes through all creation, beckons and invites us to a vision of what Gerard Manley Hopkins once described as 'the grandeur of God'. Here a new spirit is abroad which can be truly life-giving and set human hearts and minds aflame. The vision of ecofeminist spirituality is an empowering one, a real discovery which can give people hope, faith and energy for a new life. It is the vision of a seamless web, of the stream and energy of life, of its mystery of renewal and regeneration, but it is not a vision without questions. How to cope with differences, inequalities, conflicts and divisions in the world? The ecological paradigm works in nature, it works as a vision and idea, but it is quite another matter how to restructure and transform our institutions and govern our world so that it becomes a place of justice and peace.

Women's voices call on us to revision and reshape the world which is our home. At their largest and most universal they speak about both women and men, about redrawing the boundaries of gender in a non-exclusive way so that we can all, women and men, become fully human and relate to each other in a new spirit where we respect each other as people.

We need to see the world with both eyes, female and male, and ultimately go beyond gender divisions to find the spiritual wholeness for which we all yearn. It is the task of our generation to take up the challenge of inner and outer transformation and be empowered by the spirit who is the breath of life.

Further Reading

Prologue

For a general background to feminism and a broad understanding of the term see Banks (1981), Bouchier (1983), Deckland (1979), Eisenstein (1984) and Evans (1982). The material on spirituality may be difficult to get hold of but helpful discussions are found in the articles by Principe (1983) and Webster (1982) and in the books by Muller (1982) and Zappone (1991). The main themes of the book are briefly touched on by King (1984a). For bibliographical guides on women and religion see Bass, Boyd and Hughes (1986) and Carson (1986); for sources on women's spirituality Wynne (1988); for resources on women, religion and development in the third world see Carroll (1983) and Fenton and Heffron (1987).

Chapter 1: Voices of Protest and Anger

In addition to the works on feminism already mentioned see Beauvoir's classic (1972 edition or later) and Mitchell and Oakley (1986). Rendall (1985) examines the historical origins of modern feminism and Richards (1982) and Midgley and Hughes (1983) analyse the philosophical problems inherent in feminism. Most helpful and wideranging on all aspects, ideas, movements and publications of feminism up to 1980 is the annotated bibliography by Warren (1980). The best introduction to the feminist critique of religion is found in the Reader edited by Christ and Plaskow (1979) whilst documents on sexism in the Christian churches have been published from a conference of the WCC (1975). See also Ruether's (1987) discussion of androcentrism. On new patterns in feminist spirituality see Plaskow and Christ (1989).

Chapter 2: Voices of Challenge

The effect of Women's Studies on religion is discussed in the articles by Doyle (1974), Ruether (1981b), Gross (1983) and Buchanan (1987). One of the earliest and best known feminist challenges to Christianity comes from Daly (1974a). For a historical treatment of woman in the Christian tradition see Tavard (1973); for new perspectives on women in Judaism see Plaskow (1990) whilst crosscultural perspectives on women in different world religions are discussed in Gross (1977a), Carmody (1979), Falk and Gross 1980, Holden (1983), Sharma (1987), King (1987a), Cooey *et al.* (1991). For women in early Christianity see Aspregen (1990), Witherington (1990), Børresen (1991).

Chapter 3: Voices of Experience

This chapter discusses the pluralism and international dimension of women's experience. Crosscultural perspectives on women, religion and social change are explored by Haddad and Findly (1985), Eck and Jain (1986) whilst Webster and Webster (1985) deal with Christian women in the third world. A mine of information on black women and religion is found in Richardson's (1980) bibliography. The experience of black women and feminism is studied by Hooks (1983) and documented in the anthology edited by Moraga and Anzaldúa (1981). For the spiritual dimension of woman's understanding of self and body see the fine studies by Washbourn (1977) and Kolbenschlag (1979). An insightful account of woman's psychological development is provided by Gilligan (1982). For women's experience in the third world see Fabella and Oduyoye (1988) and the bibliographies in Carroll (1983) and Fenton and Heffron (1987).

Chapter 4: Voices of Spiritual Power

Women saints and mystics are found in East and West (Ramakrishna Vedanta Centre 1955) but this chapter looks in particular at Christian women mystics in medieval times. Easily accessible extracts of primary sources can be found in Dronke (1984), Wilson (1984), Bowie (1989) and Zum Brunn and Epiney-Burgard (1989) whereas Ruether and McLaughlin (1979) are concerned with women spiritual leaders in the Jewish and Christian traditions. Sölle (1984) discusses important themes of Christian feminist identity whilst Giles (1982) looks at the feminist mystic and presents a book of essays on contemporary women and spirituality, as do Garcia and Maitland (1983), Hurcombe (1987) and Bancroft (1989). A helpful general book for understanding mysticism is Woods (1981). Christian feminist spirituality is explored in Fischer (1989) and Zappone (1991), and Jewish women's spirituality in Umansky and Ashton (1992).

Chapter 5: Voices of a New Spirituality

This chapter is explicitly concerned with the new feminist spirituality outside existing religious institutions. Well-known, influential studies relating to the understanding of the goddess are by Harding (1982) and Stone (1979). Important historical data on goddesses in Old Europe have been collected by Gimbutas (1982, 1991) whereas a general introduction to the religion of the goddess is found in Olson (1983) and Gadon (1989); material on Hindu goddesses is given in Kinsley (1986). Jewish material on the goddess is found in Pirani (1991) and Long (1992). A full-length study on androgyny is by Heilbrunn (1973), but most material on androgyny and matriarchy exists in the form of articles in journals or collective works such as *Womanspirit Rising* edited by Christ and Plaskow (1979) or *The Politics of Women's Spirituality* edited by Spretnak (1982) with a long bibliography on feminist spirituality. Both works have articles on feminist rituals; more information is found in Budapest (1979a and 1980) and Starhawk (1979a). Very helpful are *Weaving the Visions* edited by Plaskow and Christ (1989), *Dance of the Spirit* by Harris (1991), the catalogue on Womanspirit resources by Wynne (1988) and the rich documentation in Goodison (1990).

Chapter 6: Voices of a New Theology

Most accessible is the Reader on *Feminist Theology* edited by Loades (1990). Other introductions to the major perspectives of Christian feminist theology are Moltmann-Wendel (1986), Furlong (1984a) and Carr (1990); also helpful are Dowell and Hurcombe (1981) and Maitland (1983). For a feminist interpretation of biblical texts see Russell (1985) and Trible (1984). A detailed scholarly analysis of New Testament texts is found in Schüssler Fiorenza's *In Memory of Her* (1983), a feminist reconstruction of early Christian origins. Heine (1987) disagrees with the feminist interpretation of early Christian data and Hayter (1987) examines the use of biblical passages in the debate for and against the ordination of women. For debates about the ordination of women see Field-Bibb (1991) and Furlong (1991).

For the different theological orientations of Mary Daly and Rosemary Radford Ruether see Heyward (1979), Daly (1971, 1974a, 1974b, 1979b) and Ruether (1974b, 1975, 1979a, 1983). An overview from a post-Christian perspective is given by Hampson (1990). Valuable material on women in different Christian churches is published by the World Council of Churches (WCC, 1975, 1977; Herzel, 1981; Parvey, 1980, 1983). For the women-church movement and women liturgical communities see Schüssler Fiorenza (1983) and Ruether (1985) and the texts of celebration in Morley (1988) and Winter (1987, 1991).

For feminist theology in the third world see Fabella and Oduyoye (1988), Russell (1988), Fabella and Lee Park (1989), Tamez (1989) and Chung (1991a). Mollenkott (1988) and O'Neill (1990) discuss women in interfaith dialogue.

Chapter 7: Voices of Prophecy and Integration

Important connections exist between women's spirituality and political action, best documented by Spretnak (1982, 1986). For women's work in the peace movement see Jones (1983), Brown (1984), Cambridge Women's Peace Collective (1983) and Brock-Utne (1987); for the connections between feminism and non-violence McAllister (1982), and for ecological issues Caldecott and Leland (1983) and Capra and Spretnak (1984). New perspectives on feminism, Christianity and ecology are explored by Primavesi (1991), Ruether (1992) and Halkes (1991). A substantial study on Christian spirituality with brief reference to some other religious traditions, but no mention at all of women's spirituality is Jones, Wainwright and Yarnold (1986) whereas Muller (1982, 1991) and King (1989a) explore ideas about shaping a global spirituality. Works on women's spirituality include Washbourn (1979), Giles (1982), Garcia and Maitland (1983), Iglehardt (1983), Ochs (1983), Kalven and Buckley (1984), Hurcombe (1987), Harris (1991) and Zappone (1991).

Bibliography

A Centennial Tapestry (1983) *The Continuing Journey of Women in Mission: Program Resources*, New York: General Board of Global Ministries, The United Methodist Church, Women's Division.

Aarnink, Laetitia (1983) 'Frauen, die ihrer Erfahrung treu blieben' in *Mystik, Band 1, Ihre Struktur und Dynamik*, Düsseldorf: Patmos Verlág, pp. 189–211.

Adler, Margot (1982) 'Meanings of Matriarchy', in C. Spretnak (ed.), *The Politics of Women's Spirituality*, New York: Anchor Press; Doubleday, pp. 127–37.

Allen, Paula Gunn (1986) *The Sacred Hoop. Recovering the Feminine in American Indian Tradition*, Boston: Beacon Press.

Amoah, Elizabeth (1986) 'Women, Witches and Social Change in Ghana', in Diana L. Eck and Devaki Jain (eds), *Speaking of Faith*, New Delhi: Kali for Women, pp. 77–87.

Andrews, William L. (ed.) (1986) *Sisters of Spirit. Three Black Women's Autobiographies of the Nineteenth Century*, Bloomington: Indiana University Press.

Archbishop Runcie and Cardinal Hume, Basil (1987) *Prayers for Peace: an Anthology of Readings and Prayers*, London: SPCK.

Arthur, Rose Horman (1984) *The Wisdom Goddess*, Washington DC: The University Press of America.

—— (1987) 'The Wisdom Goddess and the Masculinization of Western Religion', in U. King (ed.) *Women in the World's Religious, Past and Present*, New York: Paragon House, pp. 24–37.

Asen, Bernhard A. (1981) 'Women and the ministerial priesthood: an annotated bibliography', *Theology Digest*, 29/4, pp. 329–42.

Aspegren, Kerstin (1990) *The Male Woman. A Feminine Ideal in the early Church*, (ed. René Kieffer), Uppsala Women's Studies, Stockholm: Almqvist & Wiksell International.

Atkinson, Clarissa W. (1983) *Mystic and Pilgrim: The Book and the World of Margery Kempe*, Ithaca: Cornell University Press.

Atkinson, Clarissa W., Buchanan, Constance H. and Miles, Margaret R. (eds) (1985) *Immaculate and Powerful: The Female in Sacred Image and Social Reality*, The Harvard Women Studies in Religion Series, Boston: Beacon Press.

—— (1987) *Shaping New Visions. Gender and Values in American Culture*, Ann Arbor, Michigan: UMI Research Press.

Aubert, Jean Marie (1975) *La Femme, Antiféminisme et Christianisme*, Paris: Cerf/Desclée.

Bachofen, J. J. (1861) *Das Mutterrecht: Eine Untersuchung über die Gynaikokratie der Alten Welt nach ihrer Religiösen und Rechtlichen Natur*, Stuttgart: Krais and Hoffman; trans Ralph Manheim, *Myth, Religion and Mother Right*, Princeton NJ: Princeton University Press 1967.

Bacon, Mary Hope (1986) *Mothers of Feminism. The Story of Quaker Women in America*, San Francisco: Harper & Row.

Badham, Linda (1984) 'The Irrationality of the Case Against Ordaining Women', *The Modern Churchman, New Series*, 27/1, pp. 13–22.

Bailey, Derrick Sherwin (1959) *The Man–Woman Relationship in Christian Thought*, London: Longman.

Bancroft, Anne (1987) 'Women in Buddhism', in U. King (ed.), *Women in the World's Religions, Past and Present*, New York: Paragon House, pp. 81–104.

—— (1989) *Weavers of Wisdom. Women Mystics of the Twentieth Century*, London: Penguin Arkana.

Banks, Olive (1981) *Faces of Feminism*, Oxford: Martin Robertson.

Barrett, David B. (ed.) (1982) *World Christian Encyclopedia: A comparative study of churches and religions in the modern world AD 1900–2000*, Nairobi, Oxford, New York: Oxford University Press.

Bass, Dorothy, C. Boyd and Sandra Hughes (1986) *Women in American Religious History. An annotated bibliography and guide to sources* (568 entries) Boston: G. K. Hall.

Bazin, Nancy Topping (1974) 'The concept of androgyny: A working bibliography', *Women's Studies*, 2, pp. 217–35.

Beauvoir, Simone de (1972) *The Second Sex*, Harmondsworth: Penguin Books, 1952; 1949 French original, *Le Deuxième Sexe*.

Becher, Jeanne (ed.) (1990) *Women, Religion and Sexuality, Studies on the Impact of Religious Teachings on Women*, Geneva: WCC Publications.

Bekkenkamp, J., Droes, F. and Korte, A. M. (eds) (1986) *Van Zusters, Meiden en Vrouwen: Tien jaar feminisme en theologie op fakulteiten en hogescholen en Nederland*, Leiden-Utrecht: Interuniversitair Institut voor Missiologie en Oecumenica (IIMO/IWFT, No. 19).

Bell, Diane (1984) *Daughters of the Dreaming*, Melbourne: McPhee Gribble Publishers in association with George Allen & Unwin, Australia.

Bennett, Anne McGrew (1989) *From Woman-Pain to Woman-Vision*, edited by Mary E. Hunt, Minneapolis: Fortress Press.

Berger, Peter L. (1979) *Facing up to Modernity*, Harmondsworth: Penguin Books.

—— (1980) *The Heretical Imperative: Contemporary Possibilities of Religions Affirmation*, London: Collins.

Berkman, Joyce Avrech (1979) *Olive Schreiner: Feminism on the Frontier*, St Alban's, Vermont: Eden Press.

Bernstein, Marcelle (1976) *Nuns*, London: Collins.

Binford, Sally R. (1981) 'Myths and Matriarchies', *Anthropology*, 1, pp. 150–3.

Bishop, Margaret (1982) 'Feminist Spirituality and Non-violence', in P. McAllister (ed.), *Reweaving the Web of Life*, Philadelphia: New Society Publishers, pp. 156–61.

Børresen, Kari Elisabeth (1977) 'Male–Female, a Critique of Traditional Christian Theology', *Temenos*, 13, pp. 31–42.

—— (1981) *Subordination and Equivalence: The Nature and Role of Woman in Augustine and Thomas Aquinas*, Lanham: University Press of America.

—— (ed.) (1991) *Images of God and Gender Models in Judaeo-Christian Tradition*, Oslo: Solum Forlag.

Boucher, Sandy (1988) *Turning the Wheel. American Women Creating the New Buddhism*, San Francisco: Harper & Row.

Bouchier, David (1983) *The Feminist Challenge: The Movement for Women's Liberation in Britain and the United States*, London: Macmillan.

Boulding, Elise (1981) 'Peace Making as an Evolutionary Capacity: Reflections on the Work of Teilhard de Chardin, Martin Buber and Jane Addams', cyclostyled lecture, Dartmouth College.

Bowie, Fiona (ed.) (1989) *Beguine Spirituality, An Anthology*, London: SPCK.

Bregman, Lucy (1977) 'Women and Ecstatic Religious Experience', *Encounter* (Christian Theological Seminar, Indianapolis), 38, pp. 43–53.

Briffault, Robert (1927) *The Mothers: A Study of the Origins of Sentiments and Institutions*, 3 vols, London: George Allen & Unwin, 1952, abridged by Gordon R. Taylor, New York, 1977.

Brock, Rita Nakashima (1988) *Journeys by Heart. A Christology of Erotic Power*, New York: Crossroad.

Brock-Utne, Birgit (1987) *Educating for Peace. A Feminist Perspective*, New York, Oxford, Frankfurt: Pergamon Press.

Brooten, Bernadette J. (1982) *Women Leaders in the Ancient Synagogue: Inscriptional Evidence and Background Issues*, Chico, California: Scholars Press, Brown Judaic Studies, No. 36.

Brown, Cheever Mackenzie (1974) *God as Mother: A Feminine Theology in India: An Historical and Theological Study of the Brahmavaivarta Purāna*, Hartford, Vermont: Claude Stark.

Brown, Wilmette (1984) *Black Women and the Peace Movement*, Bristol: Falling Wall Press, 2nd edn.

Bruner, Charlotte H. (ed.) (1983) *Unwinding Threads: Writing by Women in Africa*, London: Heinemann.

Buchanan, Constance H. (1987) 'Women's Studies', *The Encyclopedia of Religion*, 15, pp. 433–40, New York: Macmillan, London: Collier Macmillan.

Budapest, Zsuzsanna E. (1979a and 1980) *The Holy Book of Women's Mysteries*, vols I and II, Los Angeles: Susan B. Anthony Coven, No. 1.

—— (1979b) 'Self-Blessing Ritual', in Carol P. Christ and Judith Plaskow (eds), *Womanspirit Rising*, New York: Harper & Row, pp. 269–782.

Bührig, Marga (1985) 'The Role of Women in Ecumenical Dialogue', *Concilium, 182: Women – Invisible in Church and Theology*, pp. 91–8.

Burfield, Diana (1983) 'Theosophy and Feminism: Some Explorations in Nineteenth Century Biography', in Pat Holden (ed.), *Women's Religious Experience*, London: Croom Helm, pp. 27–56.

Burman, Rickie (1986) '"She Looketh Well to the Ways of Her Household": The Changing Role of Jewish Women in Religious Life, c. 1880–1930', in

G. Malmgreen (ed.), *Religion in the Lives of English Women 1760–1930*, London: Croom Helm, pp. 234–59.

Burmeister, Elisabeth (1982) *Frauen machen Frieden*, Berlin: Burkhardthaus Verlag, Laetare Frauenprogramm.

Butler-Bowden, W. (ed.) (1936) *The Book of Margery Kempe, a modern version by W. Butler-Bowden*, London: Jonathan Cape.

Bynum, Caroline Walker (1982) *Jesus as Mother: Studies in the Spirituality of the High Middle Ages*, Berkeley, Los Angeles, London: University of California Press.

—— (1987) *Holy Feast and Holy Fast: The Religious Significance of Food to Medieval Women*, Berkeley, Los Angeles, London: University of California Press.

Cady Stanton, Elizabeth (1985) *The Woman's Bible: The Original Feminist Attack on the Bible*, Edinburgh: Polygon Books, repr. of 1898 edition.

Caldecott, Leonie (1983) 'At the Foot of the Mountain: The Shibokusa Women of Kita Fuji', in L. Jones (ed.), *Keeping the Peace*, London: The Women's Press, pp. 98–107.

Caldecott, L. and Leland, S. (eds) (1983) *Reclaim the Earth: Women speak out for Life on Earth*, London: The Women's Press.

Cambridge Women's Peace Collective (1983) *My Country is my Whole World*, London: Pandora.

Cameron, A. and Kuhrt, A. (eds) (1983) *Images of Women in Antiquity*, London and Canberra: Croom Helm.

Canham, Elizabeth (1983) *Pilgrimage to Priesthood*, London: SPCK.

Cardman, Francine (1978) 'The Medieval Question of Women and Orders', *The Thomist*, 42, pp. 582–99.

Capra, F. and Spretnak, C. (1984) *Green Politics: The Global Promise*, New York: E. P. Dutton.

Carmody, Denise Lardner (1979) *Women and World Religions*, Nashville, Tennessee: Abingdon, 1979.

Carr, Anne, B. V. M. (1980) 'Theological Anthropology and the Experience of Women', *Chicago Studies*, 19/2, Summer, pp. 113–25.

—— (1982) 'Is a Christian Feminist Theology Possible?', *Theological Studies*, 43/2, pp. 279–97.

—— (1990) *Transforming Grace. Christian Tradition and Women's Experience*, San Francisco: Harper & Row.

Carroll, Theodora Foster (1983) *Women, Religion and Development in the Third World*, New York: Praeger.

Carson, Anne (1986) *Feminist Spirituality and the Feminine Divine. An annotated bibliography* (739 entries), Trumansburg, New York: Crossing Press.

Chatterji, Jyotsna (ed.) (1979) *Good News for Women*, Delhi: ISPCK.

—— (ed.) (1982) *Women in Praise and Struggle*, Delhi: ISPCK.

—— (ed.) (1986) *Vision and Service*, 12 Bible Studies for Women, Delhi: ISPCK.

Chopp, Rebecca S. (1989) *The Power to Speak. Feminism, Language, God*, New York: Crossroad.

Christ, Carol (1975) 'Spiritual Quest and Women's Experience', *Anima*, 1/2, pp. 4–15.

—— (1976) 'Feminist Studies in Religion and Literature: A Methodological Reflection', *Journal of the American Academy of Religion*, 2, pp. 317–25.

—— (1979) 'Why Women Need the Goddess: Phenomenological, Psychological and Political Reflections', in Carol Christ and Judith Plaskow (eds), *Womanspirit Rising*, New York: Harper & Row, pp. 273–87.

—— (1983) 'Symbols of Goddess and God in Feminist Theology', in C. Olson (ed.), *The Book of the Goddess*, New York: Crossroad, pp. 231–51.

—— (1986) *Diving Deep and Surfacing: Women Writers on Spiritual Quest*, Boston: Beacon Press, 1980; new preface in 1986 edition.

—— (1987) *Laughter of Aphrodite. Reflection on a Journey to the Goddess*, San Francisco: Harper & Row.

—— (1991) 'Mircea Eliade and the Feminist Paradigm Shift', *Journal of Feminist Studies in Religion*, 7/2, pp. 75–94.

—— and Plaskow, J. (eds) (1979) *Womanspirit Rising. A Feminist Reader in Religion*, New York: Harper & Row.

Christian Conference of Asia (1985/6) *In God's Image*, journal published from Singapore.

Chung Hyun Kyung (1991a) *Struggle to be the Sun Again. Introducing Asian Women's Theology*, London: SCM Press; also 1990, Maryknoll, New York: Orbis Books.

—— (1991b) 'Come, Holy Spirit – Renew the Whole Creation', in M. Kinnamon (ed.), World Council of Churches, *Signs of the Spirit*, official report Seventh Assembly, Canberra, 7–20 February 1991, Geneva: World Council of Churches, pp. 37–47.

Clark, E. and Richardson, H. (eds) (1977) *Women and Religion: A Feminist Source-Book of Christian Thought*, New York: Harper & Row.

Clinebell, Charlotte Holt (1973) *Meet Me in the Middle: On Becoming Human Together*, New York: Harper & Row.

Coghill, M. and Redmond, S. (1983) 'Feminism and Spirituality', in J. Holland (ed.), *Feminist Action*, 1, London: Battle Axe Books.

Colegrave, Sukie (1979) *The Spirit of the Valley: The Masculine and Feminine in the Human Psyche*, Los Angeles: J. P. Tarcher, Inc.

Coll, Regina (ed.) (1982) *Women and Religion: A Reader for the Clergy*, New York: Paulist Press.

Collins, Sheila D. (1974) *A Different Heaven and Earth*, Valley Forge, Pennsylvania: Judson Press.

—— (1982), 'The Personal is Political', in C. Spretnak (ed.), *The Politics of Women's Spirituality*, New York: Anchor Press, Doubleday, pp. 362–7.

Concilium (1980) No. 134, *Women in a Men's Church*, Virgil Elizondo and Norbert Greinacher (eds), Edinburgh: T & T Clark.

—— (1981) No. 143, *God as Father?*, Edward Schillebeeckx and Johannes Baptist (eds), Metz, Edinburgh: T & T Clark.

—— (1985) No. 182, *Women – Invisible in Church and Theology*, Elisabeth Schüssler Fiorenza and Mary Collins (eds), Edinburgh: T & T Clark.

—— (1989) No. 206, *Motherhood: Experience, Institution, Theology*, Anne Carr and Elisabeth Schüssler Fiorenza (eds), Edinburgh: T & T Clark.

Condren, Mary (1989) *The Serpent and the Goddess. Women, Religion and Power in Celtic Ireland*, San Francisco: Harper & Row.

Conn, Joann Wolski (1980) 'Women's Spirituality: Restriction and Reconstruction', *Cross Currents*, 30, pp. 293–308; also in J. W. Conn, *Women's Spirituality* (1986), pp. 9–30.
—— (ed.) (1986) *Women's Spirituality: Resources for Christian Development*, New York: Paulist Press.
Cooey, Paula M., Eakin, William R. and McDaniel, Jay B. (eds) (1991) *After Patriarchy. Feminist Transformations of the World Religions*, Maryknoll, New York: Orbis Books.
Cook, Alice and Kirk, Gwyn (1983) *Greenham Women Everywhere: Dreams, Ideas and Actions from the Women's Peace Movement*, London: Pluto Press.
Cooper, Fiona (1983) 'Women in the Peace Movement', in Jo Garcia and Sara Maitland (eds), *Walking on the Water*, London: Virago Press, pp. 132–8.
Cox, Harvey (1974) *The Seduction of the Spirit: The Use and Misuse of People's Religion*, London: Wildwood House.
Craighead, Meinrad (1982) 'Immanent Mother', in Mary E. Giles (ed.), *The Feminist Mystic and Other Essays on Women and Spirituality*, New York: Crossroad, pp. 71–83.
Crawford, J. and Kinnamon, M. (eds) (1983) *In God's Image: Reflections of Identity, Human Wholeness and the Authority of Scripture*, Geneva: World Council of Churches.
Culver, Elsie Thomas (1967) *Women in the World of Religion*, New York, Doubleday (authorised fascimile by United Microfilms, Ann Arbor, Michigan, London, 1981).
Curle, Adam (1976) *Mystics and Militants: A Study of Awareness, Identity and Social Action*, London: Tavistock.
Daly, Mary (1968) *The Church and the Second Sex*, New York: Harper & Row.
—— (1971) 'The Women's Movement: An Exodus Community', in E. Clark and H. Richardson (eds), *Women and Religion: A Feminist Sourcebook of Christian Thought*, New York: Harper & Row, pp. 259–71.
—— (1974a) *Beyond God the Father: Toward a Philosophy of Women's Liberation*, Boston: Beacon Press: Beacon Paperback.
—— (1974b) 'Theology after the Demise of God the Father: A Call for the Castration of Sexist Religion', in A. L. Hageman (ed.), *Sexist Religion and Women in the Church: No More Silence!*, New York: Association Press, pp. 125–42.
—— (1979a) *Gyn/Ecology: The Metaethics of Radical Feminism*, London: The Women's Press, Boston: Beacon Press, 1978.
—— (1979b) 'After the Death of God the Father: Women's Liberation and the Transformation of Christian Consciousness', in C. P. Christ and E. J. Plaskow (eds), *Womanspirit Rising*, New York: Harper & Row, pp. 53–67.
—— (1984) *Pure Lust: Elemental Feminist Philosophy*, Boston: Beacon Press, London: The Women's Press.
—— (1992) *Outercourse. The Be-Dazzling Voyage*, San Francisco: HarperSanFrancisco.
Daniélou, Jean (1974) *The Ministry of Women in the Early Church*, Leighton Buzzard: The Faith Press.
Davaney, Sheila Greeve (ed.) (1981) *Feminism and Process Thought*, The Harvard

Divinity School/Claremont Center for Process Studies Symposium Papers, New York and Toronto: The Edwin Mellen Press.

Davis, Elizabeth Gould (1973) *The First Sex*, Baltimore, Maryland: Penguin Books; G. P. Putnam & Sons, 1971.

Davis, J. and Weaver, J. (1975) 'Dimensions of Spirituality', *Quest: A Feminist Quarterly*; also in C. Spretnak (ed.), *The Politics of Women's Spirituality* (1982) pp. 368–72.

De Pizan, Christine (1983) *The Book of the City of Ladies*, trans Earl Jeffrey Richards, London: Pan Books, Picador.

Deckland Sinclair, Barbara (1979) *The Women's Movement: Political Socioeconomical and Psychological Issues*, New York, Hagerstown, San Francisco, London: Harper & Row.

Deen, Elizabeth (1959) *Great Women of Faith*, London: Independent Press.

Diamond, Irene and Orenstein, Gloria Feman (eds) (1990) *Reweaving the World: The Emergence of Ecofeminism*, San Francisco: Sierra Club Books.

Dickason, Anne (1982) 'The Feminine as Universal', in M. Vetterling-Braggin (ed.), *'Femininity', 'Masculinity' and 'Androgyny'*, Totawa, NJ: Rowman & Allanheld, pp. 10–30.

Donnelly, Dody H. (1982) 'The Sexual Mystic: Embodied Spirituality', in Mary E. Giles (ed.), *The Feminist Mystic*, New York: Crossroad, pp. 120–41.

—— (1984) *Radical Love: An Approach to Sexual Spirituality*, Minneapolis: Winston Press.

Dowell, S. and Hurcombe, L. (1981) *Dispossessed Daughters of Eve: Faith and Feminism*, London: SCM.

Downing, Christine (1984) *The Goddess: Mythological Images of the Feminine*, New York: Crossroad.

—— (1988) *Psyche's Sisters. ReImaging the Meaning of Sisterhood*, San Francisco: Harper & Row.

—— (1989) *Myths and Mysteries of Same-Sex Love*, New York: Continuum.

Doyle, Patricia Martin (1974) 'Women and Religion: Psychological and Cultural Implications', in R. Radford Ruether (ed.), *Religion and Sexism*, New York: Simon & Schuster, pp. 15–40.

Driver, Anne Barstow (1976) 'Religion', Review Essay in *Signs*, 2/2 (Winter 1976) pp. 434–42.

Dronke, Peter (1984) *Women Writers of the Middle Ages: A Critical Study of Texts from Perpetua (+203) to Marguerite Porete (+1310)*, Cambridge: Cambridge University Press.

Dumais, Monique (1985) *Les femmes dans la Bible: Expériences et interprétations*, Montreal: Les éditions Paulines and Paris: Mediaspaul.

—— and Roy, Marie-Andrée (eds) (1989) *Souffles de femmes. Lecures féministes de la religion*, Montréal: Editions Paulines and Mediaspaul.

Eck, Diana L. and Jain, Devaki (eds) (1986) *Speaking of Faith: Cross-cultural Perspectives on Women, Religion and Social Change*, New Delhi: Kali for Women, London: The Women's Press.

Eckhardt, A. R. (1986) 'Christians, Jews and the Women's Movement', *Christian Jewish Relations*, 19/2, pp. 13–22, London: Institute of Jewish Affairs.

Ehrenreich, B. and English, D. (1973) *Witches, Midwives and Nurses: A History of Women Healers*, London: Writers and Readers Publishing Cooperative.

Eisenstein, Hester (1984) *Contemporary Feminist Thought*, London, Sydney: Unwin Paperbacks.

Eisler, Riane (1987) *The Chalice and the Blade. Our History and Our Future*, San Francisco: Harper & Row.

Elwes, Teresa (ed.) (1992) *Women's Voices. Essays in Contemporary Feminist Theology*, London: HarperCollins.

Evans, Mary (ed.) (1982) *The Woman Question: Readings on the Subordination of Women*, London: Collins Fontana Paperbacks.

—— (1985) *Simone de Beauvoir: A Feminist Mandarin*, London and New York: Tavistock.

Fabella M. M., Virginia and Oduyoye, Mercy Amba (eds) (1988), *With Passion and Compassion. Third World Women Doing Theology*, Maryknoll, New York: Orbis Books.

—— and Lee Park, Sun Ai (eds) (1989) *We dare to dream. Doing Theology as Asian Women*, Hongkong: Asian Women's Resource Centre for Culture and Theology and the EATWOT Women's Commission in Asia.

Falk, Nancy A. and Gross, Rita M. (eds) (1980) *Unspoken Worlds: Women's Religious Lives in Non-Western Cultures*, San Francisco: Harper & Row.

Faria, S. Alexander, A. V. and Tellis-Nayak, J. B. (eds) (1984) *The Emerging Christian Woman: Church and Society Perspectives*, Bangalore: Satprakashan Sanchar Kendra/Ishvani.

Fenton, Thomas P. and Heffron, Mary J. (eds) (1987) *Women in the Third World. A Directory of Resources*, Maryknoll, New York: Orbis Books.

Ferguson, John (1977) *War and Peace in the World's Religions*, London: Sheldon Press.

Ferm, Deane W. (1981) 'Feminist Theology in America', *Scottish Journal of Theology*, 34, pp. 157–78.

Field, Barbara (ed.) (1989) *Fit For This Office. Women and Ordination*, Melbourne: Collins Dove.

Field-Bibb, Jacqueline (1991) *Women Towards Priesthood. Ministerial Politics and Feminist Praxis*, Cambridge: Cambridge University Press.

Figes, Eva (1986) *Patriarchal Attitudes*, London: Macmillan 1970.

Fischer, Kathleen (1989) *Women at the Well. Feminist Perspectives on Spiritual Direction*, London: SPCK.

Friedan, Betty (1983) *The Second Stage*, London: Abacus.

Furlong, Monica (ed.) (1984a) *Feminine in the Church*, London: SPCK.

—— (1984b) 'What is Dr Oddie afraid of?', *The Tablet*, 27 October 1984, p. 1046.

—— (1991) *A Dangerous Delight. Women and Power in the Church*, London: SPCK.

Gaba, Christian R. (1987), 'Women and religious experience among the Anlo of West Africa', in U. King (ed.), *Women in the World's Religions, Past and Present*, New York: Paragon House, pp. 177–95.

Gadon, Elinor W. (1989) *The Once and Future Goddess. A Symbol of Our Time*, San Francisco: Harper & Row.

Gage, Matilda Joslyn (1982) *Woman, Church and State: A Historical Account of the Status of Woman through the Christian Ages: with Reminiscences of the Matriarchate*, Arno Press Inc:, repr., New York: The Truth Seeker Co.; 2nd edn, 1900, 1st edn 1893.

Garcia, J. and Maitland, S. (eds) (1983) *Walking on the Water: Women talk about spirituality*, London: Virago.

Gateley, Edwina V. M. M. (1986) *Psalms of a Laywoman*, Hertfordshire: Anthony Clarke.

Gaube, K. und Von Pechman, A. (1986) *Magie, Matriarchat und Marienkult*, Hamburg: Rowholt Taschenbuch.

Gerber, Uwe (1984) 'Feministische Theologie – Selbstverstädnis-Tendenzen-Fragen', *Theologische Literaturzeitung*, 109, Jhg No. 8, August, pp. 563–92.

Giles, Mary E. (ed.) (1982) *The Feminist Mystic and Other Essays on Women and Spirituality*, New York: Crossroad.

Gilligan, Carol (1977) 'In a Different Voice: Women's Conceptions of Self and Morality', *Harvard Educational Review*, 47/4, pp. 481–517.

—— (1982) *In a Different Voice: Psychological Theory and Women's Development*, Cambridge, Mass.: Harvard University Press.

Gimbutas, Marija (1982) *The Goddesses and Gods of Old Europe 6500–3500 BC: Myths and Cult Images*, Berkeley and Los Angeles: University of California Press.

—— (1991) *The Language of the Goddess*, San Francisco: HarperCollins paperback.

Goldberg, Steven (1977) *The Inevitability of Patriarchy*, London: Temple Smith.

Goldenberg, Naomi R. (1976) 'A Feminist Critique of Jung', *Signs*, 2/2, Winter, pp. 443–9.

—— (1977) 'Jung after Feminism', in R. M. Gross, (ed.), *Beyond Androcentrism: New Essays on Women and Religion*, American Academy of Religion, Missoula, Montana: Scholars Press, pp. 53–66.

—— (1979) *Changing of the Gods: Feminism and the End of Traditional Religion*, Boston: Beacon Press.

—— (1982) *The End of God. Important Directions for a Feminist Critique of Religion in the Works of Sigmund Freud and Carl Jung*, Ottawa: University of Ottawa Press.

—— (1990) *Returning Words to Flesh. Feminism, Psychoanalysis, and the Resurrection of the Body*, Boston: Beacon Press.

Goodison, Lucy (1990) *Moving Heaven and Earth. Sexuality, Spirituality and Social Change*, London: The Women's Press.

Gössmann, E., Moltmann-Wendel, E., Pissarek-Hudelist, H., Praetorius, I., Schottroff, L. and Schüngel-Straumann, H., (eds) (1991) *Wörterbuch der Feministischen Theologie*, Gütersloh: Verlagshaus Gerd Mohn.

Göttner-Abendroth, Heide (1980) *Die Göttin und ihr Heros, Die matriarchalischen Religionen in Mythos, Märchen und Dichtung*, München: Frauenoffensive.

—— (1984) *Die tanzende Göttin: Prinzipien einer matriachalischen Ästhetik*, München: Frauenoffensive.

Grant, Jacquelyn (1989) *White Women's Christ and Black Women's Jesus, Feminist Christology and Womanist Response*, Atlanta, Georgia: Scholars Press.

Green, Deirdre (1989) *Gold in the Crucible. Teresa of Avila and the Western Mystical Tradition*, Longmead, Shaftesbury, Dorset: Element Books.

Grey, Mary (1989) *Redeeming the Dream. Feminism, Redemption and Christian Tradition*, London: SPCK.

Griffin, Susan (1982) 'The Way of All Ideology', in Keohane, N. O. Rosaldo, M. Z. and Gelpi, B. C. (eds), *Feminist Theory: A Critique of Ideology*, Brighton: Harvester Press, pp. 273–92.

—— (1984) *Woman and Nature: The Roaring Inside Her*, London: The Women's Press, New York: Harper & Row, 1978.

Griffith, Elizabeth (1984) *In Her Own Right: The Life of Elizabeth Cady Stanton*, New York, Oxford: Oxford University Press.

Gross, Rita M. (1974) 'Methodological Remarks on the Study of Women in Religion: Review, Criticism and Redefinition', in J. Plaskow and J. A. Romero (eds), *Women and Religion*, American Academy of Religion, Missoula, Montana: Scholars Press: pp. 153–65.

—— (ed.) (1977a) *Beyond Androcentrism: New Essays on Women and Religion*, American Academy of Religion, Missoula, Montana: Scholars Press.

—— (1977b) 'Androcentrism and Androgyny in the Methodology of History of Religions', in R. M. Gross (ed.), *Beyond Androcentrism*, pp. 7–19.

—— (1978) 'Hindu Female Deities as a Resource for the Contemporary Rediscovery of the Goddess', *Journal of the American Academy of Religion*, XLVI/3, pp. 269–91.

—— (1979) 'Female God Language in a Jewish Context', in Carol P. Christ and Judith Plaskow (eds), *Womanspirit Rising*, New York: Harper & Row, pp. 167–73.

—— (1980) 'Menstruation and Childbirth as Ritual and Religious Experience among Native Australians', in N. Auer Falk and R. M. Gross (eds), *Unspoken Worlds: Women's Religious Lives in Non-Western Cultures*, San Francisco: Harper & Row, pp. 277–92.

—— (1981) 'Steps Toward Feminine Imagery of Deity in Jewish Theology', *Judaism: A Quarterly Journal*, 30/2, pp. 183–93.

—— (1983) 'Women Studies in Religion: The State of the Art, 1980', in P. Slater and D. Wiebe (eds), *Traditions in Contact and Change: Selected Proceedings of the XIVth Congress of the International Association for the History of Religions*, Waterloo/Ont: Wilfrid Laurier University Press, pp. 579–91.

—— (1984) 'The Feminine Principle in Tibetan Vajrayana Buddhism: Reflections of a Buddhist Feminist', *Journal of Transpersonal Psychology*, 16/2, pp. 179–92.

—— (1986) 'Buddhism and Feminism: Toward Their Mutual Transformation', *The Eastern Buddhist*, New Series, XIX/I, pp. 44–58.

—— (1987) 'I will never forget to visualise that Vajrayoginī is my body and mind', *Journal of Feminist Studies in Religion*, 3/1, pp. 77–89.

—— and Falk, N. A. (1980) 'Patterns in Women's Religious Lives', Introduction to Nancy A. Falk and Rita M. Gross (eds), *Unspoken Worlds: Women's Religious Lives in Non-Western Cultures*, San Francisco: Harper & Row, pp. xi–xviii.

Gupta, Bina (ed.) (1987) *Sexual Archetypes East and West*, New York: Paragon House.

Hackett, Rosalind I. J. (1985) 'Sacred Paradoxes: Women and Religious Plurality in Nigeria', in Y. Yazbeck Haddad and E. Banks Findly (eds), *Women, Religion and Social Change*, New York: State University of New York Press, pp. 247–71.

Haddad, Y. Y. and Findly E B. (eds) (1985) *Women, Religion and Social Change*, New York: State University of New York Press.

Hadewijch, (1981) *The Complete Works*, trans Mother Columba Hart, London: SPCK, New York: Paulist Press, 1980.

Hageman, Alice L. (ed.) (1974) in collaboration with the Women's Caucus of Harvard Divinity School, *Sexist Religion and Women in the Church: No More Silence!*, New York: Association Press.

Halkes, Catherina J. M. (1980a) *Gott hat nicht nur starke Söhne: Grundzüge einer feministischen Theologie*, Gütersloh: Gerd Mohn; trans of *Met Mirjam is het begonnen*, Barn: Ten Have, 1980.

—— (1980b) 'Feminist Theology: An Interim Assessment', *Concilium, 134 – Women in a Men's Church*, pp. 110–21.

—— (1981) 'The Themes of Protest in Feminist Theology against God the Father', *Concilium, 143 – God as Father*, pp. 103–10.

—— (1985) *Suchen, was verloren ging: Beiträge zur feministischen Theologie*, Gütersloh: Gütersloher Verlagshaus Gerd Mohn, trans of *Zoekend naar wat verloren ging*, Baarn: Ten Have, 1984.

—— (1986) *Feminisme en Spiritualiteit*, Barn: Ten Have.

—— (1991) *New Creation. Christian Feminism and the Renewal of the Earth*, London: SPCK.

Hampson, Daphne (1984) 'Women, Religion and Social Change', *The Modern Churchman*, XXVI/4, pp. 19–22.

—— (1986a) 'Women, Ordination and the Christian Church', in Diana L. Eck and Devaki Jain (eds), *Speaking of Faith: Cross-cultural Perspectives on Women, Religion and Social Change*, New Delhi: Kali for Women, pp. 129–38.

—— (1986b) 'Feminism: its nature and implications', *The Month*, March, pp. 69–9.

—— (1990) *Theology and Feminism*, Oxford: Basil Blackwell.

—— and Ruether, R. R. (1987) 'Is there a place for Feminists in a Christian Church?', *New Blackfriars*, January, pp. 7–24.

Harding, Esther M. (1982) *Woman's Mysteries, Ancient and Modern: A Psychological Interpretation of the Feminine Principle as Portrayed in Myth, Story and Dreams*, Introduction by C. G. Jung, 1955.

Harding, S. and Hintikka M. B. (eds) (1983) *Discovering Reality – Feminist Perspectives on Epistemology, Metaphysics, Methodology and Philosophy of Science*, Dordrecht, Boston, London: D. Reidel.

Harris, Maria (1991) *Dance of the Spirit. The Seven Steps of Women's Spirituality*, New York: Bantam Books.

Hawley, John Stratton and Wulff, Donna Maria (eds) (1982) *The Divine Consort: Rādhā and the Goddesses of India*, Berkeley Religious Studies Series, Berkeley: Graduate Theological Union.

Hayter, Mary (1987) *The New Eve in Christ: The Use and Abuse of the Bible in the Debate about Women in the Church*, London: SPCK.

Haywood, Carol Lois (1983) 'The Authority and Empowerment of Women among Spiritualist Groups', *Journal for the Scientific Study of Religion*, 22/2, pp. 157–66.

Hebblethwaite, Margaret (1984) *Motherhood and God*, London: Geoffrey Chapman.

Heeney, Brian (1986) 'The Beginnings of Church Feminism: Women and the Councils of the Church of England, 1897–1919', in G. Malmgreen (ed.), *Religion in the Lives of English Women, 1760–1930*, London: Croom Helm, pp. 260–84.

Heilbrunn, Carolyn G. (1973) *Toward a Recognition of Androgyny*, New York: Alfred A. Knopf. 1964.

Heiler, Friedrich (1977) *Die Frau in den Religionen der Menschheit*, Berlin, New York: Walter de Gruyter.

Heine, Susanne (1987) *Women and Early Christianity: Are the feminist scholars right?*, London: SCM.

—— (1989) *Matriarchs, Goddesses and Images of God. A Critique of Feminist Theology*, Minneapolis: Augsburg Fortress; also London: SCM, 1988, published as *Christianity and the Goddesses*.

Heinsohn, Gunnar and Steiger, Otto (1986) *Die Vernichtung der Weisen Frauen*, Hexenverfolgung-Menschenproduktion-Kinderwelten, Herbstein: März Verlag.

Herzel, Susannah (1981) *A Voice for Women: The women's department of the World Council of Churches*, Geneva: World Council of Churches.

Heschel, Susannah (1986) 'Current Issues in Jewish Feminist Theology', *Christian Jewish Relations*, 19/2, pp. 23–32, London: Institute of Jewish Affairs.

Heyward, Carter (1979) 'Ruether and Daly: Theologians Speaking and Sparking, Building and Burning', *Christianity and Crisis*, 39/5, pp. 66–72.

—— (1989) *Touching our Strength. The Erotic as Power and the Love of God*, San Francisco: Harper.

Holden, Pat (ed.) (1983) *Women's Religious Experience: Cross-Cultural Perspectives*, London: Croom Helm.

hooks, bell (1983) *Ain't I a Woman: Black Women and Feminism*, London: Pluto Press; Boston: South End Press, 1981.

Hoover, Theressa (1974) 'Black Women and the Churches: Triple Jeopardy', in A. L. Hageman (ed.), *Sexist Religion and Women in the Church: No More Silence!*, New York: Association Press, pp. 63–76; also in G. S. Wilmore and J. H. Cone (eds), *Black Theology*, pp. 377–88.

Horner, I. B. (1975) *Women under Primitive Buddhism: Laywomen and Almswomen*, Delhi: Motilal Banarsidass repr.; 1st edn, 1930.

Horowitz, Maryanne Cline (1976) 'Aristotle and Woman', *Journal of the History of Biology*, 9/2, pp. 183–213.

Hopko, Thomas (ed.) (1983) *Women and the Priesthood*, New York: St Vladimir's Seminary Press.

Howard, Christian (1984) *General Synod – The Ordination of Women to the Priesthood: Further Report*, London: Church Information Office Publishing, Church House.

Hubbard, Barbara Marx (1983) *The Evolutionary Journey. A Personal Guide to a Positive Future*, Wellingborough: Turnstone Press.

Hunt, Mary E. (1991) *Fierce Tenderness. A Feminist Theology of Friendship*, New York: Crossroad.

Hurcombe, Linda (ed.) (1987) *Sex and God – Some Varieties of Women's Religious Experience*, London: Routledge & Kegan Paul.

Iglehart, Hallie (1983) *Womanspirit. A Guide to Women's Wisdom*, New York: Harper & Row.

Irvin, Dorothy (1980) 'The Ministry of Women in the Early Church: The Archaeological Evidence', *Duke Divinity School Review*, 45, pp. 76–96.

ISIS Women's International Bulletin (1978), *Women in Southern Africa*, Bulletin 9, Geneva: Women's International Resource Centre.

—— (1983) *Women for Peace*, Bulletin 26, Geneva: Women's International Resource Centre.

Jacobson, Doranne and Wadley, Susan S. (eds) (1977) *Women in India. Two Perspectives*, Delhi: Manohar.

Jannberg, Judith (1983) *Ich bin eine Hexe; Erfahrungen und Gedanken,* aufgeschrieben von Gisela Meussling, Bonn: Verlag Gisela Meussling Edition die Maus.

Jantzen, Grace M. (1987) *Julian of Norwich. Mystic and Theologian*, London: SPCK; also New York: Paulist Press, 1988.

Jayakar, Pupul (1990) *The Earth Mother, Legends, Ritual Arts and Goddesses in India*, San Francisco: Harper & Row.

Johnson, Patricia Altenberd and Kalven, Janet (eds) (1988) *With Both Eyes. Seeing Beyond Gender*, New York: The Pilgrim Press.

Jones, Lynne, (ed.) (1983) *Keeping the Peace*, London: The Women's Press.

Jones, Cheslyn, Wainwright, Geoffrey and Yarnold, Edward, S. J. (eds) (1986) *The Study of Spirituality*, London: SPCK.

Journal of Feminist Studies in Religion (1991), 7/2, 'Special Section on Feminist Anti-Judaism', pp. 95–133.

Julian of Norwich (1978) *Showings*, trans Edmund Colledge and James Walsh, *The Classics of Western Spirituality*, London: SPCK, New York: Paulist Press.

Jung, Carl Gustav (1982) *Aspects of the Feminine*, trans R. F. C. Hull, Bollingen Series, XX, Princeton: Princeton University Press.

Kalven, Janet and Buckley, Mary I. (eds) (1984), *Women's Spirit Bonding*, New York: The Pilgrim Press.

Kaplan, Alexandra G. and Bean, Joan P. (eds) (1976) *Beyond Sex-Role Stereotypes: Readings Toward a Psychology of Androgyny*, Boston and Toronto: Little, Brown & Co.

Katoppo, Marianne (1979) *Compassionate and Free. An Asian Woman's Theology*, Geneva: World Council of Churches, repr., 1981.

Keller, Catherine (1986) *From a Broken Web: Separation, Sexism and Self*, Boston: Beacon Press.

—— (1987) 'Walls, Women and Intimations of Interconnection', in U. King (ed.), *Women in the World's Religions, Past and Present*, New York: Paragon House, pp. 232–50.

Kennally, Christine (1986) 'The Debate about the Ordination of Women in the Roman Catholic Church since Vatican II with special reference to Britain', University of Leeds, MA thesis.

Keohane, Nanerl O., Rosaldo, Michelle Z. and Gelpi, Barbara C. (eds) (1982) *Feminist Theory: A Critique of Ideology*, Brighton: Harvester Press.

King, Ursula (1976) 'Women and Religion: Prospects for Liberation', *The Way*, 16, pp. 3–14.

—— (1977) 'The Role of Woman in Today's Society', Cardinal Bea Memorial Lecture, *The Month*, August, pp. 268–72.

—— (1980) 'Women and Religion: The Status and Image of Women in Some Major Religious Traditions', in A. Souza (ed.), *Women in Contemporary India and South Asia*, Delhi: Manohar, pp. 181–97.

—— (1981a) 'Towards an Integral Spirituality. Sexual Differentiation and the Christian Doctrine of Man', *Vidyajyoti*, Delhi, pp. 358–71.

—— (1981b) 'Mysticism and Feminism or Why Look at Women Mystics?', in M. A. Rees (ed.), *Teresa de Jesús and her World*, Leeds: Trinity and All Saints' College, pp. 7–17.

—— (1982) 'Current Perspectives in the Study of Mysticism', *Studies in Mystical Literature*, 2/1, pp. 1–17.

—— (1984a) *Voices of Protest, Voices of Promise: Exploring Spirituality for a New Age*, The Hibbert Lecture, London: The Hibbert Trust.

—— (1984b) 'The Effects of Social Change on Religious Self-Understanding: Women Ascetics in Modern Hinduism', in K. Ballhatchet and D. Taylor (eds), *Changing South Asia: Religion and Society*, Hong Kong: Asian Research Service, pp. 69–83.

—— (1985a) 'Women in Dialogue: A New Vision of Ecumenism', Cardinal Heenan Memorial Lecture, *The Heythrop Journal*, XXVI/2, pp. 125–42.

—— (1985b) 'Spirituality in Secular Society: Recovering a Lost Dimension', *British Journal of Religious Education*, Special Issue on 'Spirituality across the Curriculum', pp. 135–9.

—— (1986a) 'Female Identity and the History of Religions', in Victor C. Hayes (ed.), *Identity Issues and World Religions. Selected Proceedings of the Fifteenth Congress of the International Association for the History of Religions*, Bedford Park: Australian Association for the Study of Religions, pp. 83–92.

—— (1986b) 'Feminismus', *Evangelisches Kirchenlexikon*, I, Göttingen: Vandehoeck & Ruprecht, pp. 1280–4.

—— (ed.) (1987a) *Women in the World's Religions, Past and Present*, New York: Paragon House.

—— (1987b) 'Goddesses, Witches, Androgyny and Beyond? Feminism and the Transformation of Religious Consciousness', in U. King (ed.), *Women in the World's Religions, Past and Present*, New York: Paragon House, pp. 201–18.

—— (1987c) 'World Religions, Women and Education', *Comparative Education*, 23/1, pp. 35–49.

—— (1989a) *The Spirit of One Earth. Reflections on Teilhard de Chardin and Global Spirituality*, New York: Paragon House.

—— (1989b) 'The Divine as Mother', *Concilium*, 206: *Motherhood: Experience, Institution, Theology*, pp. 128–37.

—— (1990a) 'Religion and Gender', in U. King (ed.), *Turning Points in Religious Studies*, Edinburgh: T & T Clark, pp. 275–86.

—— (1990b) 'Women Scholars and the *Encyclopedia of Religion*', *Method and Theory in the Study of Religion*, 2/1, pp. 91–7.

—— (ed.) (1991a) *Liberating Women. New Theological Directions*, Conference Reader of the Fourth Conference of the European Society of Women in Theological Research, Bristol: Department of Theology and Religious Studies.

—— (1991b) 'Frauen in den Weltreligionen: Hinduismus', in E. Gössman *et al.* (eds), *Wörterbuch der feministischen Theologie*, Gütersloh: Verlaghaus Gerd Mohn.

—— (1991c) 'Der feministische Aufbruch und die Ökumene', *Orientierung*, 30 June, pp. 139–43.

—— (1992) 'Women and Christianity – A Horizon of Hope', in Teresa Elwes (ed.), *Women's Voices*, London: HarperCollins, pp. 149–60.

King, Ynestra (1984a) 'Eco-feminism – Where the Spiritual and the Political come together', *Women for Life on Earth*, Winter, pp. 4–7.

—— (1984b) 'Making the World Live: Feminism and the Domination of Nature', in J. Kalven and M. I. Buckley (eds), *Women's Spirit Bonding*, New York: The Pilgrim Press, pp. 56–64.

Kinsley, David (1986) *Hindu Goddesses. Visions of the Divine Feminine in the Hindu Religious Tradition*, Berkeley: University of California Press.

Knott, Kim (1987) 'Men and Women, or Devotees? Krishna Consciousness and the Role of Women', in U. King (ed.), *Women in the World's Religions, Past and Present*, New York: Paragon House, pp. 111–27.

Kolbenschlag, Madonna (1979) *Kiss Sleeping Beauty Good-bye. Breaking the Spell of Feminine Myths and Models*, New York: Doubleday.

Koltun, Elizabeth (ed.) (1978) *The Jewish Woman*, New York: Schocken Books, 1976.

Komatsu, Kayoko (1986) 'An Empirical Study of Matriarchy Groups in Contemporary Britain and their Relationship to New Religious Movements', University of Leeds, MA thesis.

Koppers, Christiane (1986) 'Die dreimal Geborene . . . Dimensionen "weiblicher" Spiritualität', in Ch. Schaumberger and M. Maassen (eds), *Handbuch feministischer Theologie*, Münster: Morgana Frauenbuchverlag.

Kramrisch, S. (1975) 'The Indian Goddess', *History of Religions*, 14/4, pp. 235–65.

Krattiger, Ursa (1984) *Die perlmutterne Mönchin. Reise in eine weibliche Spiritualität*, Zürich: Kreuz Verlag.

Lampe, Geoffrey W. H. (1974) *The Church's Tradition and the Question of the Ordination of Women to the Historic Ministry*, Midhurst, Sussex: Anglican Group for the Ordination of Women to the Historic Ministry of the Church, 2nd edn; 1st edn 1967.

Lampe, Philip E. (1981) 'Androgyny and Religiosity', *International Journal of Women's Studies*, 4/1, pp. 27–34.

Larner, Christine (1983) *Enemies of God. The Witch-hunt in Scotland*, Oxford: Basil Blackwell.

—— (1984) *Witchcraft and Religion. The Politics and Popular Belief*, Oxford: Basil Blackwell.

Laut, Renate (1983) *Weibliche Züge im Gottesbild Isrealitisch-Jüdischer Religiosität*, Materials for the Study of the History of Religions, 9, Köln: Brill.

Lerner, Gerda (1986) *The Creation of Patriarchy*, New York, Oxford: Oxford University Press.

Lerner, Robert E. (1972) *The Heresy of the Free Spirit in the Later Middle Ages*, Berkeley, Los Angeles, London: University of California Press.

Leslie, Julia (1983) 'Essence and Existence: Women and Religion in Ancient Indian Texts', in P. Holden (ed.), *Women's Religious Experience*, London: Croom Helm, pp. 89–112.

—— (1989) *The Perfect Wife: The Status and Role of the Orthodox Hindu Woman as described in the Strīharmapaddhati of Tryambakayajvan*, Delhi: Oxford University Press, South Asian Monograph Series.

—— (ed.) (1991) *Roles and Rituals for Hindu Women*, London: Pinter Publishers.

Lewis, Alan F. (ed.) (1984) *The Motherhood of God. A Report by a Study Group appointed by the Woman's Guild and the Panel on Doctrine on the Invitation of the General Assembly of the Church of Scotland*, Edinburgh: The Saint Andrew Press.

Li, Florence Tim Oi with Harrison, Ted, (1985) *Much Beloved Daughter, Florence Tim Oi Li*, London: Darton, Longman & Todd.

Lipman, Beata (1984) *We Make Freedom. Women in South Africa*, London: Pandora Press.

Loades, Ann (ed.) (1990) *Feminist Theology, A Reader*, London: SPCK and Louisville, Kentucky: Westminster/John Knox Press.

Long, Asphodel P. (1981) Review of M. Sjöö and B. Mor, *The Ancient Religion of the Great Cosmic Mother of All, Women Speaking*, July–December, pp. 17–18.

—— (1982) 'Feminism and Spirituality: A Review of Recent Publications 1975–1981', *Women's Studies International Forum*, 5/1, pp. 103–08.

—— (1992) *In a Chariot Drawn by Lions. The Search for the Female in Deity*, London: The Women's Press.

Lovelock, J. E. (1979) *Gaia. A New Look at Life on Earth*, Oxford: Oxford University Press.

Luke, Helen (1981) *Woman, Earth and Spirit*, New York: Crossroad.

Lüthi, Karl (1978) *Gottes Neue Eva. Wandlungen des Weiblichen*, Stuttgart: Kreuz Verlag.

MacDonald, Sharon, Holden, Pat and Ardener, Shirley (eds) (1987) *Images of Women in Peace and War, Cross-Cultural and Historical Perspectives*, London: Macmillan.

Maitland, Sara (1983) *A Map of the New Country. Women and Christianity*, London: Routledge & Kegan Paul.

Malmgreen, Gail (ed.) (1986) *Religion in the Lives of English Women, 1760–1930*, London and Sydney: Croom Helm.

Mbon, Friday M. (1987) 'Women in African Traditional Religions', in U. King (ed.), *Women in the World's Religions, Past and Present*, New York: Paragon House, pp. 7–23.

McAllister, Pam (ed.) (1982) *Reweaving the Web of Life. Feminism and Non-violence*, Philadelphia: New Society Publishers.

McFague, Sallie (1983) *Metaphorical Theology. Models of God in Religious Language*, London: SCM.

—— (1987) *Models of God. Theology for an Ecological, Nuclear Age*, London: SCM.

McLaughlin, Eleanor (1974) 'Equality of Souls, Inequality of Sexes: Woman in Medieval Theology', in R. Radford Ruether (ed.), *Religion and Sexism: Images of Woman in the Jewish and Christian Traditions*, New York: Simon & Schuster, pp. 213–66.

—— (1979) 'Women, Power and the Pursuit of Holiness', in R. Ruether and E. McLaughlin (eds), *Women of Spirit. Female Leadership in the Jewish and Christian Traditions*, New York: Simon & Schuster, pp. 100–30.

McMillan, Carol (1982) *Women, Reason and Nature, Some Philosophical Problems with Feminism*, Oxford: Basil Blackwell.

Meeks, Wayne A. (1974) 'The Image of the Androgyne: Some Uses of a Symbol in Earliest Christianity', *History of Religions*, 13/3, pp. 165–208.

Merchant, Carolyn (1982) *The Death of Nature. Women, Ecology and the Scientific Revolution*, London: Wildwood House; New York: Harper & Row, 1980.

Michalowski, Helen (1976) 'Connecting Feminism and Non-Violence', in *Womanspirit*, 2/8, pp. 42–3.

Midgley, Mary and Hughes, Judith (1983) *Women's Choices. Philosophical Problems Facing Feminism*, London: Weidenfeld & Nicolson.

Miles, Margaret M. (1989) *Carnal Knowing. Female Nakedness and Religious Meaning in the Christian West*, Boston: Beacon Press.

Millett, Kate (1971) *Sexual Politics*, London: Rupert Hart-Davis, 1st edn, 1969.

Mitchell, Juliet (1986) *Psychoanalysis and Feminism. A radical reassessment of Freudian psychoanalysis*, Harmondsworth: Penguin Books, repr.; 1st edn, 1974.

—— and Oakley, Ann (eds) (1986) *What is Feminism?*, Oxford: Basil Blackwell.

Mollenkott, Virginia Ramey (1983) *The Divine Feminine. The Biblical Imagery of God as Female*, New York: Crossroad.

—— (ed.) (1988) *Women of Faith in Dialogue*, New York: Crossroad.

—— (1992) *Sensuous Spirituality. Out from Fundamentalism*, New York: Crossroad.

Moloney, Francis J. (1985) *Woman. First among the Faithful. A New Testament Study*, London: Darton, Longman & Todd; Blackburn, Victoria: Dove Communications, 1984.

Moltmann-Wendel, Elisabeth (1982) *The Women around Jesus*, London: SCM Press; New York: Crossroad.

—— (1986) *A Land Flowing with Milk and Honey. Perspectives on Feminist Theology*, London: SCM Press.

Moore, Robert L. and Meckel, Daniel J. (eds) (1990) *Jung and Christianity in Dialogue. Faith, Feminism and Hermeneutics*. New York: Paulist Press.

Moorehouse, Geoffrey (1969) *Against All Reason*, London: Weidenfeld & Nicolson.

Moraga, Cherríe and Anzaldúa, Gloria (1981) *This Bridge Called My Back. Writings by Radical Women of Color*, New York: Kitchen Table, Women of Color Press, 1983.

Morgan, Robin (ed.) (1970) *Sisterhood is Powerful. An Anthology of Writings from the Women's Liberation Movement*, New York: Vintage Books.

—— (1982) *The Anatomy of Freedom. Feminism, Physics and Global Politics*, Oxford: Martin Robertson, New York: Anchor Press; Doubleday.

Morley, Janet (1984) '"The Faltering Words of Men": Exclusive Language in the Liturgy', in M. Furlong (ed.), *Feminine in the Church*, London: SPCK, pp. 56–70.

—— (1988) *All Desires Known*, London: Movement for the Ordination of Women.

—— and Ward, Hannah (eds) (1986) *Celebrating Women*, London: Women in Theology and Movement for the Ordination of Women.

Morris, Joan (1974) *Against Nature and God. The History of Women with Clerical Ordination and the Jurisdiction of Bishops*, London and Oxford: Mowbrays, New York: Macmillan, 1973 (*The Lady was a Bishop*).

Mühlmann, Wilhelm E. (1984) *Die Metamorphose der Frau. Weiblicher Schamanismus und Dichtung*, Berlin: Dietrich Reimer.

Mulack, Christa (1983) *Die Weiblichkeit Gottes. Matriarchalische Voraussetzungen des Gottesbildes*, Frankfurt: Kreuz Verlag.

Muller, Robert (1982) *New Genesis – Shaping a Global Spirituality*, New York: Doubleday.

—— (1991) *The Birth of a Global Civilization. With proposals for a New Political System for Planet Earth*, Anacortes, WA: World Happiness and Cooperation.

Murray, Margaret A. (1929) 'Witchcraft', *Encyclopaedia Britannica*, 14th edn, London, New York: William Benton.

—— (1970) *God of the Witches*, New York: Oxford University Press; 1st edn 1931.

—— (1971) *The Witch-Cult in Western Europe*, Oxford: Oxford University Press: Clarendon Press; 1st edn 1921.

Murray, Pauli (1978) 'Black Theology and Feminist Theology: A Comparative View', *Anglican Theological Review*, 60/1, pp. 3–24; also in G. S. Wilmore and J. H. Cone (eds), *Black Theology* (1979), pp. 398–417.

Neuberger, Julia (1987) 'Needing the Ministry of Women', *The Times*, 28 March.

Neumann, Erich (1955) *The Great Mother: An Analysis of the Archetype*, New York: Pantheon Books (Bollingen series, 47); 2nd edn, 1963; repr., 1991.

Newman, Barbara (1987) *Sister of Wisdom. St Hildegard's Theology of the Feminine*, Berkeley and Los Angeles: University of California Press.

Nornengast, Urda (1970) *Der Androgyne Mensch*, Bellnhausen, Hessen: Verlag Hinder and Deelman.

Nunnally-Cox, Janice (1981) *Foremothers. Women of the Bible*, New York: Seabury Press.

Oakley, Ann (1982) *Subject Women*, London: Fontana Paperbacks.

Ochs, Carol (1977) *Behind the Sex of God. Towards a New Consciousness – Transcending Matriarchy and Patriarchy*, Boston: Beacon Press.

—— (1983), *Women and Spirituality*, Totowa, NJ: Rowman & Allanheld.

—— (1986), *An Ascent to Joy. Transforming Deadness of Spirit*, Notre Dame, Indiana: University of Notre Dame Press.

Ochshorn, Judith (1981) *The Female Experience and the Nature of the Divine*, Bloomington: Indiana University Press.

Oddie, William (1984) *What Will Happen to God? Feminism and the Recon-struction of Christian Belief*, London: SPCK.

O'Faolain, Julia and Martines, Lauro (1979) *Not in God's Image. Women in History*, London: Virago, 1st edn, 1973.

O'Flaherty, Wendy O. and Eliade, Mircea (1987) 'Androgynes', *The Encyclope-dia of Religion*, 1, pp. 276–81, New York: Macmillan, London: Collier Macmillan.

Ohler, Annemarie (1987) *Frauengestalten der Bibel*, Würzburg: Echter Verlag.

—— (1992) *Mutterschaft in der Bibel*, Würzburg: Echter Verlag.

Okano, Haruko (1976) *Die Stellung der Frau im Shinto. Eine religions-phänomenologische und -soziologische Untersuchung*, Wiesbaden: Otto Harrassowitz.

Oldfield, Sybil (1989) *Women against the Iron Fist. Alternatives to Militarism 1900–1989*, Oxford: Blackwell.

Olson, Carl (ed.) (1983), *The Book of the Goddess Past and Present. An Intro-duction to Her Religion*, New York: Crossroad.

O'Neill, Maura (1990) *Women Speaking, Women Listening. Women in Interreligious Dialogue*, Maryknoll, New York: Orbis Books.

Open University (1983) Course U221, *The Changing Experience of Women* (16 units), Milton Keynes: The Open University Press.

Owen, Alex (1989) *The Darkened Room. Women, Power and Spiritualism in Late Victorian England*, London: Virago.

Pagels, Elaine (1979) *The Gnostic Gospels*, London: Weidenfeld & Nicolson.

—— (1988) *Adam, Eve and the Serpent*, New York: Random House.

Pahnke, Donate (1991) *Ethik and Geschlecht. Menschenbild und Religion in Patriarchat und Feminismus*, Marburg: Diagonal Verlag.

Papa, Mary Bader (1981) *Christian Feminism. Completing the Subtotal Women*, Chicago: Fides/Claretian.

Parrinder, Geoffrey (1980) *Sex in the World's Religions*, London: Sheldon Press.

Parker, Roszsika and Pollock, Griselda (1981) *Old Mistresses, Women, Art and Ideology*, London: Routledge & Kegan Paul.

Parvey, Constance F. (ed.) (1980), *Ordination of Women in Ecumenical Per-spective. Workbook for the Church's Future*, Faith and Order Paper 105, Geneva: World Council of Churches.

—— (1983) *The Community of Women and Men in the Church. The Sheffield Report*, Geneva: World Council of Churches. A Report of the WCC's Confer-ence, Sheffield, England, 1981.

Paul, Diane Y. (1979) *Women in Buddhism. Images of the Feminine in Mahayana Tradition*, Berkeley: Asian Humanities Press.

Pepper, Mary and Hebblethwaite, Margaret (1984) 'Finding God in Mother-hood: Release or Trap?', *New Blackfriars*, September, pp. 372–84.

Perera, Sylvia Binton (1981) *Descent to the Goddess. A Way of Initiation for Women*, Studies in Jungian Psychology by Jungian Analysts, Toronto: Inner City Books.

Pernoud, Régine (1980) *La Femme au temps des Cathédrales*, Paris: Stock.

Pierson, Ruth Roach (ed.) (1987) *Women and Peace, Theoretical, Historical and Practical Perspectives*, London: Croom Helm.

Pirani, Alix (ed.) (1991) *The Absent Mother. Restoring the Goddess to Judaism and Christianity*, London: Mandala, HarperCollins.

Plant, Judith (ed.) (1989) *Healing the Wounds: The Promise of Ecofeminism*, Philadelphia: New Society.

Plaskow, Judith (1977) 'The Feminist transformation of theology', in Rita M. Gross (ed.), *Beyond Androcentrism: New Essays on Women and Religion*, Missoula, Montana: Scholars Press, pp. 23–31.

—— (1979) 'The Coming of Lilith: Toward a Feminist Theology', in Carol P. Christ and Judith Plaskow (eds), *Womanspirit Rising*, New York: Harper & Row: pp. 198–209.

—— (1980) *Sex, Sin and Grace. Women's Experience and the Theologies of Reinhold Niebuhr and Paul Tillich*, Washington: University Press of America.

—— (1990) *Standing Again at Sinai. Judaism from a Feminist Perspective*, San Francisco: Harper & Row.

—— and Christ, Carol P. (eds) (1989) *Weaving the Visions. New Patterns in Feminist Spirituality*, San Francisco: Harper & Row.

—— Arnold, Joan and Romero, J. A. (eds) (1974) *Women and Religion*, American Academy of Religion: Aids for the Study of Religion, Missoula, Montana: Scholars Press.

Pobee, John S. and von Wartenburg-Potter, Bärbel (eds) (1986) *New Eyes for Reading. Biblical and Theological Reflections by Women from the Third World*, Geneva: World Council of Churches.

Pomeroy, Sarah B. (1976) *Goddesses, Whores, Wives and Slaves. Women in Classical Antiquity*, London: Robert Hale.

—— (1984) 'Selected Bibliography on Women in Classical Antiquity', Part I to 1973, Part II 1973–1981, in J. Peradotto and J. P. Sullivan (eds), *Women in the Ancient World. The Arethusa Papers*, Albany: State University of New York Press, pp. 315–72.

Portefaix, Lilian (1988) *Sisters Rejoice. Paul's Letter to the Philippians and Luke–Acts as Received by First-Century Philippian Women*, Stockholm: Almqvist & Wiksell International.

Prelinger, Catherine M. (1986) 'The Female Diaconate in the Anglican Church: What Kind of Ministry for Women?', in J. Malmgreen (ed.), *Religion in the Lives of English Women, 1760–1930*, London: Croom Helm, pp. 161–92.

Preston James J. (ed.) (1982) *Mother Worship: Theme and Variations*, Chapel Hill: The University of North Carolina Press.

—— (1987) 'Goddess Worship: Theoretical Perspectives', *The Encyclopedia of Religion*, 6, pp. 53–59, New York: Macmillan, London: Collier Macmillan.

Primavesi, Anne (1991) *From Apocalypse to Genesis. Ecology, Feminism and Christianity*, Tunbridge Wells, Kent: Burns & Oates.

Principe, Walter (1983) 'Toward defining Spirituality', *Studies in Religion/Sciences Religieuses*, 12/2, pp. 127–41.

Pro Mundi Vita Bulletin (1980) 'The Situation of Women in the Catholic Church – Developments since International Women's Year', by Marc Luyckx, Bulletin 83, Brussels.

Pruett, Kyle D. (1987) *The Nurturing Father*, New York: Warner Books.

Quebedeaux, Richard (1987) '"We're on our Way, Lord!": The Rise of "Evangelical Feminism" in Modern American Christianity', in U. King (ed.), *Women in the World's Religions, Past and Present*, New York: Paragon House, pp. 129–44.

Rabuzzi, Kathryn A. (1982) *The Sacred and the Feminine: Toward a Theology of Housework*, New York: Seabury Press.

Ramakrishna Vedanta Centre (1955) *Women Saints East and West*, Hollywood, California: Vedanta Press.

Raming, Ida (1976) *The Exclusion of Women from the Priesthood: Divine Law or Sex Discrimination*, Metuchen, New Jersey: Scarecrow Press.

Ratte, Lou (1985) 'Goddesses, Mothers, and Heroines: Hindu Women and the Feminine in the Early Nationalist Movement', in Y. Y. Haddad and E. Banks Findly (eds), *Women, Religion, and Social Change*, New York: State University of New York Press, pp. 351–76.

Rebecca, Meda, Hefner, Robert and Oleshansky, Barbara (1976), 'A Model of Sex-Role Transcendence', in A. G. Kaplan and J. E. Bean (eds), *Beyond Sex-Role Stereotypes: Readings Towards a Psychology of Androgyny*, Boston, Toronto: Little, Brown & Co, pp. 90–97.

Rebera, Ranjini (ed.) (1990) *We cannot dream alone. A story of women in development*, Geneva: World Council of Churches.

Rendall, Jane (1985) *The Origins of Modern Feminism: Women in Britain, France and the United States, 1780–1860*, London: Macmillan.

Ricci, Carla (1991) *Maria di Magdala e le Molte Altre. Donne sul cammino di Gesu*, Naples: M. D'Auria.

Richards, Janet Radcliffe (1982) *The Sceptical Feminist. A Philosophical Enquiry*, Harmondsworth: Penguin Books.

Richardson, Marilyn (1980) *Black Women and Religion, A Bibliography*, Boston: G. K. Hall.

Robins, Wendy S. (1986) *Through the Eyes of a Woman. Bible studies on the experience of women*, World YWCA.

Ross, Isabel (1984), *Margaret Fell. Mother of Quakerism*, York: William Sessions Book Trust; The Ebor Press (1st edn 1949, Longman, Green & Co.).

Ruether, Rosemary Radford (1972) *Liberation Theology: Human Hope Confronts Christian History and American Power*, New York: Paulist Press.

—— (1974a), *Faith and Fratricide. The Theological Roots of Anti-Semitism*, New York: Seabury.

—— (ed.) (1974b), *Religion and Sexism. Images of Woman in the Jewish and Christian Traditions*, New York: Simon & Schuster.

—— (1975) *New Woman, New Earth. Sexist Ideologies and Human Liberation*, New York: Seabury Press.

—— (1979a) *Mary – the Feminine Face of the Church*, London: SCM Press; Philadelphia: Westminster 1977.

—— (1979b) 'Motherearth and the Megamachine: A Theology of Liberation in a Feminine, Somatic and Ecological Perspective', in Carol P. Christ and J. Plaskow, (eds), *Womanspirit Rising*, New York: Harper & Row, pp. 44–52.

—— (1979c) 'Crisis in Sex and Race: Black Theology *vs.* Feminist Theology', in G. H. Anderson and T. F. Stransky (eds), *Mission Trends, No. 4: Liberation Theologies in North America and Europe*, Grand Rapids: W. B. Eerdmans, pp. 175–87.

—— (1980a), 'A Religion for Women', *Womanspirit*, 6/24, pp. 22–25; also *Christianity and Crisis*, 10 December 1979.

—— (1980b) 'The Preacher and the Priest: Two Typologies of Ministry and the Ordination of Women', in C. F. Parvey (ed.), *Ordination of Women in Ecumenical Perspective*, Geneva: World Council of Churches, pp. 67–73.

—— (1981a) 'The Female Nature of God: A Problem in Contemporary Religious Life', *Concilium, 143 – God as Father?*, pp. 61–6.

—— (1981b) 'The feminist critique in religious studies', *Soundings*, 64, pp. 388–402.

—— (1982) 'Goddesses and Witches', in *One More Eve – Christian Action Journal*, Spring, pp. 6–9.

—— (1983) *Sexism and God-Talk. Towards a Feminist Theology*, London: SCM Press.

—— (1984) 'Are Women Today's Prophets?', address given for the Catholic Women's Network, London, 23 August 1984.

—— (1985) *Womanguides. Readings Toward a Feminist Theology*, Boston: Beacon Press.

—— (1986a) *Women-Church. The Theology and Practice of Feminist Liturgical Communities*, New York: Harper & Row.

—— (1986b) 'Emerging Feminist Liturgical Communities', *Concilium, 186 – Popular Religion*, pp. 52–9.

—— (1987) 'Androcentrism', in *The Encyclopedia of Religion*, 1, pp. 272–6, New York: Macmillan, London: Collier Macmillan.

—— (1989) 'Toward an Ecological–Feminist Theology of Nature', in J. Plant (ed.), *Healing the Wounds. The Promise of Ecofeminism*, Philadelphia: New Society, pp. 145–50.

—— (1992) *Gaia and God. An Ecofeminist Theology of Earth Healing*, San Francisco: HarperSanFrancisco.

—— and McLaughlin, Eleanor A. (eds) (1979) *Women of Spirit: Female Leadership in the Jewish and Christian Traditions*, New York: Simon & Schuster.

Rudd, Inger Marie (1981) *Women's Status in the Muslim World. A Bibliographical Survey*, Materials for the Study of the History of Religions, 6, Köln: Brill.

Russell, Letty M. (1974), *Human Liberation in a Feminist Perspective – A Theology*, Philadelphia: The Westminster Press.

—— (1979) 'Women and Freedom', in G. H. Anderson and Th. F. Stransky (eds), *Mission Trends, No. 4: Liberation Theologies in North America and Europe*, Grand Rapids: W. B. Eerdmans, pp. 234–43.

—— (ed.) (1985) *Feminist Interpretation of the Bible*, Oxford: Basil Blackwell.

—— *et al.* (eds) (1988) *Inheriting Our Mother's Gardens. Feminist Theology in Third World Perspective*, Louisville: The Westminster Press.

St Hilda Community (1991) *Women Included. A Book of Services and Prayers*, London: SPCK.

Saiving, Valerie (1979) 'The Human Situation: A Feminine View', in Carol P. Christ and Judith Plaskow (eds), *Womanspirit Rising*, San Francisco: Harper & Row, pp. 25–42, first published in *The Journal of Religion*, April 1960.

Sayers, Janet (1982) *Biological Politics. Feminist and Anti-Feminist Perspectives*, London and New York: Tavistock.

Schaumberger, Christine and Maassen, Monika (eds) (1986) *Handbuch der feministischen Theologie*, Münster: Morgan Frauenbuchverlag.

Schimmel, Annemarie (1975) *Mystical Dimensions of Islam*, Chapel Hill: University of North Carolina Press.

—— (1982), 'Women in Mystical Islam', *Women's Studies International Forum*, 5/2, pp. 145–51.

Schreiner, Olive (1895) *Dreams*, London: T. Fisher Unwin, 1890.

—— (1983) 'Three Dreams in a Desert', in *Dreams*, pp. 67–85; reprinted in Charlotte H. Bruner (ed.), *Unwinding Threads: Writing by Women in Africa*, London: Heinemann, pp. 102–8.

Schüssler Fiorenza, Elisabeth (1979a) 'Feminist Spirituality, Christian Identity, and Catholic Vision', in Carol P. Christ and Judith Plaskow (eds), *Womenspirit Rising*, San Francisco: Harper & Row: 1979, pp. 136–48.

—— (1979b) 'Feminist theology as a critical theology of liberation', in G. H. Anderson and T. F. Stransky (eds), *Mission Trends, No. 4: Liberation Theologies in North America and Europe*, Grand Rapids: W. B. Eerdmans, pp. 188–216.

—— (1979c) '"You are not to be called Father": Early Christian History in a Feminist Perspective', *Cross Currents*, 29/3, pp. 301–23.

—— (1983) *In Memory of Her: A Feminist Theological Reconstruction of Christian Origins*, London: SCM.

—— (1984) *Bread not Stone: The challenge of feminist biblical interpretation*, Boston: Beacon Press.

—— (1985) 'Breaking the Silence – Becoming Visible', *Concilium, 182 – Women, Invisible in Church and Theology*, pp. 3–16.

Scottish Churches Council (1977) *Working Party Report on 'Spirituality'*, Dunblane: Scottish Churches House.

Setta, Susan M. (1984) '*In Memory of Her. A Symposium on an Important Book*', *Anima*, 10/2, pp. 95–112.

Sewell, Marilyn (ed.) (1991) *Cries of the Spirit. A Celebration of Women's Spirituality*, Boston: Beacon Press.

Shântâ, N. (1985) *La Voie Jaina. Historie, spritualité, vie des ascètes pèlerines de l'Inde*, Paris: OEIL – Les deux rives: collection dirigée par M. M. Davy.

Sharma, Arvind (ed.) (1987) *Women in World Religions*, Albany: State University of New York Press.

Shiva, Vandana (1988) *Staying Alive. Women, Ecology and Development in India*, London: Zed Books.

Siegele-Wenschkewitz, Leonore and Schottroff, Luise (1986) 'Feministische Theologie', in *Evangelisches Kirchenlexikon* (EKL), Göttingen Bd I: Vandenhoeck & Ruprecht, pp. 1284–91.

Singer, June (1976) *Androgyny: Toward a New Theory of Sexuality*, Garden City, New York: Anchor Press.

Sjöö, Monica and Mor, Barbara (1981) *The Ancient Religion of the Great Cosmic Mother of All*, Trondheim, Norway: Rainbow Press.

—— (1987) *The Great Cosmic Mother. Rediscovering the Religion of the Earth*, San Francisco: Harper & Row.

Smith, Margaret (1928) *Rabi'a the Mystic and her Fellow saints in Islam*, Cambridge: Cambridge University Press.

—— (1976) *The Way of the Mystics. The Early Christian Mystics and the Rise of the Sufis*, London: Sheldon Press.

Snyder, Mary Hembrow (1988) *The Christology of Rosemary Radford Ruether*, Mystic, Connecticut: Twenty-Third Publications.

Sölle, Dorothee (1981a) 'Mysticism, Liberation and the Names of God', *Christianity and Crisis*, 41/11, pp. 179–85; also in D. Sölle, *The Strength of the Weak* (1984), pp. 79–105.

—— (1981b) 'Paternalistic Religion as Experienced by Woman', *Concilium. 143 – God as Father?*, pp. 69–74.

—— (1984) *The Strength of the Weak. Toward a Christian Feminist Identity*, Philadelphia: The Westminster Press.

Sorge, Elga (1985) *Religion und Frau. Weibliche Spiritualität im Christentum*, Stuttgart: W. Kohlhammer Taschenbuch Bd 1038; 3rd edn, 1987.

Spretnak, Charlene (1981) *Lost Goddesses of Early Greece. A Collection of Pre-Hellinic Myths*, Boston: Beacon Press, 1st edn, 1978.

—— (ed.) (1982) *The Politics of Women's Spirituality. Essays on the Rise of Spiritual Power within the Feminist Movement*, New York: Anchor Press; Doubleday.

—— (1986) *The Spiritual Dimension of Green Politics*, Santa Fe, New Mexico: Bear & Co.

—— (1991) *States of Grace. The Recovery of Meaning in the Postmodern Age*, San Francisco: HarperSanFrancisco.

Sri Sarada Math (1974–6), *The General Report of the Sri Sarada Math and Ramakrishna Sarada Mission, April 1974–March 1976*, Calcutta.

Starhawk (1979a) *The Spiral Dance: A Rebirth of the Ancient Religion of the Great Goddess*, San Francisco: Harper & Row.

—— (1979b) 'Witchcraft and Women's Culture', in C. P. Christ and J. Plaskow (eds), *Womanspirit Rising*, New York: Harper & Row, pp. 259–68.

Steffenson Hagen, June (1990) *Gender matters. Women's Studies for the Christian Community*, Grand Rapids, Mich.: Academie Books.

Stenger, Mary Ann (1982) 'A Critical Analysis of the Influence of Paul Tillich on Mary Daly's Feminist Theology', *Encounter*, Summer, pp. 219–38.

Stone, Merlin (1978) 'The Three Faces of Goddess Spirituality', *Heresies*, Spring, pp. 2–4; also in C. Spretnak (ed.), *The Politics of Women's Spirituality* (1982), pp. 64–70.

—— (1979) *The Paradise Papers. The Suppression of Women's Rites*, London: Virago: new edn, American edn, *When God was a Woman*, New York: Dial Press, 1976.

—— (1979 and 1980) *Ancient Mirrors of Womanhood: Our Goddess and Heroine Heritage*, New York: New Sybilline Press, 2 vols.

Strachan, Elspeth and Gordon (1985) *Freeing the Feminine*, Dunbar: Labarum Publications.

Tamez, Elsa (ed.) (1989) *Through Her Eyes. Women's Theology from Latin America*, Maryknoll, New York: Orbis Books.

Tavard, George H. (1973) *Woman in Christian Tradition*, Notre Dame, Indiana, London: University of Notre Dame Press.

Teilhard de Chardin, Pierre (1975) *Toward the Future*, London: Collins.

The Encyclopedia of Religion (1987) 'Goddess Worship', vol. 6, pp. 35–59, New York: Macmillan, London: Collier Macmillan.

The Friends' Quarterly (1986), 'Sexism and the Society of Friends', January, Ashford, Kent: Headley Brothers.

The Woman in the Church – La Femme dans l'Eglise, International Bibliography (1972–), RIC Supplement, Strasburg: CERDIC.

Thompson, Betty (1982) *A Chance to Change. Women and Men in the Church*, Geneva: World Council of Churches.

Trevett, Christine (1983) '"The lady vanishes": sexism by omission in religious education', *British Journal of Religious Education*, Spring, pp. 81–3.

—— (1984a) 'Religious Education and Sexism: a challenge ignored?', *Quaker Social Responsibility and Education Journal*, VI/2, Summer, pp. 6–18.

—— (1984b) 'Woman, God and Mary Baker Eddy', *Religion*, 14, pp. 143–53.

—— (1991) *Women and Quakerism in the Seventeenth Century*, York: The Ebor Press, Sessions Book Trust.

Trible, Phyllis (1978a) *God and the Rhetoric of Sexuality*, Philadelphia: Fortress Press.

—— (1978b) 'Depatriarchalizing in Biblical Interpretation', in Elizabeth Koltun (ed.), *The Jewish Woman. New Perspectives*, New York: Schocken Books, pp. 217–40.

—— (1984) *Texts of Terror. Literary – Feminist Readings of Biblical Narratives*, Philadelphia: Fortress Press.

Turner, Kay (1978) 'Contemporary Feminist Rituals', in *Heresies. A Feminist Publication on Art and Politics*, Spring, pp. 20–6. Also in C. Spretnak *The Politics of Women's Spirituality* (1982), pp. 219–33.

Umansky, Ellen M. (1984) 'Creating a Jewish Feminist Theology. Possibilities and Problems', *Anima*, 10/2, pp. 26–35.

—— and Ashton, Diane (eds) (1992), *Four Centuries of Jewish Women's Spirituality*, Boston: Beacon Press.

Valenze, Deborah M. (1985) *Prophetic Sons and Daughters. Female Preaching and Popular Religion in Industrial England*, Princeton, NJ: Princeton University Press.

Vetterling-Braggin, Mary (ed.) (1982), *'Femininity', 'Masculinity' and 'Androgyny'. A Modern Philosophical Discussion*, Totowa, NJ: Rowman & Allanheld.

Viljoen, S. (1984) 'The role of women in society – a sociological perspective', in W. S. Vorster (ed.), *Sexism and Feminism*, Pretoria: University of South Africa, pp. 106–18.

Von Kellenbach, Katharina (1986) 'Jewish–Christian Dialogue on Feminism and Religion', *Christian–Jewish Relations*, 19/2, pp. 33–40, London: Institute of Jewish Affairs.

Vorster, W. S. (ed.) (1984) *Sexism and Feminism in Theological Perspective*, Proceedings of the Eighth Symposium of the Institute for Theological Research (UNISA) held at the University of South Africa in Pretoria, 5 and 6 September 1984, Pretoria: University of South Africa.

Wadley, Susan S. (1977) 'Women and Symbolic System: Women and the Hindu Tradition', *Signs*, Autumn, pp. 113–125; also in D. Jacobson and S. S. Wadley, *Women in India* (1977), pp. 113–39.

Walker, Alice (1983) *The Color Purple*, London: The Women's Press.

Walker, Barbara J. (1983) *The Woman's Encyclopedia of Myths and Secrets*, San Francisco: Harper & Row.

Ward, Lester F. (1914) *Pure Sociology. A Treatise on the Origin and Spontaneous Development of Society*, New York, London: Macmillan, 1903; repr. 1914.

Warner, Marina (1985) *Alone of all her Sex. The Myth and Cult of the Virgin Mary*, London: Pan Books; Picador, London: Weidenfeld & Nicolson, 1976.

Warren, Mary Ann (1980) *The Nature of Woman. An Encyclopedia and Guide to the Literature*, Inverness, California: Edgepress.

—— (1982) 'Is Androgyny the Answer to Sexual Stereotyping?', in M. Vetterling-Braggin (ed.), *'Femininity', 'Masculinity' and 'Androgyny'*, Totowa, NJ: Rowman & Allanheld, pp. 170–96.

Washbourn, Penelope (1977) *Becoming Woman. The Quest for Wholeness in Female Experience*, New York: Harper & Row.

—— (1979) *Seasons of Woman. Song, Poetry, Ritual, Prayer, Myth, Story*, San Francisco: Harper & Row.

WCC (1975) *Sexism in the 1970s. Discrimination Against Women*, A Report of a World Council of Churches Consultation, West Berlin 1974, Geneva: World Council of Churches.

—— (1977) *Orthodox Women: Their Role and Participation in the Orthodox Church*, Report on the Consultation of Orthodox Women, 11–17 September 1976, Agapia, Rumania, Geneva: World Council of Churches.

—— (1983) *Nairobi to Vancouver, 1975–1983*, Report of the Central Committee to the Sixth Assembly of the World Council of Churches, Geneva: World Council of Churches.

—— (1985) *By Our Lives. Stories of Women – Today and in the Bible*, Geneva: World Council of Churches.

Weaver, Mary Jo (1985) *New Catholic Women. A Contemporary Challenge to Traditional Religious Authority*, San Fracisco: Harper & Row.

Webster, Derek H. (1982) 'Spiritual Growth in Religious Education', *Religious Education and the Imagination. Aspects of Education*, 28, pp. 85–95.

Webster, John C. B. and Webster, Ellen Low (eds) (1985) *The Church and Women in the Third World*, Philadelphia: The Westminster Press.

Weidmann, Judith L. (ed.) (1984), *Christian Feminism. Visions of a New Humanity*, San Francisco: Harper & Row.

Weiler, Gerda (1985) *Der enteignete Mythos. Eine notwendige Revision der Archetypenlehre C. G. Jungs and Erich Neumanns*, München: Frauenoffensive.

Welch, Sharon D. (1990) *A Feminist Ethic of Risk*, Minneapolis: Fortress Press.

White, Erin and Tulip, Marie (1991) *Knowing Otherwise. Feminism, Women and Religion*, Melbourne: David Lovell Publishing.

Whitmont, Edward C. (1983) *Return of the Goddess. Femininity, Aggression and the Modern Grail Quest*, London, Boston: Routledge & Kegan Paul; New York: Crossroad, 1982.

Wilber, Ken (1983) *Up from Eden*, London: Routledge & Kegan Paul.

Wilmore, Gayraud, S. and Cone, James H. (eds) (1979) *Black Theology: A Documentary History, 1966–1979*, New York: Orbis Books.

Wilson, Katharina M. (ed.) (1984) *Medieval Women Writers*, Manchester: Manchester University Press, Athens, Georgia: University of Georgia Press.

Wilson-Kastner, Patricia (1983) *Faith, Feminism and the Christ*, Philadelphia: Fortress Press.

Winter, Miriam Therese (1987) *Woman Prayer, Woman Song. Resources for Ritual*, Oak Park, Illinois: Meyer Stone Books.

—— (1991) *WomanWisdom. A Feminist Lectionary and Psalter*, New York: Crossroad.

Winter, Urs (1983) *Frau und Göttin. Exegetische und ikonographische Studien zum weiblichen Gottesbild im Alten Israel und in dessen Umwelt*, Göttingen; Vandenhoeck & Ruprecht.

Witherington III, Ben (1990) *Women and the Genesis of Christianity*, Cambridge: Cambridge University Press.

Women and Religion, A Bibliography selected from the *ATLA Religion Database*; 3rd revised edn, October 1983, Chicago: American Theological Library Association Religion Indexes.

Women, Status of (1974) *Encyclopaedia Britannica*, 5th edn, Chicago: Macropaedia, 19, pp. 906–16.

Woods, Richard (ed.) (1981) *Understanding Mysticism*, London: The Athlone Press, New York: Doubleday.

Wren, Brian (1989) *What Language Shall I Borrow? God-Talk in Worship: A Male Response to Feminist Theology*, London: SCM Press.

Wulff, David M. (1982) 'Prolegomenon to a Psychology of the Goddess', in J. S. Hawley and Donna M. Wulff (eds), *The Divine Consort: Rādhā and the Goddesses of India*, Berkeley: Graduate Theological Union, pp. 283–97, New Delhi: Motilal Banarsidass, 1984.

Wynne, Patrice (1988) *The Womanspirit Sourcebook. A Catalog of Books, Periodicals, Music, Calendars and Tarot Cards, Organizations, Video and Audio Tapes, Bookstores, Interviews, Meditations, Art*, San Francisco: Harper & Row.

Yates, Gayle Graham (1983) 'Spirituality and the American Feminist Experience', *Signs, Journal of Women in Culture and Society*, 9/1, pp. 59–72.

You Can't Kill the Spirit. Yorkshire Women go to Greenham (1983), Wakefield: Bretton Women's Book Fund – People's Library History of Yorkshire, 4.

Young, Katherine K. and Sharma, Arvind (1974) *Images of the Feminine – Mythic, Philosophic and Human – in the Buddhist, Hindu, and Islamic Traditions. A Bibliography of Women in India*, Chico, California: New Horizons Press.

Young, Pamela Dickey (1990) *Feminist Theology/Christian Theology. In Search of Method*, Minneapolis: Fortress Press.

Zappone, Katherine (1991) *The Hope for Wholeness. A Spirituality for Feminists*, Mystic, Connecticut: Twenty-Third Publications.

Zum Brunn, Emilie and Epiney-Burgard, Georgette (1989) *Women Mystics in Medieval Europe*, New York: Paragon House.

Index